NOT

Health Services Management

Series Editors:
Chris Ham, Professor of health policy and management at the Health Services Management Centre, University of Birmingham and director of the strategy unit at the Department of Health
Chris Heginbotham, Chief Executive, East and North Hertfordshire Health Authority

The British National Health Service is one of the biggest and most complex organizations in the developed world. Employing around one million people and involving high levels of public expenditure, the Service is of major concern to both the public and politicians. Management within the NHS faces a series of challenges in ensuring that resources are deployed efficiently and effectively. These challenges include the planning and management of human resources, the integration of professionals into the management process, and making sure that services meet the needs of patients and the public.

Against this background, the Health Services Management series addresses the many issues and practical problems faced by people in managerial roles in health services.

Current and forthcoming titles

Judith Allsop and Linda Mulcahy: *Regulating Medical Work: Formal and Informal Controls*
Steve Cropper and Paul Forte (eds): *Enhancing Health Services Management: The Role of Decision Support Systems*
Valerie Iles: *Really Managing Health Care*
Richard Joss and Maurice Kogan: *Advancing Quality: Total Quality Management in the National Health Service*
Justin Keen (ed.): *Information Management in Health Services*
Maurice Kogan, Sally Redfern *et al.*: *Making Use of Clinical Audit: A Guide to Practice in the Health Professions*
Carol Lupton *et al.*: *Managing Public Involvement in Healthcare Purchasing*
Gordon Marnoch: *Doctors and Management in the National Health Service*
John Øvretveit: *Purchasing for Health*
Amanda Reynolds and Graham Thornicroft: *Managing Mental Health Services*
Rod Sheaff: *Responsive Healthcare: Marketing for a Public Service*

Responsive Healthcare

Marketing for a public service

Rod Sheaff

Open University Press
Buckingham · Philadelphia

Open University Press
Celtic Court
22 Ballmoor
Buckingham
MK18 1XW

email: enquiries@openup.co.uk
world wide web: www.openup.co.uk

and

325 Chestnut Street
Philadelphia, PA 19106, USA

First Published 2002

Copyright © Rod Sheaff, 2002

A catalogue record of this book is available from the British Library

ISBN   0 335 19966 6 (pb)   0 335 19967 4 (hb)

Library of Congress Cataloging-in-Publication Data
Sheaff, Rod.
   Responsive healthcare : marketing for a public service / Rod Sheaff.
      p. cm. – (Health services management series)
   Includes bibliographical references and index.
   ISBN 0–335–19967–4 – ISBN 0–335–19966–6 (pbk.)
   1. Medical care–Marketing.   2. Health maintenance organizations–
Marketing.   3. Preferred provider organizations (Medical care)–Marketing.
I. Title.   II. Health services management

RA410.56 .S543 2001
362.1′068′8–dc21
                                                              2001032137

Typeset by Graphicraft Limited, Hong Kong
Printed in Great Britain by Biddles Limited, Guildford and King's Lynn

Contents

Preface

Public services are often slow to respond to users' demands about what services should be available, about when and where they should be provided, and about what standards of staff behaviour, information provision, accommodation and service outcomes are acceptable to the public. One would have thought that attempts to diagnose and solve this problem would form a large and central part of the literature on public management, but few works consider it in much depth. Fewer still start by considering the marketing literature and practice dealing with analogous problems and solutions in the commercial sphere. Those works that do so are frequently quite uncritical of existing marketing practice, tending to assume that public services should copy commercial marketing practice rather than learn from it. This book argues the opposite; that public services can learn from both the positive and the negative aspects of commercial marketing, but should not just copy it. The following text differs from its predecessor, *Marketing for Health Services*, in attempting to dismantle commercial marketing theory and practice more systematically; and in attempting to rebuild the components which are worth salvaging into a coherent, distinct theory suggesting how to make public services responsive to their users. Like its predecessor, this book examines some practical attempts to improve the responsiveness of publicly funded health services, as a large and distinctive part of the public sector. If this book is an improvement on its predecessor, that is due partly to this more systematic approach, and partly to the stimulus of discussion with the people acknowledged below.

Choosing marketing as a topic for study risks giving the impression that the author advocates either dismantling and privatizing the public sector or, as second best, imitating private sector management. That impression would be false. Learning how to make public services responsive is a step towards inventing better alternatives than the private corporation as the organizational basis for producing consumer services in the future.

Acknowledgements

I am grateful for a multitude of ideas and improvements to this text suggested by Rachel Brooks, Naomi Chambers, Gary Coleman, Linda Gask, Ashish Gopakumar, Philip Jones, Sue Kirk, Louise Locock, Adrian Mercer, Susan Pickard, Martin Roland, Amanda Squires, Bruce Wood, numerous MBA, MA and MSc course members, many colleagues in the NHS and the series editors Chris Heginbotham and Chris Ham. *Health Which* gave me the chance to review some of its articles early in their preparation. The National Primary Care Research and Development Centre is funded by the (English) Department of Health. NPCRDC's Primary Care Group database was created by Deborah Baker, Mark Hann and Andrew Wagner, collaborating with Robert Barr, Justin Hayes and Neil Matthews of the Department of Geography, Manchester University, UK. Its Tracker Survey core team are Brenda Leese, Keri Smith and David Wilkin. None of these people or organizations, however, should be held responsible for any opinions or mistakes that appear in what follows.

1 | Health services, public management and users

Chapter overview

Illustrating from the British National Health Service, this chapter indicates the type of problems in service design and public image which have led people to consider applying marketing methods in public services. But what is marketing, and what relevance has it to making public services more responsive to their users? The obvious starting point are the archetypal forms of marketing which firms use in commercial settings. A model of commercial marketing provides the raw material for later chapters to adapt for publicly funded health systems.

A marketing crisis?

During January 1999, British newspapers were again criticizing National Health Service management. Patients arriving at hospital accident and emergency departments faced long waits, in some cases passing their first night in hospital on a trolley because of a bed shortage. Journalists were unsure whether to blame this 'crisis' on underfunding of the NHS; on shortages of nurses due to low salaries; on the locum GPs who cover out-of-hours services and allegedly refer many patients to hospitals; or on patients themselves for presenting with increasingly trivial illnesses (Ungoed-Thomas and Dignan 1999). Such reports of NHS unresponsiveness to patients' reasonable demands have become increasingly politically visible. *The NHS Plan* states as a principle that in future:

> The NHS will shape its services around the needs and preferences of individual patients, their families and carers.
>
> (Department of Health 2000: 4)

Many commentators on the NHS and public management generally argue that such problems have a deep-rooted cause in the way in which the NHS and other publicly funded services are structured and managed (see, for example, Osborne and Gaebler 1992). Allegedly the NHS and other publicly funded and managed systems are structured, managed and financed in ways that allow managers and professions to pursue their own interests without needing to take notice of their users' reasonable demands, let alone satisfy them. Excess demand and the fact that those who finance the system are also insulated from users' control allow staff to adopt patronizing, condescending, self-important attitudes towards consumers (Baker 1988). The 'New Public Management' and 'reforms' of the 1990s repositioned the demarcations between managers and doctors but still left publicly funded health systems relatively insensitive to users' demands (Smith *et al.* 1999). Here we are not speaking of extravagant or irrational demands, but such moderate desires as being treated within an hour of admission to an accident and emergency department, and having access to a bed without an overnight wait on a trolley in a corridor before a bed becomes available. The critics also allege that publicly funded services tend to be poor at inventing and applying new management methods and technologies. Such a critic might observe that the NHS is only now adopting automated, flexible booking systems which other producers (for example, airlines) have used for decades, or that some of the most important organizational innovations in healthcare (for example, hospices) originated outside the NHS.

In the 1980s the 'new right' proposed that the solution was to privatize public services as far as possible. But one should see the above criticisms in perspective. Whatever its other failings, the NHS and similar services have solved the market entry problem: that those who most need healthcare (education, housing and so on) tend for that very reason to be badly placed to participate in the labour or other markets to get the money to buy it. For most healthcare consumers, the 'remedy' of privatization is far worse than the original disorders of public management.

Another solution is to encourage public managers to adopt marketing methods because, marketers say:

> The marketing concept represents an 'outside-in' view of the organisation, in that a deliberate attempt is made to look at the organisation and its products and services from the viewpoint of the customer. In doing this, a far greater emphasis is placed on meeting the customer's needs, emphasising the products' benefits . . . and generally achieving a far better match between what the customers needs [sic] and what the organisation provides.
>
> (Gilligan and Lowe 1995: 18)

Marketing is much more developed outside the health sector than in it. Modern marketing originated from large firms in Germany and the USA as a refinement of selling techniques in mass markets. These commercial origins have coloured the language of marketing, not to mention marketing theory and practice. At the very least, any transfer of these marketing practices into publicly funded healthcare should be selective. Healthcare has its peculiarities. It is more technically complex than most consumer services and its workpiece is the consumer themself, mind and body. Commercial marketing practice has been criticized (see Chapter 2) on grounds that anyone contemplating healthcare marketing would be foolish to ignore. Conversely, commercial marketers may simply lack techniques which a publicly funded health system needs. For public health system purposes it may be necessary to adapt commercial marketing techniques, adding some materials and discarding others.

This text considers what that project involves and how it might be taken further, emphatically without privatizing healthcare. Whilst this book focuses on the English NHS, it tries to use that example to illuminate what marketing methods also apply to other services with post-market forms of organization (in much of Europe, education, housing, public transport and so on). It therefore starts by outlining what marketing is in its archetypal, commercial form. That outline will serve as raw material for adapting the archetype for the purposes of publicly funded health systems.

Marketing – the commercial model

Dozens of textbooks describe the archetypal commercial forms of marketing. To use a marketing buzzword, each 'differentiates' itself by using somewhat different terminology, by subdividing the marketing cycle described below in different ways, by advocating specific techniques and in its choice of examples. Yet beneath these differences, most such models are essentially similar. They usually start by pointing out – correctly – that a firm undertakes marketing as a means of meeting its particular strategic objectives. These objectives are the criteria by which commercial marketers decide which marketing activities to undertake and develop, and which not. However, it is much rarer for marketing textbooks to point out that these objectives themselves reflect the market structures within which the firm works (see Chapter 2). Because we shall be transposing marketing into different organizational structures and using it for different objectives, we must begin by understanding how the market structure which a firm inhabits influences its objectives and thus the marketing activity by which the firm pursues those objectives.

Market structures – incentives and actors

For firms in a market economy the fundamental objective is, familiarly, profit maximization. The single term, however, covers two different imperatives. One is simply to maximize the distributable profits available to the firm's owners, or shareholders, and senior managers; in other words, to maximize stockholder value. However, to maximize stockholder value over anything but the shortest period, requires, in most markets, that a second imperative be met: that of accumulating capital to reinvest. The firm's owners and managers have little control over these intermediate objectives because they arise from the firm's 'environment', or, more precisely, from structural characteristics of the economy external to the firm. These are:

1 The firm derives its income from sales, whether to the end-users of its products or services or to intermediaries.
2 Other firms are competing to sell to these end-users or intermediaries.
3 Investment in developing new products, methods of production and indeed marketing gives a firm competitive advantage in gaining or at minimum, maintaining, sales.
4 Ultimately the only way a firm can invest is out of its own profits, whether its past profits or, if it must raise external finance, its future profits; and these profits are realized through sales of the goods or services which it produces.

The imperative to reinvest, and therefore to earn the profits from which to reinvest, results from the combination of all four.

This incentive structure does not remove all leeway for a firm's owners and managers to choose the firm's objectives and strategy, but it does constrain them. Indeed, in the medium term it constrains them absolutely, to cover the firm's day-to-day operating costs. Consequently, firms' fundamental 'corporate', i.e. company-wide, *objectives* for profit optimization (i.e. long-term profit maximization, all things considered) are usually expressed in a range of standard indicators such as:

- ROI (return on investment) or ROTA (return on total assets);
- operating margin, for example 16–20 per cent on capital employed in UK;
- dividend rates – earnings per share is a critical indicator in Britain, where firms commonly rely on external finance (Hutton 1996);
- share price;
- turnover;
- break-even period, i.e. the length of time from the start of a project until the income it generates just covers the costs to that point. This is an important indicator in high-technology sectors such as pharmaceuticals because even after a new product is patented, another 10–12 years' development may be required to make it saleable (allowing for testing, licensing and so on). Since a UK patent lasts 20 years, the product must break even in the remaining 8–10 years before competitors imitate it and drive down the price;
- ratio of profit to sales;
- ratio of sales to capital;
- ratio of sales to fixed assets;
- ratio of sales to stocks;
- sales per employee;
- profit per employee.

These conditions and objectives are so familiar and taken-for-granted, so fundamental and stable, that marketing textbooks rarely give them a second thought, although the incentive structure outlined above is of fundamental explanatory importance. For everyday practical marketing purposes it has simply to be taken as given.

Marketing textbooks pay greater attention to a second aspect of market structures – the 'channels' or 'publics' from which flow the money, resources or power on which the firm depends in order to realize its objectives – for this aspect of market structures tends to be much less stable than the incentive structures and to vary more between different sectors of the economy. A firm such as Coca-Cola producing consumer goods on an international scale is unlikely to be able or willing to sell directly to the millions of end-consumers of its products. Instead it constructs distribution channels, for instance selling its products to wholesalers or other distributors, who in turn sell its products to retailers, who in their turn sell to the eventual consumer (whether over-the-counter, by mail order etc.). There are many ways in which this can be done. Whichever the firm chooses, its marketing activity must ensure that each actor in its distribution channels is willing to buy its produce and able to sell the produce on to their own (direct) customers. Consequently, the firm's marketing activity must succeed in managing all these actors' behaviour coherently and simultaneously. Figure 1.1 shows in simplified form the channels for a firm making cookers, refrigerators, washing machines and other 'white goods'. Each of these routes for selling the product counts as one market when the time comes for situation analysis, market research and marketing planning (see below). Health insurers in the USA, for example, must influence both the employer who pays for the insurance and the worker who uses it (Helms *et al.* 1992). Further actors also influence the process, for instance the mass media, government, consumer groups and researchers (such as those involved in the controversy over genetically modified foods).

Taken together, these actors are the target audiences or 'publics'. The firm's marketing activity has to manage their behaviour and beliefs sufficiently to

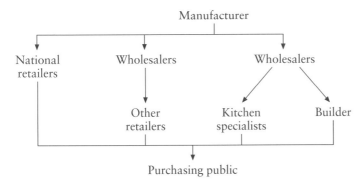

Figure 1.1 Channels for a white goods manufacturer (simplified).

achieve the firm's own, more fundamental objectives. Not all these audiences are equally influential. Marketing activity has to concentrate on those who are both critical for the firm's success and whose behaviour it cannot guarantee to control. They typically include, in descending order of influence: consumers, government, financiers, distributors, staff, media, pressure groups and the general public. A firm requires somewhat different marketing techniques for managing each of these audiences. Consequently the discipline of marketing contains the sub-specialities of industrial marketing, consumer marketing, public relations, social marketing and so on. Gilligan and Lowe (1995) suggest concentrating on the powerful and interested audiences, keeping the powerful but uninterested ones satisfied (and by implication benignly passive), the interested but powerless groups well-informed, and minimizing marketing attention for those who are both low power and uninterested.

Familiar as these points are in market contexts, they are worth spelling out because some actors that play rather marginal roles in ordinary markets (for example voluntary workers, the state) play bigger roles in quasi-markets, in the public and voluntary sectors. Conversely, some actors that dominate ordinary markets (for example financial institutions) are more marginal in the public, voluntary and quasi-market sectors whilst other agents, above all consumers, play an equally large but different role.

Situation analysis

The most important characteristics of the firm's environment that are likely to change on a year-by-year basis are not its incentive structures nor, to a lesser extent, its target audiences but the particular configuration of customers, competitors and business collaborators that the firm faces. These changes are what the firm's strategy and marketing activity have to adjust to periodically, and what pose the greatest opportunities and threats to it, for they further constrain a firm's objectives and hence its marketing objectives.

To adjust their objectives and marketing activities to these conditions many firms periodically carry out a situation analysis. One situation analysis

- Market characteristics
  - Market size
  - Market trends
  - Segments
  - Who buys
  - Buying decisions
- Competitors
- Technology
- Legal setting
- Social setting

Figure 1.2   Situation analysis – contents.

is necessary for each distinct market. The precise content, how it is organized and presented vary from firm to firm, as does the specific market research on which it is based. Generally, though, a situation analysis will contain the types of information listed in Figure 1.2.

Market size concerns trends in the growth or decline of effective demand, i.e. the number of people who are able to buy, and the amount of money they bring to the market. This information indicates which markets it might be worth entering or investing more in. Under 'who buys' one would list the main target audiences (see above), covering the whole channel including the intermediaries (wholesalers, retailers and so on) who sell the product on to the final consumer. Each target audience can often be divided into segments, each segment being a sub-population which requires a distinct set of benefits, hence different products and services, in short (to anticipate a concept explained below) a distinct marketing mix. Yankelovich (1964) and Berkowitz (1996) give the uses of segmentation as being to:

- identify profitable segments;
- allow segment-specific product design;
- give early warning of market changes;
- enable tailoring of advertisements;
- allow choice of advertising medium;
- aid the timing promotions and advertisements;
- facilitate understanding market demography;
- prevent 'cannibalization' (i.e. launching a new product which attracts one's existing customers rather than new ones);
- prevent competitors providing services more closely tailored to a given market than one's own.

A given market can be segmented in various ways. Consumer markets, for instance, can be segmented according to:

- product type – for instance vegans buy different snacks from non-vegans;
- the consumer's motivation for buying the product, reflecting the use to which they will put the product. An electronics company would thus produce different radios for young children, hi-fi enthusiasts and other adults;
- scale of purchase or distribution channel. Thus a travel company would offer different pricing regimes to individuals and to large groups (for example schools);
- psycho-social differences, for example life-cycle stage, class, adopter phase (see below), values and life styles;
- proxies for consumption patterns, for example education, car ownership;
- geographically, for example for travel, tourism;
- frequency of use, for example air travel;
- payer – car repairs often appear to be priced higher for an 'insurance job' than when the customer pays personally;
- gender, obviously important for markets such as clothing or pharmaceuticals, and in healthcare.

Marketing literature contains various disputes about what types of segmentation are most useful to firms and under which conditions. In any event, the point of segmentation is to find market segments which are measurable, accessible to the firm's marketing efforts, large, profitable and require a distinct marketing mix (see below).

It is critically necessary for firms to know on what grounds the buyer decides to buy. This depends, firstly, on who actually makes the decision to buy. It is not always the final consumer (for example in markets for toys or petfood). The other fundamental question is why they buy; that is, what benefits they are trying to obtain. To say simply that the consumer is getting the practical benefits of the good or service assumes too much in some circumstances. Many goods are valued not in themselves but only as means to an end. For instance, insurance is bound to be a waste of money for most people who buy it. They need it only as a means to (say) be allowed to drive a car. 'Distress goods' such as repair services and healthcare are largely in this category too. If possible, people would prefer not to have to use them. But in other cases it is saying too little just to point to the practical benefits or a product or service. Some goods provide more than these benefits, for instance as a mark of social position (for example the hospital consultant's Rolls-Royce), or as a means of self-expression ('lifestyle' goods such as clothes). Many products thus serve both functional and symbolic purposes for their buyers (Douglas and Isherwood 1996). Marketers use the term 'benefit' for this mixture of uses (Levitt 1976). The grounds on which customers buy determine what benefits it is necessary to persuade them that they will gain by purchasing.

Customers also decide what to buy with an eye to related markets. A firm's situation analysis typically notes changes in demand for complementary goods, because rises (or falls) in demand for them will induce (or reduce) demand for its own products. Thus activity in the housing market tends to produce a slightly lagged increase in demand for furnishings and for DIY materials; demand for house extensions is counter-synchronized (people improve their existing house instead of moving).

An obvious determinant of demand for a firm's products are its competitors' activities. Most firms face two kinds of competitor. Direct competitors provide a similar product (for example Lufthansa and British Airways compete directly). However, the notion of benefit implies that firms face wider competition than that, because they are in effect competing also with firms who provide the same benefit by another means (usually, another technology). So British Airways faces indirect competition, inside the UK, from train operating companies. Consequently, firms use market research to identify which their competitors and substitutes are (including firms likely to enter or leave the market), their market strength, pricing and discount strategies, R&D intentions, activity levels, cost structures, profit sources, new products, what benefits they offer. The relative importance of different markets to these competitors will influence how they are likely to respond to one's own activity, for example which markets they will defend most fiercely. To make such analyses, portfolio analysis (business grids – see below) can be applied to competitors' activity besides a firm's own. Porter's (1981) 'five forces' analysis is one of the best-known ways of analysing a firm's market strength.

Behind all these determinants of demand lie larger but less direct determinants. A well-known way of enumerating these is under the headings 'political', 'economic', 'social' and 'technological'; hence, 'PEST analysis'. For most firms, the political climate matters chiefly because of possible changes in the legal framework (for example through changes in EU regulations on product safety or labelling). For some, governments are major buyers in their own right (for example the arms industry). Governments also pursue policies which expand or restrict demand for specific goods (through taxation, housing or transport policy and so on). The relevance of economic events such as levels of employment, economic growth and inflation are obvious. Social changes are relevant in so far as they influence demand patterns and buyers' requirements. Rising divorce rates create demand for small or medium-sized cars for single mothers. Technological developments are relevant in so far as they promise methods of producing new saleable benefits which can be incorporated in existing or new products, if not by one's own firm then by competitors. From this perspective, 'technology' should not be interpreted too narrowly. Organizational innovations (for example time-sharing, franchising) sometimes have similar implications.

All the foregoing methods analyse the situation outside the firm. Sometimes on the basis of a SWOT analysis (see below), many firms also make periodic internal evaluations of how competent their current marketing practice is and what factors determine its success or failure. All these are summarized as a *marketing audit*. Its purposes are to let the firm re-evaluate its objectives, the assumptions on which it has based its marketing, forecast the effects of its marketing activity, identify how it can exploit opportunities and convert its marketing weaknesses into strengths and invent 'preventative as well as curative marketing practices' (Berkowitz 1996: 373).

Again, firms differ in what content they include, the balance between items, what data are cited and the formulations used (Davidson 1987). Typically, the audit will cover each main market (or segment or product-group), under such headings as:

- Where sales and profit originate, including a 'contribution analysis' showing which products lines make the highest proportional contributions to fixed costs once the direct (variable) costs of production have been met.
- Market shares by firm and brand.
- The firm's marketing assets (brands, technologies, skills, people, physical resources including spare capacity, networks of consumers, customers and suppliers, its cost base).
- Factors causing the firm's own marketing successes or failures, such as its cost profile and the causes of any recent mis-marketing or competitive advantage.

- Public image and profile, the firms promotional and advertising effectiveness (which is especially important where public image directly promotes the product, for example The Body Shop), and the positioning (see below) of its own products and services compared with competitors'.
- Product range and quality, and its 'unique selling points' or 'unique selling propositions' (either way, USPs), including the balance between differentiated products (which give a marketing advantage) and undifferentiable 'commodity' products (such as baked beans, petrol) and how the product range compares with consumer characteristics and segmentation.
- Information – the firm's market research and forecasting competence.
- Distribution system – its reliability, costs, frequency of stockouts, calibre of salesforce.
- Innovation – the firm's capacity for R&D, its intellectual property and patents.
- Costs and effectiveness of the marketing and sales function. The ratio of marketing costs to sales varies greatly between sectors: 1.4 per cent for cars, 14 per cent for US airlines, 17.2 per cent for toys (Davidson 1987).

Some writers treat marketing audit as part of SWOT analysis (see below).

Marketing strategy and objectives

A firm's fundamental objectives are themselves determined by the wider market structures within which it operates, structures which are relatively stable and durable. Its marketing objectives and strategy articulate how it will use its marketing activity to pursue its fundamental objectives in the current market situation. Although it is possible to derive a marketing strategy directly from a situation analysis, many firms derive their marketing objectives and strategy from a situation analysis by way of a SWOT analysis, sometimes supplemented with a TOWS analysis, and a portfolio analysis ('business grid').

A situation analysis provides the raw material for a marketing strengths, weaknesses, opportunities and threats (SWOT) analysis which summarizes its practical marketing implications; indeed situation analyses and SWOT analyses are often conflated. Strengths and weaknesses are defined as strengths or weaknesses, relative to competitors, in securing customers (and thereby realizing the firm's more fundamental objectives). They are enumerated in the marketing audit. Opportunities and threats are respectively defined as potentials for the firm to make itself stronger, and for circumstances to make it weaker, in the same terms. These opportunities and threats are implications of changes in competitors' behaviour and implications of the PEST analysis outlined above. A SWOT analysis is then used to indicate marketing strategies. One way is by systematically deriving a marketing strategy for each SWOT combination in turn, resulting in a TOWS analysis (Figure 1.3).

Another way to derive a marketing strategy is by using a strategy grid (or 'matrix' or 'business grid', 'portfolio analysis') for deciding investment

	Strengths	Weaknesses
Opportunities	Opportunities strategies	Opportunities to reduce or correct weaknesses
Threats	Use strenths to remove threats	Avoid threats, minimize weaknesses

Figure 1.3 TOWS analysis.
Source: Gilligan and Lowe (1995).

		Firm's market share	
		High	Low
Market growth	High	Stars – invest and promote	Problem child – Strengthen or withdraw
	Low	Cash cow – extract profits to invest elsewhere	Dog – withdraw

Figure 1.4 Boston Consulting Group grid.

and development priorities for each market that a firm serves. One can illustrate the principle with the well-known Boston grid (Boston Consulting Group 1968) – see Figure 1.4.

In the Boston grid, as most of the others, information from the situation analysis is used to position each of the firm's products or subsidiaries or markets on each axis. The corresponding cell within the grid states what business and therefore marketing strategy should be followed in such cases. Many other grids are available. Most marketing texts adumbrate Porter's (1981) Generic Strategy Model, Ansoff's (1957), Little's, the McKinsey (or General Electric or Shell) and the Profit Impact of Marketing Strategies (PIMS) grids, and others.

The precise content of a marketing strategy depends on the nature of the firm and the situation in which it is formulated. That said, a marketing strategy generally states, firstly, which markets to enter or leave. For many years British Rail tried to leave the small-consignment (one or two wagonloads) freight business, preferring to concentrate on moving whole trainloads of single commodities (coal, china clay or whatever) – misguidedly, since EWS and others have since managed to start building this market up again. However, it is equally risky for a firm to enter markets outside its original competence, as Procter & Gamble found when it tried to enter the food market (Davidson 1987). A sounder strategy is to use a firm's existing strengths when entering new markets, for instance by 'brand stretching' or 'line extension' (as Laura Ashley did in diversifying from clothes to fabrics to interior decoration to furniture).

Another strategic decision is whether to adopt defensive (imitative) or offensive (initiative-taking) marketing. Partnerships can be used to reduce competition, or as a form of integration with firms supplying complementary products such as air travel with car hire and hotel accommodation (for example Lufthansa with Kempinski, British Airways with Hertz). A marketing strategy will also state how the firm will use market positioning and product differentiation, including whether to pursue price or non-price competition. Marketers usually reckon product differentiation and branding to be good marketing strategies. Each firm can reduce the competition it faces by positioning its products for sale to market segments which other firms cannot attract so successfully. Thus Aldi sells a limited range of foodstuffs from basic premises at low cost; Marks and Spencer sells a smaller, higher quality, more expensive range. Until the 'Asda price' campaign, Asda tended to sell a middling-to-large range of products at middling prices, and so on. Occasionally, though, differentiation is a mistake. Apple's refusal to license its operating system to other firms let Microsoft dominate the microcomputer market by distributing its operating systems (MS-DOS, Windows) widely. The opposite of differentiation is to offer 'lookalike' or 'me-too' products such as PC clones.

Marketing strategies tend to emphasize quality for one of three reasons. One is to differentiate the products, especially at the luxury end of consumer goods markets, by emphasizing the exclusiveness or prestige of the product (so that the product functions primarily as a badge of social status). Putatively high quality can then legitimate high prices which then become a further symbol – in extreme cases, a guarantee – of the product's 'exclusiveness' (for example, 'designer' clothes in the 1980s). A second use for quality strategies is in response to marketing crises or as remedial marketing, for example McDonald's marketing during the 1996 BSE scare, or Skoda cars' shift from a low-price strategy to quality competition after the Volkswagen takeover. Thirdly, competing on product quality is less financially risky than price competition, especially for firms with high costs or narrow profit margins and during times of inflation.

Although firms tend to be more wary about publicizing them, many do pursue anti-marketing ('spoiling') strategies against competitors. For instance, Davidson (1987) records:

- Mars sold a branded low-priced cat food (Katkins) to pre-empt shops' cheaper, own-label competition.
- Perverse as it may seem, it is a lesser evil for a firm to produce the own-label product itself under the shop's branding than for a genuine competitor to do so. Thus Boots own-brand indigestion tablet is Settlers under another label.

- Playtex increased its marketing spend ten-fold in Rochester (USA) to distort test marketing of new tampon by Procter & Gamble.
- 'Encirclement' strategies: one firm produces a complete range of products to 'crowd out' competitors. Toys 'R' Us has adopted this strategy. Seiko at one time marketed 2300 models of watch.

A firm's marketing strategy would include a selling strategy, whether a 'pull' strategy of getting end-users to demand the firm's products from intermediaries, or a 'push' strategy of selling the product to wholesalers, retailers and other distributors and leaving it to them to promote the product to the final consumer. US pharmaceutical firms promote their drugs to consumers, so that patients will demand their products by name from the doctor. UK pharmaceutical firms, by contrast, concentrate on getting the doctor to prescribe their products to the patient.

A firm's marketing objectives are often expressed in its business plan. Here, 'business plan' means 'plan for getting business, i.e. income' rather than (as in parts of the UK public sector) 'plan of productive activity'. For each market, segment or product (depending on case), a firm's main marketing targets are likely to be stated in terms of intended market share, sales, repeat sales, consumer mix, cost ratios (sales/costs ratios and so on). Concomitantly, it is also likely to specify what behaviours, beliefs and attitudes the firm is trying to produce in each target audience.

For public and staff consumption, a firm's mission statement usually contains a simplified and more euphemistic version of its marketing objectives. David (1989) recommends that mission statements specify customers, products or services, location, technology, economic objectives, basic aspirations of the firm, self-concept of the firm's strengths and weaknesses, desired public image, attitude towards staff.

Marketing plan

A marketing plan states what firm will do in order to realize its marketing objectives. It typically recapitulates the preceding elements but its new and essential elements are a statement of the firm's intended marketing mix and an implementation plan. The situation analysis provides the raw material and assumptions for the marketing plan. Figure 1.5 shows what a marketing plan's headings would typically be.

A marketing mix is the set of activities which a firm can use for marketing purposes. (Some writers conflate the terms 'marketing mix' and 'marketing strategy'.) The first practical applications of the idea of marketing mix were in the US motor industry, whose marketers regarded their four marketing variables as product, price, promotions and place of sale (the 4Ps) (McCarthy 1978). Firms use their marketing mix primarily for selling purposes, but not exclusively – occasionally firms also use their marketing mix for social marketing purposes (trying to influence social attitudes and behaviour). For instance, firms sometimes undertake marketing in support of political

- Executive summary
- Situation analysis
  - Background
  - Normal forecast
  - Opportunities and threats
  - Strengths and weaknesses
- Objectives and goals
- Marketing strategy
- Action programmes
- Budgets
- Controls

Figure 1.5   Instance of marketing plan headings.
Source: Kotler and Clarke (1987: 194).

parties, for anti-marketing purposes and for demarketing. Demarketing is the use of marketing methods to discourage or divert demand for products that firms no longer wish to sell, for example making it harder for passengers to obtain or use discounted rail tickets.

Within each market (and segment within it) the marketing mix must meet the demands of each actor in the channel between producer and consumer. Consider food packaging. Supermarkets need such characteristics as tessellation (to minimize space requirements), quick availability, long product shelf-life and to minimize special storage requirements (for example refrigeration). Consumers, by contrast, might value clear labelling, handles for heavy or bulky items and child-proof openings. Manufacturers want it to be cheap and to stimulate sales.

Many firms will produce a specific marketing mix for each market or even each segment, and consider alternative plans and mixes. Majaro (1982) suggests that a specific element should appear in a marketing mix only if it represents a substantial expenditure for a firm, if customers respond to it and if it is possible to allocate responsibility for implementing it. 'Differentiated marketing' consists of using one distinct mix for each segment or product. One problem that firms face in doing this is to achieve consistency and coherence across their different markets and segments. 'Concentrated' or 'undifferentiated marketing' is the practice of using only one marketing mix without regard to segmentation.

The other element which a marketing plan usually contains is an implementation programme, whose main elements will normally be an account of how the marketing plan will be implemented through the firm's own workforce. Typically these would include:

- Specific deadlines and targets for activities (sales, advertising campaigns and so on).
- Training and other internal 'communications', with an eye to achieving consistency between these messages and the external promotions aimed at purchasers (see below).

- Resourcing – staffing, physical inputs, budgets.
- Incentives.
- Management of day-to-day working practices and any concomitant changes to organizational structure. For instance, a firm might decide to shift from a regional or functional organizational structure to one based on market segments or specific products or services ('product-line management'). Thus a chemical firm might have different divisions for producing pharmaceuticals, food additives, agricultural chemicals and so on.
- How the purchasing of inputs and any subcontracting of work will be managed so as to contribute to realizing the marketing plan. In particular, many firms (for example McDonald's) rely heavily on franchising. Independent firms or individuals pay the franchiser for being allowed to use the franchiser's marketing mix (especially the brand name, other promotions, production processes and quality specifications).
- Marketing department tasks and its budget, what salesforce is required, and how to train and reward them. One variation is to recruit customers as sellers by offering rewards for introducing new customers.

Marketing mix

The next step is to implement the plan by actually creating and using the marketing mix. Here we outline the main points of a marketing mix based on the original 4Ps (Chapter 5 expands and refines the idea of marketing mix).

Product

Product (or service) design is a fundamental marketing activity. The essential point of product design is not to design an object as such, but to design a vehicle for providing the benefits which customers want to buy. Because many consumer goods serve a symbolic besides a practical purpose, they have to be designed with both in view. This is most evident in products such as cars, whose ease of use and appearance count for more, with most customers, than technical specifications. Product design for a car would then cover not only the vehicle itself but also dealer support and customer services (providing servicing, repairs or replacements, resolving complaints). Further, the product can be designed to be differentiated from competing products, in effect reducing competition.

Marketing value analysis consists in using market research to discover what product benefits matter most to the consumer. The product can then be designed to satisfy these requirements, and specifications reduced to a minimum (if cheaper) for the others. A corollary of specifying product design is that one specifies both its quality standards and, by implication, its production process (which may have to be 're-engineered' to meet the new design and quality standards) and costs.

Marketers continually redesign firms' products, partly to gain competitive advantage, partly to create new products which will make their predecessors obsolete. This practice leads to the idea of a product life cycle, the end of

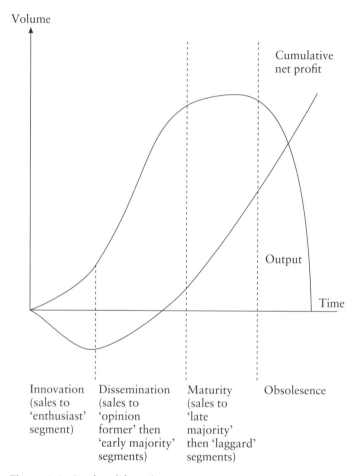

Innovation | Dissemination | Maturity | Obsolesence
(sales to | (sales to | (sales to |
'enthusiast' | 'opinion | 'late |
segment) | former' then | majority' |
| 'early majority' | then 'laggard' |
| segments) | segments) |

Figure 1.6   Product life cycle.

one product's life cycle resulting from the start of another's. Figure 1.6 shows its four phases, the associated level of marketing activity (and spending) usually associated with each and the names of the corresponding consumer segments. Over time, the duration of this life cycle tends to shorten – the product life cycle of microchips is a good example.

Price
In pricing its products a firm has first of all to cover its costs and normal profits, at least in the medium term. Provided this requirement is satisfied, price can be used to help sell products in various ways, most obviously by undercutting competitors' prices. Some firms, for instance grocery retailers such as Aldi and KwikSave, use price as their main marketing tool. This is

most feasible for firms which have high productivity per unit of capital or labour, low overhead costs, low wages, capacity to purchase inputs cheaply, a limited product range, cheap distribution systems (for example telephone banking), and can achieve economies of scale.

In the long term this strategy will be viable only if economies of scale in production reduce average costs of production sufficiently to increase profits, and – crucially – if buyers' demand is price elastic (i.e. buyers are so price-sensitive that increased total sales more than compensate for the reduction in income for each item sold). Firms can adjust the methods and time of payment to increase sales. For instance, by providing consumers with loans, a firm can create a further profit centre (for financial services), capture future buyers (for example Ford promotions in the early 1990s based on com-mitting customers to future part-exchanges) or divide a high-cost purchase into smaller and less daunting instalments. For certain goods, especially luxuries, a high price also is used to promote sales by suggesting a high quality or an exclusive (high-status) product.

In the shorter term, price discounting can be used to maintain sales volume and market share in a buyers' market, or to increase market share (i.e. a part of a market penetration strategy) in the middle and late dissemination stage of the product's life cycle. An indirect way of reducing prices with less risk of provoking price competition is by making 'three-for-two' and similar offers. Early in the dissemination stage it may instead be possible to set prices high, for 'cream-skimming' income from the first purchasers of new product who, as enthusiasts or fashion-conscious buyers (for consumer goods) or firms under competitive pressure (for producer goods), are likely to price-insensitive. At the maturity stage, pricing has generally to be on a cost-plus basis to recoup the initial investment, generate profit and finance future reinvestment.

Place
Place refers to the ways in which products are distributed and hence the places where they are sold. Thus a firm would select whether to distribute its products via wholesalers, retailers (supermarkets, corner-shops or specialists), brokers, franchises (for example Coca-Cola in Malta, Schweppes in UK public houses), an exclusive distributor, tenants (for example in restaurants, pubs), mail order, by a salesforce ('direct sales'), to other manufacturers or services (for example airline or train caterers), consumer networks (Tupperware, Ann Summers, pyramid selling), and so on. An unusual feature of Daewoo's marketing in the early 1990s was that it used 'place' as a marketing tool by selling its cars direct to the public, presenting this as a way of reducing prices and chicanery by 'getting rid of an obsolete com-ponent – the salesman'. Internet shopping is the biggest recent extension of 'places' of sale. The choice of outlets can be used to reinforce the product's image (for example, delicatessen rather than supermarket sales). The 1990s saw an expansion of direct selling through 'clubs' and mail order catalogues. Supermarkets are experimentally reintroducing delivery to customers' homes (which grocers abandoned in 1950s).

Promotions

Promotions are what most people understand by 'marketing'. Davidson (1987) mentions some ninety methods and more will doubtless be invented. The commonest are:

- Adverts, whose chief aim is typically to communicate the benefits of a product, using, besides direct information, such techniques as association, innuendo, cues (i.e. using a few product characteristics to indicate its overall quality, for example by emphasizing that this chocolate is Belgian).
- Branding serves as an aid to consumer recognition, a cue and a barrier to competition. One need only mention such brand names as Coca-Cola or Virgin to illustrate this, or the fad for designer labels in the 1980s.
- Free samples of products, including 'cross-ruff sampling' where one product carries a free sample of another made by the same firm.
- Merchandising, i.e. point-of-sale displays, above all packaging, for example bubble-packs, which at once display the product, give space for text and can be used to make the product look larger than it really is.
- Product placement, i.e. ensuring that one's product appears being used by characters in television programmes or films.
- Sponsorships, for instance charity promotions where the customer is promised that a proportion of their spending by credit will be donated to a good cause.
- Events (such as Hewlett-Packard's Golden Helix award for deserving healthcare projects).
- Public relations and lobbying.

Communications theory explores how these methods work (see Chapter 3). The fundamental promotional task is to develop a mix of methods (a 'promotional mix') which is capable of conveying the messages about product benefits that the firm wishes to convey, which succeeds in reaching the desired audience of potential purchasers, and which appears credible to them. Measuring the effectiveness of promotions is, however, notoriously difficult.

Distribution, sale and consumption

Distribution, sale and consumption of the product occurs next. Sales is a discipline in itself, but in services a recent development is relationship marketing (Christopher *et al.* 1993), whose aim is to produce high customer commitment and contact with the provider through the provider focusing on product benefits over the long term and an emphasis on customer services (Payne 1993). This of course is intended to 'increase profitability through improved customer retention' (Payne 1993: 29).

All preceding stages in the marketing cycle are aimed at producing and managing one event: sales. In addition, the firm can include instructions to try to ensure that consumers use complex products correctly, and provide guarantees, refunds or repairs to rectify faults. Nevertheless, the sale and product consumption remain the most uncertain and unmanageable part of the marketing cycle for a firm. They are fundamentally outside the firm's direct control, always liable to disruption by changes in consumers' own preferences or circumstances (for example, changes in their personal income), by competitors' activities, not to mention the activities of governments and pressure groups, and finally by consumers themselves. By this stage, all that the firm can do is to hope that the benefit received appears to the consumer no less than the benefit which the firm promised in its promotions and no less than the benefit which the consumer was seeking.

Tracking

The last stage in the cycle is to monitor how far the marketing plan was actually implemented and to identify the causes of any success or failures. Tracking is the routine collection, by various methods, of data about the main marketing targets. Most firms have ready-made two systems for collecting data on the most important targets: the cash register (or its electronic equivalents) and the reordering system. In addition, however, many firms set up routine data collection systems to monitor the more qualitative aspects of marketing mix implementation which escape the two basic systems. Vignette 1 illustrates the tracking process of a high street supermarket.

Vignette 1.1   Tracking in a supermarket

What Somerfield checks the till operator for:

- make eye contact;
- smile;
- greet the customer;
- state total (i.e. bill);
- state change given;
- give receipt (offer savings stamps);
- offer Premier Points;
- place card in machine;
- say thank you and good-bye.

The resulting data are usually fed back to:

- managers of each shop, branch, office or other workplace;
- marketing and other functional managers responsible for implementing the marketing plan;
- in larger firms, to regional, national or international headquarters or, for franchises, to the franchiser;
- marketing and other staff responsible for preparing the next situation analysis and marketing audit.

Note that the feedback is to the situation analysis stage not the structural stage of the cycle. As noted, the fundamental structural characteristics of

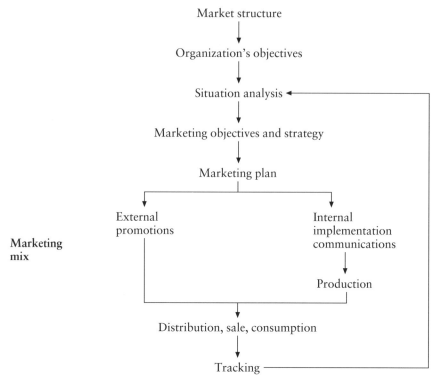

Figure 1.7   Marketing – the commercial archetype.

the market are relatively stable and taken for granted for everyday market-ing purposes. What matters for those purposes is that the firm be able to recognize and respond to unforeseen changes in consumer demand and behaviour, especially those when consumers decide, despite its efforts, not to buy its products. In response to tracking feedback, or simply on a routine timetable, the firm then repeats the marketing cycle, with any necessary adaptations.

Figure 1.7 summarizes this overview of how firms go about marketing in commercial contexts.

In conclusion

Marketing is done in the interests of the organization doing the marketing. How far consumers' interests have to be accommodated depends how demand and supply balance in the market at the time. Marketing occurs on two fronts: externally to purchasers and consumers (and perhaps other audiences such as shareholders or governments), and internally to the firm's own staff. Different firms emphasize and specialize in different aspects of the marketing process, according to the nature of their products or services, and the characteristics of the markets in which they operate. Marketing is not just about selling. It also involves environmental scanning, consumer research, planning, communications and the many other activities noted above.

Questions

1 In what market conditions do firms not face the four conditions which impel them to maximize profits?
2 What does situation analysis contribute to the rest of the marketing process?
3 What is the value of portfolio analysis to firms?
4 What is marketing?

For discussion

To what extent is there a natural community of interest between marketers and 'consumerists' trying to strengthen consumers' influence over what goods are produced and how they are marketed?

Further reading

Christopher, M., Payne, A. and Ballantyne, D. (1993) *Relationship Marketing.* Oxford: Butterworth Heinemann.
Kotler, P. (1991) *Marketing Management.* Englewood Cliffs, NJ: Prentice Hall.
Payne, A. (1993) *The Essence of Services Marketing.* Hemel Hempstead: Prentice Hall.
Porter, M.E. (1981) *Competitive Strategy: Techniques for Analysing Industries and Competition.* New York: Free Press.

2 Marketing – for, against and beyond

Chapter overview

Many people find the idea of healthcare marketing objectionable. This chapter examines the achievements and defects of commercial marketing, showing how both stem from the incentives and organization structures found in conventional markets. It analyses the differences between acceptable and objectionable forms of marketing as a difference between informing and misleading consumers. The structural differences between the quasi-markets found in many public services and conventional markets, and the different objectives which public organizations pursue, necessitate a different marketing model for quasi-market contexts. It outlines that model as a framework for healthcare marketing.

The mass production of taste

Modern marketing derives the design of consumer goods and services from evidence about why users want them and what uses consumers put them too. This approach focuses product design on providing benefits which consumers themselves actually do desire, or can readily be persuaded to. Neither are these benefits limited to the physical, practically functional characteristics of goods and services (for example, how clearly and loudly the radio plays). The benefits which products and services are designed to offer also include more subtle, indirect benefits of a social, symbolic and even emotional nature. A familiar example is that soap, cosmetics, deodorants and other cleansers are designed not only to cleanse and recolour the skin, but also to offer the benefits of presenting oneself as attractive, sophisticated and fashionable, of raising one's self-confidence and apparent social status, and so on.

Commercial consumer marketing succeeds in commodifying quite abstract psychological benefits, such as improving a person's self-image, into a saleable object or service. Over the 1990s, for instance, DIY has been reinvented as a way of making the interior decoration of one's home a fashion statement, not just of effecting routine maintenance and redecoration. A single product or service is thus designed to provide the consumer with many benefits at once, both functional and symbolic.

Because consumers can usually choose alternative products, marketers have to make (or at least, persuade consumers that) these multi-dimensional benefits are distinct from and greater than, those of alternative products. Thus the marketing process results in a requisite variety of products and innovation. Partly for this reason, product design is continually critically reviewed and repeated, resulting in periodic renewal of product designs. Technical innovations are continually converted into consumer goods and services; thus stereo replaced monophonic records, CDs replace records, cassettes replace spool-to-spool tape, digital cassettes replace analogue cassettes and so on. Product design extends to the construction of reliable distribution and maintenance systems (in stark contrast to, say, consumer services in the former USSR), for besides being as attractive as a competing product, a firm's product must be as easily obtainable and maintainable if users are to take it up.

A concomitant of product redesign is continual revision of the product users' consumption habits, of how they use products and their reasons for buying them. Marketers therefore undertake, and continually revise, promotional activity in parallel with the design and redesign of products. At best, this promotional activity informs users how to get the latest products, how to use them and to what benefit. Over time, the cumulative effect is to widen consumers' product knowledge and tastes, making consumers more demanding. The claim that adverts inform the consumer is more true in some domains than others, but most true where promotions concentrate on conveying the technical and performance characteristics of products, and how to obtain and use them. For example, Richer Sounds' promotional material largely does this, and with a bit of humour and style. In such cases promotional materials enable consumers to articulate what goods and services they can use to obtain a given benefit, inform of the alternative possibilities and their respective merits, and what the user has to do to obtain the corresponding benefit. To that extent, promotions educate consumers and enable them to choose more rationally.

The mass production of stupidity

Many forms of marketing give people good reason to doubt the value of marketing for publicly funded health systems. By examining which marketing activities are objectionable from a consumer's standpoint we can distinguish which marketing activities are worth considering for use in publicly funded health systems from those which are not. We can also diagnose what conditions cause the objectionable forms of marketing, so as to prevent their infecting the health sector.

One objectionable activity is that of developing and promoting 'high value-added' services. To increase the sale of extras, marketers try to persuade consumer to purchase the most highly specified and highly processed products that the market will bear, in some cases overspecified to an extent which reduces (other) benefits. For instance, 'top of the range' cars' bodywork 'extras' frequently decrease performance and increase fuel consumption. In the food sector, marketers promote high value-added fatty and sugary processed foods instead of fresh, minimally processed food. A large proportion of marketing promotes not consumer goods but what can be called consumer 'bads': goods such as tobacco, alcohol, fatty foods and cars which if overconsumed, or in some cases consumed at all, positively harm the consumer. A survey of city-centre advertising in Belfast in 1987 showed that 36 per cent (by number) and 40 per cent (by poster area) of city centre adverts promoted processed foods, confectionery, alcohol and tobacco (Boydell *et al.* 1991). This pattern of advertising activity remains.

With wasteful production comes inefficient consumption. Long-known examples include wasteful packaging; not only redundant packaging (for example, the sealed bottle within a bubble-pack or box) but packaging intended to prevent the consumer using all the product, such as the brush or aerosol tube which does not reach the bottom of the bottle (Packard 1960), meaning that the consumer must buy a replacement sooner. Disposables are another example. There is, for example, no evidence that cross-infection is lower with disposable than with multi-use (autoclavable) syringes. Planned obsolescence enables marketers to shorten the product life cycle – and thus raise the volume of replacement sales – of functionally adequate goods. Computer software, particularly for relatively simple purposes such as office software or operating systems is a good example, in which marginal 'developments' are gradually added to outdate the basic product. The purpose is to induce the consumer to purchase a greater volume of goods and services than necessary to deliver a particular benefit, and at a greater cost. Both these forms marketing have obvious implications for the rate at which natural resources are wasted.

Although marketers make much of consumer 'choice', the range of consumer choice of goods and services is strictly limited to what firms decide to offer. The fundamental limitation of this range is to the goods which can be sold on a profitable scale and which consumers can afford to buy. Other consumers get little choice or none. Of 1223 new pharmaceutical products marketed between 1975 and 1997, for instance, 4 were designed for use in developing countries and another 13 for treating tropical infections (Davis 2000). But even among the consumers who do have a choice, marketers tend to converge on designing essentially similar products to appeal to mass markets ('me-too' products). As time passes, product differentiation diminishes (the mass car market is a good example), leading to convergence on lowest-common-denominator, 'middlebrow' design.

This brings us to marketers' habit of promoting product on entirely specious grounds, for instance by associating smoking with sporting prowess or habitual chocolate-eating with attractiveness. Not only are these marketers using entirely the symbolic, not its functional, aspect to promote the product but the only connection between the symbol itself and the product is the one the advert makes by association – and a pretty ludicrous association too, in many cases. Branding is largely the attempt to establish such associations in the consumer's mind, giving the firm a monopoly in the goods which carry those associations (Klein 2000). The claim that adverts inform consumers is palpable nonsense in the case of those adverts which rely on such spurious or false associations as, say, most car adverts do. The success of this strategy is most visible when a technically inferior product outsells a technically better product (VHS versus Betamax video formats is a case often cited; and Microsoft versus Linux computer operating systems). The marketing of McDonald's foods, for instance, is a triumph of image promotion over nutrition, of symbol over function.

The extreme case is when marketing involves corruption, fraud or just sharp practice (Vignette 2.1 – all real cases).

Vignette 2.1   Twelve sharp practices – management consultants

1 Sending a senior partner to sell the consultancy and gain the work, then a junior to do it.
2 Sending a junior to do the work, whilst charging the rate for a senior.
3 Sending a senior to do work which a junior could do equally well, and charging the senior's rate.
4 Pricing at a per day rate instead of a rate for the whole job. Projects show a remarkable tendency to expand under this system.
5 Using research or review work as a selling opportunity ('spivving' – the Market Research Society Ethical Code forbids this practice).
6 Charging full consultancy rates plus expenses for meetings they have proposed – which you only discover when the bill arrives. If they are sharp they will charge you for giving them lunch into the bargain.
7 Charging expenses 'as incurred' not at a predetermined rate.
8 Charging both you and another of their clients for expenses for the same round trip to visit both. A really sharp consultancy will charge both clients for the same whole day.
9 Starting at a modest daily charge then gradually increasing it unilaterally as the project continues.
10 Disparaging ostensible 'partners' with an eye to getting the next piece of work for themselves alone.
11 'Poison pills' – constructing the consultancy project so as to lead the client on to buy still more consultancy to put right problems 'found' – or caused – by the original consultancy project.
12 'Bundling' consultancy, administration, support services and expenses charges etc. into a single fee to inflate and conceal the daily consultancy rate.

Not only commercial but some charitable and not-for-profit marketers go in for 'spivving'. Oxfam's 'Public Awareness Survey' HA74 of March 1998, for instance, consisted of eight factual questions followed by a request to give, a banker's order and freepost envelope. In this case, the addresses of possible donors were apparently obtained from commercial market research surveys (another dubious ploy).

Lastly, there is the common practice of misleading the consumer, whether with half-truths or inconspicuous or obscure 'small print' conditions. In other cases, marketers attempt to deflect or pre-empt the critics' demands for higher product quality, for instance by marketing products as 'green' or 'healthy'. However, many cereal bars, for example, have similar fat and sugar levels to chocolate (Boustani and Mitchell 1990). Another example of illusory benefits is that Dixons brands its UK-made electrical goods as 'Matsui', presumably to suggest Far Eastern provenance and, by innuendo, better design and technical quality than consumers associate with British electronics. A more subtle effect is that marketing homogenizes language, weakening its capacity to distinguish the important from the banal. From one side, German commentators long ago noted the *Banalisierung* ('banalization') of language in political marketing. 'War', for instance, becomes 'conflict'. From the other side, marketers overdramatize the most trifling product changes. It is almost a rule-of-thumb that advertising phrases mean the opposite of what they say; 'new' usually means 'much the same', 'traditional' means 'invented by our marketing department', 'style' (as in 'Spanish-style') means 'unlike', 'up to' means 'less than' and so on. An old favourite is the formula; 'Save up to £590 on this computer . . . price £1319'. One could save £1319 by not buying the thing at all. (For some pithy replies to marketing nonsense, see the Adbusters website at <http://www.adbusters.org>.)

Such marketing tries to persuade consumers to buy more goods than necessary to achieve a given benefit or even to buy goods which will harm them, to buy for spurious, absurd or even fraudulent reasons, and when they would not have wanted to if they were more fully informed. To mislead consumers in this way is the mass production of stupidity.

Needs and nonsense

What differentiates the two kinds of marketing? The first kind enables the user to become better informed, more critical and demanding, and to acquire wider and more discriminating tastes and habits of consumption. It involves the design, production and distribution of more diverse goods and services which meet these requirements and serve multiple purposes for the consumer. The second kind does the opposite. One difference lies in the quality of goods and services which result. The other lies in whether marketing tends to make consumers' demands more or less rational. In attempting to bamboozle consumers, the second kind of marketing tries to make them less able to distinguish critically between goods and services that really will and those that will not produce the benefits which they want. It attempts to make the consumer less rational, in the sense of factually less well-informed about products' characteristics and benefits. Another way of expressing this is to say that the second kind of marketing tries to get consumers to demand goods which they do not actually need for the purpose of meeting their original desires or, in some cases, at all.

The difference lies, therefore, in a distinction between demands and needs, where 'needs' means 'rational demands', and 'rational' means 'consistent and well-informed'. The distinction stands out when a person wants a good or service only as the means to some further end. Healthcare provides many examples. Mostly, healthcare is not especially convenient or pleasant to consume. People usually do so only as a means to maintaining or restoring their health. What a person needs is the treatment that works most effectively. But they might ill-informedly demand a treatment that would actually be ineffective or, in the long run, harmful. In this case, the patient's demand for treatment is a purely instrumental demand. They make their demand because they hold certain assumptions about what treatment will best alleviate their disease. Depending on the case, these factual assumptions may be true or false. (Evidence-based medicine tells us which.) In this case, the patient's demand is irrational because it rests on false assumptions: they demand one treatment but need another (cp. Sheaff 1996). So, unlike most marketing theory which simply equates them (cp. Katz 1988), there is an important difference between needs and demands. People often demand services they do not need; but equally, they often fail to demand services or goods that they do need, perhaps because they are unaware of their existence or benefits. The first type of marketing thus assists in meeting users' needs for products and services. The second type frustrates these needs by promoting irrational demands.

Let us assume that the reader is interested in healthcare marketing as a health service user (as we all are, even those who need only preventive healthcare). Whatever commercial marketers may do, we shall take at face value the idea that the sole purpose and justification of marketing is as a contribution to meeting consumers' needs (here, for healthcare). Indeed this is a fundamental rationale for publicly funding health systems and for healthcare professionals' role in them. But we maintain the distinction between demands and needs (cp. Bradshaw 1972) by defining needs as *rational* demands, in contrast to the irrational demands which much (but not all) marketing creates.

The most general objection to healthcare marketing associates marketing with markets, and both with the undesirability of markets in healthcare. There are two main reasons why markets are undesirable in healthcare. One is the market entry problem. The people who most need (and demand) healthcare are for that very reason those who are least well placed to earn the money required, in a market system, to buy it. The other reason is information asymmetry. Because of the complexity of healthcare, its consumers mostly lack the knowledge necessary to choose the healthcare that will most effectively meet their desire to preserve or restore their health.

We have now seen that marketing at its worst increases the information asymmetry, but at best might reduce it. The solution to the market entry problem is either to nationalize the health system or to set up a quasi-market. This leaves the problem of how to design these post-market structures so as to incorporate the kinds of marketing activity which make consumers' demands better informed and which assist in devising the corresponding innovations in services. Such marketing activities are both compatible with and relevant to the publicly funded health systems. Indeed, they offer a positive benefit of helping the post-market institutions to meet users' healthcare needs more successfully than markets do. The other kind of marketing, which promotes irrational demands (and the corresponding products) rather than rational demands (needs) is inimical to a publicly funded health system. It should be systematically excluded from nationalized and quasi-market health systems. We have now to ask, therefore, which characteristics of a conventional market tend to stimulate the forms of marketing that reduce information asymmetry, and which stimulate the mass production of stupidity.

Marketing in markets

In conventional markets the incentives for perverse marketing activities arise from a combination of three structural characteristics. Firms have an incentive to maximize sales; sales are effected voluntarily solely by persuasion of the consumer; and firms receive all their costs, profit and other expenditure bundled up in a single sum of money which the consumer pays the firm.

To begin with the incentive to maximize sales, 'marketing activities usually precede selling activities because the purpose of marketing is to prepare the way for sales' (Helms *et al.* 1992: 6). As Berkowitz says: 'the ultimate goal of any marketing strategy is to affect a consumer's purchase decision' (Berkowitz 1996: 177). Because the consumer purchases voluntarily, what is necessary for the firm is to get the consumer to part with their money. What methods are used – producing a higher-quality project or tricking the consumer – is a subordinate, purely instrumental question. Indeed, stupefying a customer's critical faculties is more likely to achieve success than sharpening them. The incentive to sell thus motivates both good marketing practice and bad, from market research thought to product design, promotions, in short the whole marketing cycle. *Selling is not the whole of commercial marketing activity, but it is the whole point of commercial marketing activity.* Although Kotler (1991) says, 'the objective of marketing is to make selling superfluous', he does not do so to criticize maximizing sales or profits, but to advocate using other marketing tools so as to make aggressive selling unnecessary (and generate more sales rather than fewer).

In turn, the commercial motive for selling is profit maximization. In conventional markets, a firm's profit is included within the single, undifferentiated sum of money paid as the price for a product or service. From this sum the first has to meet all its production cost. The owners' and managers' disposable cash is the unspent residue. This familiar arrangement produces the following incentives, which for consumers have a mixture of perverse and beneficial effects. To maximize the residual income, firms must, as far as they can:

• maximize the quantity of units sold, i.e. sales (see above);
• maximize 'value added' to each unit. Provided customers can be persuaded to buy, each additional embellishment to a product is a further saleable entity (for example the car sunroof, CD player) from which, with judicious costing and pricing, extra profit can be made;
• maximize the price of each unit, subject to the constraints of competing firms' prices, what buyers are able to pay and how astutely they 'play the market';
• minimize input costs for each unit, whether by reducing labour inputs (good for the consumer, bad for the worker) or the quantity of raw materials (good for all except the raw materials producer) or product quality (bad for the consumer);
• concentrate on selling units with the biggest residual. Loss-leading may be possible as a short-term tactic but in the long run a firm can only market products yielding a nett residual income.

It is not simply the owners' and managers' desire for personal income that compels a firm to maximize profits (and therefore sales). The four necessary and sufficient structural conditions for profit-maximization as a firm's prime objective are that:

• firms derive their income from sales;
• firms compete for sales;
• investment is necessary to defend, let alone increase, the firm's capacity to compete for sales;
• Firms have to generate their own sources of investment.

Investment comes from profits, whether by spending saved past profits or borrowing money and repaying it from future profits. What compels profit maximization is the combination of the four conditions.

The perverse effects which this combination has upon providers' ability to meet patients' healthcare needs are well known. They include maximizing the number and intensity of treatments sold, even unnecessary or iatrogenic treatment. Illustrating both points, South Korean primary healthcare doctors receive a fee for each patient visit and each act of prescribing. Accordingly they commonly maximize the 'value added' in treating influenza by prescribing antibiotics (ineffectively, because 'flu is a viral not a bacterial disease). They frequently prescribe one day's medicine and advise the patient to return the next day (Lee 2000). A more subtle perverse effect is that in defining (and marketing) consumer benefits as the effects of buying and using the products which they sell, firms disregard benefits which cannot be made into saleable commodities. In the case of distress goods such as healthcare, the greatest benefit for a consumer is not the benefit which the commodity produces (being cured) but the benefit of not needing the commodity at all (remaining well and not needing to be cured).

There is a particularly wide scope for the healthcare consumer to be misinformed. Healthcare has:

- highly technically complex components;
- considerable uncertainty of outcome;
- technological inadequacies, making some clinical decisions a choice among evils;
- limited scope for post-treatment learning or rectification of errors;
- high emotional loading;
- ill-defined benefits, often long-term or negative and counterfactual ('His prognosis would have been worse had we not . . .');
- consumers whose critical faculties may themselves be compromised by illness.

What is more, the consequences of misinformation can be especially damaging when health is involved.

Above all, there is the market entry problem. Selling only those products, and only at such prices, as yield a residual incomes results in underprovision of services for people who cannot pay such a price (for example chronically ill people, disabled people, poorer people in general). Because they are incapacitated by illness, the people who most need healthcare are least able to undertake market transactions of their own to obtain the money to buy them. Even in the USA, about one-third of the population is in this position to some extent.

Modified markets – quasi-markets

Because the above problems result from the structural characteristics of markets, the policy solutions have tended to focus on replacing these structures with some different system for organizing healthcare. Many governments used the solution of nationalizing the health system, organizing it like a single, huge private firm (i.e. as a monopolistic, hierarchical bureaucracy) and providing healthcare practically free at the point of use. For consumers, this form of nationalization is dramatically superior to a conventional market on two counts. It solves the market entry problem at a stroke, in an administratively simple way. By substituting an expert proxy purchaser (a GP or a 'third-party payer' such as a health department) for the consumer's own information resources, it solves the information asymmetry problem.

The limitations of this solution arise largely because nationalized healthcare provision is still organized on the pattern of a single huge monopoly firm. They include sluggish responses to consumers' reasonable demands even where there is no information asymmetry, tardy innovation, and – for reasons lying outside the health sector – a tendency towards undersupply of healthcare compared with needs (see Chapter 1).

For largely unconnected policy reasons, governments in several countries began reforming such systems into quasi-markets during the 1990s, that is, as structural hybrids between the nationalized model and a conventional market. For consumers, the most important question about health system redesign is how to build upon the nationalized model in a way that not only retains its superiority over a conventional market but also attenuates or removes its most bureaucratic characteristics. Our analysis of the defensible aspects of marketing indicated certain structural characteristics of markets which promote them. Building these structures, as far as possible, into a nationalized health system could therefore be expected to attenuate some of its earlier, bureaucratic characteristics. Conversely, our analysis of the causes of the worst forms of marketing indicates structural characteristics which it is in consumers' interests to exclude from health system reform.

To design a healthcare quasi-market to promote the positive forms of marketing in the interests of patients' needs would would therefore require:

- giving providers strong, contestable incentives to satisfy users' reasonable demands, i.e. needs. Competition is not the same as commerce;
- openness to a range of alternative providers, public, charitable, voluntary, cooperative and user-provided but not commercial;
- slight overcapacity of provision;
- abundant information for users about alternative providers' services and their benefits;
- encouraging users to be aware of their ability to choose providers, and to be demanding, critical and willing to shift suppliers.

To prevent the adverse affects a quasi-market would have to:

- prevent the direct sale of services to consumers, to remove incentives to exploit consumers' information asymmetry;
- prevent profit-maximization being the main incentive facing providers;
- pay providers using pricing units which do not bundle up production costs and providers' income (as residue) into a single payment.

Taken severally, all of these design criteria are practically achievable as various nationalized and quasi-market health systems already demonstrate. What is necessary to get the best for consumers out of healthcare marketing is to implement them in combination.

Modifying marketing

The beneficial and the adverse effects of commercial marketing for consumers depend upon the incentives which firms face, and these incentives depend on the organizational structure of conventional markets. To remove the adverse effects whilst retaining the beneficial effects, at least in healthcare, various forms of quasi-market have been invented. These modified organizational structures require modified marketing practice and,

---

Vignette 2.2   Multi-sectoral marketing

The Bodmin and Wenford Railway runs steam trains for tourists and enthusiasts, and until recently commercial freight trains for a local electrical engineering firm, taking them to and from the Railtrack network. It has been negotiating to take china clay traffic and to extend its passenger line to Wadebridge and Padstow. Organizationally, the railway consists of a commercial company, a voluntary society and a charitable trust. It is operated by a core of paid staff and volunteers. It markets to three main audiences:

- Visitors, mainly holidaymakers in Cornwall, who are the majority of passengers.
- Existing and potential commercial freight customers.
- Volunteers and other enthusiasts, including other railways, the National Railway Museum and so on.

Besides the services described above, its marketing mix addresses these three audience as follows:

- For holidaymakers, over 200,000 leaflets annually containing maps, timetables and notes of what tourist attractions can be reached by the railway are distributed to self-catering establishments, hotels, guest houses, campsites and tourist information centres. Paid adverts are placed in holiday guides and free tourist newspapers, and used to attract coach parties and school visits. Cheap tickets are offered for families, with through-ticketing with Great Western and Wales and West trains.
- Promotional media to volunteers are a newsletter, publicity in railway magazines and the creation of a museum trust.
- Dealings with the engineering firm, china clay company and other potential freight customers are by personal manager-to-manager contact.

For planning reasons it is also necessary to maintain good relationships with North Cornwall Council and Cornwall County Council. Press coverage has been hostile to the china clay traffic but otherwise favourable, and the railway receives irregular but supportive radio and television coverage.

---

codifying these practices, modified marketing models. There are some precedents in the public and voluntary sector for these modified forms of marketing. These modifications use many of the concepts and practices of commercial marketing, but in different combinations, for different (and multiple audiences) and to different ends (Vignette 2.2).

Commercial marketers are adroit at adapting a repertoire of standard marketing models, concepts and practices for different types of organizational setting (industrial marketing versus consumer marketing, different selling strategies and so on). Quasi-markets also exist in many different forms, involving different actors and transactional interfaces, not least in so complex and diverse a sphere as healthcare. At the very least, one would expect different adaptations of marketing to be required for health promoters, general practice, university hospitals, health ministries and so on. We therefore have to devise new marketing models for the different purposes and contexts of quasi-markets generally and healthcare quasi-markets specifically. But how?

The previous section – and a host of marketing textbooks – present various marketing models. A marketing model consists of three elements:

- A set of prescriptions which implicitly say: if you do X, you achieve Y. Thus marketing textbooks imply – and often say explicitly – that if you go about marketing in the ways the book describes, you will sell more, make more profits, and so on. Most marketing texts are cookbooks: one is given a set of instructions and some indication of what the result of following them will be. Often, various case studies are cited to illustrate, so, as critics say, the format is often one of 'proverbs and anecdotes'. True enough; nevertheless, prescriptions of the form 'Do X to achieve Y' are implicitly proposing an (often heavily disguised) causal, predictive theory: actions such as X will, in specified circumstances, produce Y. This theory is the heart of the model. Also implicitly, it makes an empirical, factual claim. The theory can be tested by observing whether, in the stated circumstances, doing X does produce Y or a different set of outcomes. However, that is rarely done in a formal, scientifically researched way. With marketing cookbooks as with ordinary cookbooks; if the recipes often seem to work in practice, that suffices for everyday purposes. The word 'model' is then more apt than the word 'theory', because the prescriptions have been tested only in an informal, rough-and-ready, unsystematic practical way. When a marketing model is offered up as a valid prescription, its proponents are asserting that it rests upon at least informal evidence of that kind.

- In addition, marketing models tend to rely upon certain normative ('moral' or 'political' or 'ideological') assumptions. They assume either that the results of following the prescription are worthwhile, or that the activity of following the prescription is, or both. To pursue the analogy, cooks who use cookbooks assume that the dish which the recipe promises they will produce is worth eating, or at least that pleasure (or some other benefit) is to be had by the act of cooking it. Nearly all marketing textbooks assume that the desirable end or activity is that of commercial profit-maximization.

- In so far as people try to put the prescriptions – or something recognizably similar – into practice, the model also appears to be a description of everyday marketing practice, or, in some cases, practice in the firms which are 'best' at using the model to produce its intended results. Either way, it is taken for granted that the background conditions which the model assumes also hold, or nearly so. Nearly all marketing textbooks assume that the daily practice and background conditions are those of North American or west European markets. Most marketing texts mention this assumption only briefly, if at all. Yet it invariably reappears in a much more potent form in the assumptions about what the ends of marketing activity are. Marketing models (cookbooks) prescribe how to do marketing in order to produce certain effects – customer loyalty, sales, profitability, return on investment and so on. These ends are not chosen arbitrarily. As shown earlier, they are ends which satisfy the incentives which confront firms operating in conventional markets. These incentives in turn reflect the organizational structures and property-relations which make up conventional markets. The most important are the facts that: most people gain their access to goods and services through purchase because they have no other way to obtain these goods and services in such quantities; that they typically gain the money for these purchases by selling their own labour or services; there is private ownership of capital; and shareholders control the firms, through managers.

Marketing models are richer than they seem. Seldom explicitly, but nonetheless powerfully, they presuppose:

• a system of economic institutions and property relations (usually, markets), and therefore
• the incentives which these economic institutions and property relations establish for the organizations operating within them, and therefore
• the ends which the organizations' marketing activities are to serve, from which follows
• a set of assumptions – a theory – about what activities will realize these ends, and hence
• specific prescriptions about how to go about marketing in these circumstances.

For their immediate practical purposes the marketing models that appear in print concentrate on the last two items. But the last two items have a practical point only because of the first three – just as cookbooks only have a point because hungry humans enjoy eating a specific range of foods.

Many marketing texts indiscriminately jumble together these elements of prescription, description and normative standpoint. Our purposes, however, require us to disentangle them. Firstly, their normative assumptions are contestable. The objectives which publicly funded health services are interested in are, at least according to official policy statements, more to do with meeting healthcare needs than with gathering money. Further, the institutional background conditions are different. Instead of conventional markets, quasi-markets exist. Health systems do require ways of making their services responsive to users' demands and needs, but require marketing models which serve different purposes in different institutional conditions. To pursue the cookbook metaphor, health services are in the position of having to discover recipes for cooking vegetarian food using electricity whilst nearly all the available cookbooks are preoccupied with roasting meat on a spit. We have to make a similar revision with marketing models.

Some marketing writers who recognize the narrow, commercial focus of much marketing work try to correct it by broadening the definition of marketing to include public service, voluntary, political or other organizations by minimal adjustments of terms, such as replacing 'sales' with 'exchange' (for example Kotler and Levy 1969). However, this approach is defective. It uncritically equates consumers' demands with what consumers actually need. Healthworkers tend not to; information asymmetry makes the demands-versus-needs distinction important in healthcare because healthcare consumers are capable of misjudging the nature of illness, what interventions are available and their relative effectiveness. The consequences of healthcare mistakes can be painful, disabling or fatal. Further, the second definition (and others like it) can only be applied to an NHS context by stretching the meaning of 'exchange' to the point of emptiness. What, for example, do NHS accident and emergency patients actually 'exchange' for their treatment? Time? Anxiety? Discomfort? And who is accepting these things as one benefit in return for another? If money is being suggested, the route by which it is exchanged is so circuitous and the relationship between what is paid and what is received is so haphazard as hardly to resemble an exchange at all.

A more sophisticated, critical and radical approach is necessary. Realistic and radical redefinition is required, one recognizing the true extent of the differences between commercial and non-commercial settings.

The stronger method, when it is available, is inductively from quasi-market practice, deriving the model as a description of 'best' practice in healthcare quasi-markets. Whilst the criteria of 'best' differ, this aspect of the method of model-building is similar to that of marketing textbooks which abstract their marketing models from 'best' (most profitable) commercial practice. However, this method shows its limitations when, as is the case in healthcare quasi-markets, marketing practice is still scanty and primitive. It is a method which is suited to transferring marketing models rather than innovating them *de novo*.

When induction is not possible, the only method is by a critical theoretical analysis and revision of orthodox marketing models. This method starts from existing, conventional marketing models. It assumes that, at least approximately and under somewhat sanitized descriptions, they do describe practically tested commercial marketing methods. The conversion of these models into models for healthcare quasi-markets involves the following steps.

1 To abstract from the institutions and objectives of markets, and transfer to healthcare quasi-markets, we have first to identify those elements in the conventional marketing models which presuppose and reflect the institutional context of a conventional market (for instance, that consumers nearly always have to pay personally for the services that they use, firms are owned by investors, producers maximize profits, and so on).

2 We then have to respecify the model for quasi-market conditions, in two ways:

  (a) by inserting assumptions that reflect quasi-market conditions (for example where services are inter alia a means of policy implementation, services are provided free at the point of use, and so on). Then we must deduce what difference those changes would make to the content and prescriptions of the marketing model we started from. In this way we modify the conventional marketing model into one that is relevant to quasi-market settings.

  This much modification would produce a marketing model which prescribed how to go about marketing so as to maximize sales, profits and ROI in a quasi-market. Such a model would be relevant to, say, private firms that happened to seek their profits by trading within quasi-markets. Most service providers in quasi-markets, however, are publicly owned and pursue other objectives. Officially, and often actually, their prime objectives are not to maximize profits or sales but to meet consumers' needs for the services they provide (education, healthcare) and to help implement other public policies (for example labour market policy). So, we also have to:

  (b) replace the assumption that profit-maximization is the main objective with the more relevant assumption that the objective is to meet users' needs.

3 Add specific assumptions about healthcare, for example that what distinguishes healthcare is that the workpiece is the patient, mind and body.

What does this approach achieve? A marketing model makes normative assumptions expressing a desirable set of outcomes. It contains a theory stating how to bring those outcomes about. In so far as people actually apply the theory in order to produce the desired outcomes, it also describes their marketing practice. The test of the theory within a marketing model is therefore whether, by applying it, one actually does produce the desired outcomes. By comparing the marketing models for quasi-market healthcare with actual practice, one can therefore establish the following:

- How far health system organizations and managers' implement the marketing model. That reveals how far they pursue the specific outcomes which the marketing model assumes to be desirable. It also reveals how far their organizational structures and managerial practice enable them to undertake the activities which marketing theory suggests are necessary, maximally to meet service users' needs. Conversely, it reveals how practicable it is to implement the marketing models. We can find out empirically whether any practical difficulties arise in implementing the models stem from defects of the models or from other causes in healthcare management, organization and policy.
- In so far as healthcare organizations do implement the marketing models, what effects follow? For the models proposed below, whose purpose is to

meet users' healthcare needs more fully, the relevant effects are whether implementing any of the models does increase the effectiveness of healthcare, makes health services more responsive to users' reasonable demands and promotes health. By examining how far implementing the model actually has these effects (or fails to), one tests the validity of the theory which the model contains.

The first comparison shows how far these new marketing models relate to existing management and organizations in healthcare quasi-markets. The second investigates how far they can claim to be evidence based, a harder question to answer at present. Direct evidence of the effects of implementing the models is as yet scarce because healthcare quasi-markets are relatively new institutions. Much of the necessary research evidence is still missing. Further, much of the evidence that does exist is negative. It tells us more about how to fail at healthcare marketing than about how to succeed. The evidence is also unevenly available; relatively abundant about some aspects of health promotion, patchy in respect of secondary care, thinner still for primary healthcare and healthcare purchasing.

To get started, we first have to generate marketing models which are relevant to quasi-markets in healthcare for the purpose of meeting users' healthcare needs. As noted, we convert commercial marketing models into models for healthcare quasi-markets by replacing the institutional assumptions and the normative assumptions (for example the goal of long-term profit maximization) that presuppose a commercial setting with assumptions that are relevant to quasi-markets (for example goods provided free, public purchasers of services). In this way, the following section produces a marketing model for quasi-markets in general. Although it is rather abstract, the general marketing model for quasi-markets gives a framework which can then be filled out in different, more concrete and specific ways, for each of the different kinds of organization found in a *healthcare* quasi-market. Starting from the general framework, the first halves of Chapters 3–6 then construct specific marketing models for each of the four main types of public healthcare organization that exist in quasi-markets:

- public bodies which purchase healthcare (Chapter 3);
- health promotion organizations (Chapter 4);
- primary healthcare providers (general practices, local clinics and so on) (Chapter 5);
- secondary healthcare providers (hospitals and other forms of long-term inpatient care) (Chapter 6).

Because the practical experience of marketing in healthcare quasi-markets is still limited, these models have a provisional status. To a limited extent they do have direct evidential sources in healthcare practice. They also draw on the evidence on which commercial marketing models rest, but much of that evidence is informal and intuitive rather than systematic. One must therefore be duly cautious in presenting these new models.

Then we can compare theory and practice. As the first sections of Chapters 3–6 present a marketing model, so the second sections attempt to compare the model empirically with the respective practice in a healthcare quasi-market. Evidence on which the analyses draw comes from several sources. Miniature case studies (the vignettes) are used to demonstrate what has been and therefore can be done (Anderson and Near 1983). The commercial marketing model is abstracted from case studies and marketers' self-reported accounts of marketing practice. Evidence about health services structures, incentives and for the situation analyses is largely descriptive, drawing from published data. In much of the NHS, however, the necessary research is missing. There, the last resort is to the informal evidence of the author's own studies, observation, working experience and discussions with NHS colleagues; no substitute for formal research, however. Consequently most of the evidence is from the English NHS, for no better reason than that is where the author has mostly worked, has access to data and contextual knowledge. Yet the British NHS continues to stimulate interest abroad and to that extent can serve as a known reference point for readers elsewhere.

Jargon is a last hurdle. Marketing models have normative assumptions built in. They usually take for granted the beneficence of free enterprise, companies and their marketing. Many health researchers are rightly sceptical of this ideological baggage and the verbiage that carries it. Thus Allsop (1984) objects to the term 'consumer' because patients co-produce healthcare, not just consume it. Here we face a dilemma. Either we invent a new jargon for use in quasi-markets (for instance, substituting 'quasi-marketing' for 'marketing') or we use the standard terms but risk seeming to endorse the political standpoint of most marketing texts. Since this text is trying to derive a new marketing model rather than instruct the reader in a new patois, the lesser evil is to use the standard terms. They mark points of continuity between marketing and quasi-marketing, and we can spell out the differences as they arise. But a new terminology would usefully symbolize the points of no return from commercial marketing, so we briefly return to the jargon question at the end.

We can now reconstruct the standard commercial marketing models.

Marketing in quasi-markets – a general model

Now we reach the most abstract stage of the argument, but one which is necessary for producing a general marketing model for quasi-markets (Figure 2.2, see p. 51). Stepwise we replace the commercially specific elements in the conventional marketing model (see Chapter 1) with alternatives germane to quasi-markets in general. Later chapters can then qualify the resulting general model for different kinds of health organization.

Structural analysis

Firms undertake marketing as a means to realize their commercial objectives (return on investment, market share, and so on). Firms have these profit-maximizing objectives because they rely upon sales to obtain income, they compete for sales, investment gives them competitive advantage and investment is financed out of profits. These often unstated but fundamental determinants make it necessary and, *given* a market system, rational for firms to undertake marketing as they do. Just as commercial marketing reflects market structures, quasi-market structures determine what marketing activities are necessary, possible and rational in that setting. To understand how marketing might have to differ for quasi-market organizations which, we assume, pursue the satisfaction of users' needs rather than profit-maximization, we have to understand how quasi-markets' structures differ from those of conventional markets.

In quasi-markets, a 'third-party' purchaser buys services instead of users. This arrangement dismembers the exchange relationship found in conventional markets. In ordinary markets the distribution channels for goods are normally the same as those for money flowing into the firm, except that the money flows in the opposite direction. In quasi-markets the routes are usually separate (not always; in, for example, the French health system a patient pays the clinic or hospital and then reclaims the cost from a social insurer). Quasi-marketing models have to deal with users and purchasers separately lest each poses different marketing requirements.

Unlike a 'command economy' in which a single hierarchy stretches from government minister to shopfloor worker, a quasi-market organizationally separates the purchasers from the service providers. The purchasers therefore attempt to manage the providers at arm's length, usually through contracts. Quasi-market providers tend to supply three main kinds of service, each with distinct marketing implications:

- Preventive services (for example crime prevention), whose task is to forestall the need for remedial services (police investigations) by using social marketing, anti-marketing, political marketing to change individuals' behaviours, and related policy and activities in other sectors.
- Primary or 'frontline' service providers to whom users have direct access (e.g. primary schools, fire brigade). To these providers, consumer marketing to users is relevant, as is demarketing when demand exceeds service capacity.
- Specialist providers, whom users access directly only via a primary provider (for example higher education, when entry depends on passing school exams; specialist hospital care).

The organizational form of the providers ranges from independent, self-employed individuals (for example chiropractors, legal aid solicitors in the UK), to small partnerships and cooperatives, to industrial-scale hierarchies (for example universities, bus companies). The latter may be privately or publicly owned, or voluntary bodies such as the large charities (for example Médecins sans frontières).

The purchasers are free to change their service providers, using the tacit threat to motivate providers to implement the purchaser's policy objectives, innovate, contain costs and respond to consumer demands. In descending order of immediacy, quasi-markets exploit the following:

- Competition, when alternative providers using similar technology already exist in a given sector (for example, rival bus companies).
- Substitutability, when a given benefit can be provided through different types of organization or technology (for example, vocational training can be provided by college courses or apprenticeships with firms).
- Contestability, i.e. the fact that even when none currently exist, alternative competitors could be established, or permitted or invited, to enter a quasi-market (for example, when a public transport purchaser invites a new bus company to bid for a route).
- Benchmarking, when a purchaser critically compares a given provider with similar services, either elsewhere in the same sector (for example, comparing the costs of building maintenance for a school with the costs in other schools) or with comparable services in other sectors (for example, comparing the costs of building maintenance for a school with building maintenance costs for offices or shops).

Besides purchasing services such as healthcare on users' behalf, governmental purchasing organizations also use the providers to realize government policy, including policies only partially related to the sector in question (for example regional policy, labour market policy, public spending policy). Unlike a conventional market, in which firms' objectives arise spontaneously, incentives in quasi-markets are often constructed deliberately (if not always adroitly) to realize wider policy objectives (for example to raise educational standards, reduce road congestion). In this sense, quasi-markets represent 'managed' or 'planned' competition.

To construct a marketing model for quasi-markets we therefore have to make an assumption about what policy objectives are to be pursued, just as conventional marketers make assumptions about what objectives firms are trying to achieve. One widely used general policy formulation is that the public provision of services, whether through quasi-markets or other institutions, is intended to meet users' needs (Wiggins (1985) quotes some British examples). Taking such objectives at face value implies that we consider what sort of marketing activity in quasi-markets is most likely to help meet service users' needs. Outlining how quasi-marketing can be used as an alternative means to the same end gives a common basis on which to evaluate two approaches to marketing and indeed the two alternative governance structures: markets and quasi-markets. Our aim will therefore be to consider how marketing has to be done in a quasi-market if its prime purpose is to meet users' needs for public services such as healthcare.

We therefore require an account of what needs are, something requiring book-length explanation. All one can do here is state which theory of needs will be used and where the reader can find fuller discussions. The theory defines a person's 'needs' as their 'rational demands' (Sheaff 1996). A person's desires, and the demands which express them, are irrational when they are:

- based on false assumptions about means–ends relationships; for instance, if somebody demands that police patrols be concentrated in wealthy areas because they think (erroneously) that most burglaries occur there;
- inconsistent, i.e. for incompatible things (for example, voters want wider access to higher education and tougher entry standards);
- logically impossible to satisfy (for example, a desire to be someone other than who one is). However, demands which are practically impossible to satisfy at present are not necessarily unreasonable. For instance, it is rational to want a cure for stomach cancer although present-day medical technology cannot supply it.

Although the concept of needs used here places the onus of proof on the policy-maker, expert or other third party to show that a given person's desires are irrational, such a proof can often be made. Indeed, one criterion by which to judge alternative approaches to marketing is according to whether they promote consumer rationality or stupidity (see earlier this chapter). Consumers' demands do sometimes express what they need, but others are corrigible. Just as commercial marketers try to alter consumer demands to make them more profitable, marketers aiming to meet users' needs would try to make them more rational.

Given the foregoing structural characteristics of quasi-markets, the incentives it would be necessary to institute for the purpose of motivating organizations in it to meet users' needs (rational demands) maximally include the following:

- *Outcome-based incentives* rewarding organizations for directly benefiting service users rather than rewarding outputs which produce these benefits indirectly if at all. Thus schools would be rewarded for improving children's knowledge, skills, emotional development and so on, rather than for the number of child-years spent in the classroom.
- *Incentives to prevent need for distress goods*, i.e. to reward services for maintaining their users' health, civil liberties, and so on. This implies making the incentive for maintaining a person's health, safety etc. stronger than the incentive to neglect prevention and to remedy adverse events (illness, crimes, and so on) only once they occur.
- *Incentives focused on the benefit added by service providers.* Many outcome gains and losses in such domains as health and child development are produced not only by public services but also by exogenous factors such as individuals' socio-economic status, their physical environment, their parents' activities, what firms such as television companies do, and so on. This makes it necessary to focus outcome-based incentives only on the outcome *added* by service providers, in the light of how much impact providers can have in the circumstances. That requires a comparison of two measures:
  - how the observed outcome for an individual or population differs between the beginning and end of the period when the service was provided;

- a comparison with what could have been achieved using current best practice. An empirical way to estimate what best practice can achieve is by taking the highest observed levels of outcome gain as a benchmark. But then purchasers must somehow correct this benchmark to allow for the different ways in which the extraneous (confounding) factors affect different service providers' performance. Thus a school which achieved a given level of exam results for children from educationally unfavourable home backgrounds would have achieved a bigger educational gain than a school which achieved identical results for the children of wealthy, educated parents. To make this adjustment, one must firstly quantify what impacts the main confounders have on the outcome to be rewarded. Then one must standardize the figures for each provider's observed outcome gains to allow for the differences in the confounding factors.

  These principles may be relatively straightforward, but not the requisite data collection and analysis. In many domains, techniques for formulating and using such incentives remain underdeveloped. In their absence, proxy measures have to be used. Effective processes (for example, use of the correct therapies, best teaching methods) can be rewarded as a proxy for rewarding the actual outcome *provided* there is independent evidence that the process rewarded does produce the desired outcome (Donabedian 1980).

- *Consistent incentives.* Taken together, the incentives used must not conflict. Strong incentives to contain costs, for instance, can frustrate the main outcomes which providers are supposed to be achieving (for example, by preventing schools' obtaining the necessary teaching materials). Incentives to maximize outcomes should therefore be insulated from any incentives to minimize costs. This implies avoiding the system (found in conventional market) of making providers' income the residue of their income minus costs, i.e. that the direct costs of production (buildings, equipment, energy, consumables) be reimbursed separately and on a different basis from the incentive payments for producing the service's main benefits. To prevent the perverse marketing effects of profit maximization, it is also necessary to remove that incentive itself. This implies financing investment from a source other than future profits. In quasi-markets, an obvious way is to prioritize investment projects according to their predicted impact on services and thus users' needs.

Situation analysis

Customers are central for a commercial situation analysis because, as payers, they are the critical actors whom the firm has to influence in order to achieve its financial goals. Abstracting the general principle, a situation analysis identifies which main actors the marketing organization has to influence and what it has to get them to do to meet its own objectives.

For quasi-market provider organizations, the critical actors are the users of the service or goods produced, and, as a means to that, the sources of the organization's income. To these must be added, as in commercial contexts, bodies (governments, media, competitors, providers of substitute services, and so on) who indirectly influence these critical actors.

Next, the commercial marketer will typically analyse the firm's market position: its sales volumes, sales trends, market shares, the level of effective demand and the firm's bargaining power and so on. That is, it will analyse how far the critical actors are acting as the firm's objectives require. The quasi-market equivalents are the extent to which users take up (i.e. demand) the services which they need. To discover that, a quasi-market organization requires both a needs analysis and a demands analysis.

A needs analysis states what services its users would demand if their demands were well-informed and consistent. Well-informed consumers might demand more of a given service than they now do or less, depending on whether they have underestimated or overestimated what benefits it provides. A needs analysis would also segment the population in service or care groups according to their specific needs and the corresponding service requirements (for example, for schoolchildren, segmentation by age or educational attainment). A needs profile then specifies what range of services each segment needs and in what volumes (for example, how many households there are of different sizes and compositions, and what housing standards apply to each).

To influence these actors, the commercial marketer has to understand who makes the buying decision and upon what criteria of benefit. Similarly, a quasi-market organization requires an analysis based on consumer research showing what benefits its users actually demand (irrespective of whether they really need these putative benefits). It will include evidence showing why consumers prove 'resistant' or 'disloyal' or 'overdemanding'.

Firms segment markets in order to identify the profitable segments and then tailor their marketing mix accordingly. Conventional marketing texts argue that a segmentation is worth making when the resulting segments are profitable, accessible to the firm's marketing efforts and require different marketing mixes. We have assumed that organizations in quasi-markets wish to identify who needs which services, and then target their marketing mix accordingly. This implies that in a quasi-market the fundamental segmentation of users differentiates;

- *Under-users*, i.e. people who do not demand services which they actually need (for example hard-to-reach groups, 'resistant consumers', people for whom the disbenefits of using services are practically prohibitive, such as older people who recall means testing).
- *Overusers* or misusers, who demand more services than they need.
- *Normal users* whose level of demand for services closely matches their needs. They often subsegment into self-users and proxy users for friends or relatives (for example school pupils and parents, respectively).

The last two segments are practically unknown to commercial marketing. For a firm whose objective is to increase income, all potential customers are simply different kinds of underuser. Since quasi-marketers also wish to influence main actors' demands they are likely also to require further segmentations for that purpose (by income, education, lifestyle and so on). These demands depend in turn on the wider determinants which commercial marketers usually explore using PEST analysis. Quasi-markets require a similar analysis, extended to include analyses of what determines users' needs as well.

Competitors are a major determinant of a firm's customers' buying behaviour, which is why firms' situation analyses typically include competitor analyses. In general terms, a competition analysis states any structural 'barriers' to sellers of competing or substitute goods entering or leaving the market (Porter 1981), the loci of competition and non-competition (i.e. whether competitors compete over price, quality, customer service, image, and where they avoid competing), and other firms' inclination and capacity to compete. Because quasi-market providers are also liable to be supplanted by alternatives, competition analysis remains a necessary part of their situation analyses. However, in quasi-markets the nature and intensity of competition results from policy decisions, so the competition analysis has to show:

- what degree of competition occurs (whether competition, benchmarking and so on – see above);
- whether the purchasers or government decide the locus of competition themselves, or let users or their proxies (for example headmaster, GP) choose what provider to use (secondary school, hospital);
- what the loci of competition are;
- how intensively and competently other providers compete.

For firms, the practical point of a situation analysis is to discover how to increase sales and market share and to realize its other objectives. The 'technology' aspect of PEST analysis shows the technologies available for these purposes. One should therefore not interpret 'technology' in a narrow, engineering sense. Relevant technologies include selling techniques (for example e-commerce), ways of producing existing benefits more cheaply and additional saleable benefits. Organizational models of service (for example home banking) are also relevant technologies. Technology therefore includes (Levitt 1976) both 'hard' technologies which automate human work ('technology' in the everyday engineering sense) and 'soft' technologies which replace individualized work with planned, scripted working by protocol (as McDonald's processes its customers (Ritzer 1996)). For quasi-market purposes, the analysis of emergent technologies focuses, we assume, on how far new technologies offer more effective ways of meeting a given type of user need (to learn, to recover, and so on).

Firms conduct marketing audits to evaluate how adeptly they are doing their marketing, given the external market situation. Since quasi-market firms do not sell to consumers, the idea of unique selling points has to be replaced with 'unique need satisfiers' (UNSs) or an equivalent concept. Otherwise, marketing audit applies with few adjustments to quasi-market organizations.

Marketing objectives – strategy

Commercial SWOT and TOWS analyses show the strengths and weakness of a firm's current activities in managing consumers' demands so as to reach its commercial objectives. Because of their different objectives (we assume), SWOT analysis for quasi-market organizations has to assess services according to their strengths and weaknesses in managing users' demands in ways that meet users' needs. For each group of service users it compares:

- the profile of services that users demand with the profile of services that they need. This indicates what promotional objectives are necessary for each user groups;
- the profile of services now provided with the profile that the users need. This comparison indicates the main 'product' (service) objectives.

The only reason for comparing the profile of existing services with those that consumers demand is to predict areas of dissatisfaction, not for the purposes of deciding a marketing strategy.

Policy-makers and managers (for example those in UK or the Netherlands health systems) often fear that such analyses will show that users' demands are too great to meet given other policy objectives such as containing public expenditure. Certainly, firms' marketing objectives usually require them to alter their products, services and methods of provision in line with their customers' demands. But despite the rhetoric of consumer sovereignty, firms rarely respond to consumer beliefs and preferences as they are. Firms go to enormous lengths to change them, adopting promotional objectives of changing consumers' demands into forms which the firm can meet profitably (usually by stimulating demand and weakening consumer resistance). Similarly, our account of users' needs implies that quasi-market organizations do not have to accept users' demands uncritically either.

Figure 2.1 shows the possible combinations of needs and demands facing a quasi-market organization and the implied marketing strategy.

'Demarketing' means a promotional strategy of reducing service use by re-educating misinformed demands into needs. It includes social marketing aimed at changing users' knowledge, attitudes, motivations, patterns of service use and consumption. Where users need services but do not demand them, the more familiar strategy of redesigning services and promoting uptake (through advertising and so on to stimulate demand) applies. When users' demands happen to match their needs, a relatively passive strategy of informing patients of what service exists and how to use it applies, without attempting to stimulate larger demand. Quasi-market organizations' marketing strategies are likely to include more social marketing and demarketing than firms use, and to use strategies for stimulating demand more selectively than firms do.

Do users need service?

		Yes	No
	Yes	Minimal 'provide and inform' strategy	Demarketing strategy
Do users demand service?	**No**	Promotional strategy	Ignore or withdraw

Figure 2.1   Quasi-marketing SWOT analysis and strategies.

Marketing grids show firms how to convert the situation and SWOT analyses into specific marketing strategies. They vary according to what specific circumstances they take into account, how they characterize these conditions and how they articulate the range of possible marketing strategies. Commercial firms use portfolio analyses to differentiate consumer demands which they satisfy profitably from those which they cannot. The former they try to meet; the latter they either try to convert into the former using both promotions and product redesigns, or abandon. Each cell of such a grid indicates for each product or market what strategies the firm should pursue in order to meet its objectives. To generalize, business grids recommend distinct marketing strategies for each combination of values of two variables: market 'attractiveness', and the firm's capacity to exploit these opportunities. Business grids presuppose that firms can enter or leave markets and that they face competition. These assumptions apply to some quasi-market organizations and not others. Some quasi-market providers (for example infant schools) have to provide a full range of services for all their user populations. They have little freedom to enter or leave spheres of activity; others do. Some quasi-market organizations (for example public transport providers) compete directly, others not at all. Different adaptations of business grid – or none – are therefore relevant to different types of quasi-market organization. The only way to unravel this question is organizational type by organizational type in later chapters.

Marketing planning

A commercial marketing plan specifies the firms's marketing mix and how the firm will implement it. In quasi-market organizations a marketing plan serves the same purpose.

Each item in a quasi-market organization's marketing mix is likely to have some characteristics in respect of which users' demands are a good proxy for users' needs. For others the reverse will apply. Strictly speaking, the comparison of users' demands with needs has to be made empirically point by point. However, users' demands are most likely to match their needs in those aspects of services in which users' knowledge is as valid as or better than that of managers, professionals or policy-makers, namely:

- Personal costs to users of using the service – disruption to other activities, time, expense, effort.
- What users want to know about the service and whether the information they get is relevant and intelligible to them.
- Social interactions whilst using the service – whether staff were helpful, kind, polite, attentive.
- Other familiar, ancillary aspects of the service, for example the quality of meals, building cleanliness and decoration.
- What benefits or arguments will induce them to take up the service voluntarily.

Where users' demands are a good proxy for their needs, the marketing mix can be planned by 'reading off' the results of consumer research into what users demand and why (from the situation analysis, if made on the lines above). Thus far, marketing planning methods are the same in both commercial and quasi-market circumstances.

When users' demands do not reflect their needs, the way to plan marketing mix is to use technical research, not consumer research, to decide what marketing mix to use. This is most likely in respect of:

- What outcome can be achieved for users of this kind.
- What technical intervention is necessary to achieve this gain (for example, what standards of vehicle design, what pedagogical approaches).
- Legal requirements (for documentation, consent, insurance, and so on).
- What preventive measures are necessary to forestall the need for distress goods (for example health promotion, routine maintenance).
- What information the user will need to be able to access the service, make full use of it and, where necessary collaborate in providing the service itself, for example by private study.

In these areas, the method of marketing planning is to use technical advice (evidence-based teaching methods and so on) to design the benefits that services are intended to deliver, the models of services and techniques of provision, and the concomitant promotional mix.

Marketing mix

McCarthy's (1978) original list of marketing mix variables, the 4Ps, was devised for a manufacturing context. Although not so daring as to challenge the alliteration, Bitner (1989) did add the variables of people, physical resources, and psychological interaction when extending the idea of marketing mix to (commercially provided) services, making 7Ps. Being inherent characteristics of consumer products and services, the 7Ps all apply those which quasi-markets supply. The principle of deliberately planning, selecting and combining these items therefore applies to quasi-market organizations too.

In regard to its *product* (or service), a quasi-market organization has not only to decide what forms of service delivery are most effective for each segment (for example, which teaching methods are most effective at achieving literacy among primary school children, which vaccine and outreach programmes give highest immune coverage). That can be found by combining the needs analysis with the conspectus of technologies in the situation analysis. Since providers in a quasi-market are liable to replacement, they have also do decide what UNSs the product is to have, i.e. what distinctive benefits it gives the user and how this benefit is differentiated. Additionally, products' technical specification must suffice for the purposes to which users put the product (for a car, reliability, luggage space and so on). However, people also use products as symbols of their taste, lifestyle and social status. Products become such symbols whether or not their makers intend it. The same occurs with public sector services.

In services, the main *psychological impact* comes from the workers with whom the user deals. To design and manage this psychological impact (for example, promoting users' self-confidence, avoiding patronizing staff behaviour towards patients) necessitates planning how to select and train *people* to deal with users in ways that promote an organization's marketing and other, wider objectives. The same applies to the *physical resources* (food, clothes, equipment and decoration, signs, letterheads, uniforms and so on) used in providing services. *Place* of service provision is itself an important physical sign of the nature and quality of the service (compare living with support at home with living in an elderly persons' home), in quasi-markets as much as conventional markets.

The principles and methods of communicating *promotions* to consumers are also in essence the same in quasi-markets as elsewhere, although the message content is likely to differ. Quasi-market organizations are also more likely to use demarketing, social marketing and anti-marketing promotions. We have also assumed that there is no place in quasi-market organizations' promotions for the techniques of obfuscation, deception and trickery found in some commercial advertising.

Price serves four roles in commercial marketing:

- As income. In the long term (allowing for loss-leaders, marginal-cost pricing, transfer pricing and other short-term expedients), market prices must at least cover production costs. Quasi-markets, however, have a wider range of providers (see above), making a wider range of payment options available – grants, budgets, subsidies, support in kind, and so on – which do not always reflect the direct costs of production (for instance, when the provider is a voluntary body or relative).
- The pricing unit determines what incentives an organization faces. One point of constructing quasi-markets is to confront providers with incentives

(for example, to provide low-cost social housing) not available in conventional markets.

- As the cost which buyers pay to get the product or service. Firms frequently design products so that they can be produced and sold for a price which market research indicates buyers are able and willing to pay (for example by reducing the service specification). Such firms thus design their products' physical (besides financial) disbenefits to the user with a view to minimizing them given the production cost limits. Although quasi-markets remove money-prices from the relationship between provider and user, the physical disbenefits of using a product or service cannot be abolished in the same way. Quasi-market organizations must also plan to minimize them.
- As a symbol of entitlement to a certain quality of product and service or, for certain luxury goods, of status or 'exclusivity' (i.e. exclusion of poorer consumers).

In quasi-markets the money-price of services falls largely to the 'third-party' purchasers. The practical and symbolic costs fall to the users. In regard to the former, it is obviously desirable to minimize transaction costs, facilitate statistical monitoring and pool the risks of providing services for the unpredictable occasional high-cost user (the dyslexic child who needs extra one-to-one teaching, the disabled resident who needs special alterations to her house). This suggests that the unit of pricing in quasi-markets be made as large as possible consistent with focused incentives and with segmentation, i.e. that service contracts be awarded as far as possible for care groups not individual users. The real, practical cost of the services (time taken to access and use the service, disruption of the user's domestic or working regime, stigmatization and so on) falls on the user and, sometimes, their family and friends. Preserving alliteration, we might label this the 'penalty for users'.

In quasi-markets the separation of user and payer therefore implies a marketing mix of 8Ps not 7Ps.

Implementation

Most firms implement their marketing plan predominantly through their internal managerial hierarchies (bureaucracies). Most quasi-market providers (schools, hospitals and so on) have essentially the same organizational structure: hierarchies of salaried employees.

Quasi-markets also use two further governance structures which firms use too (but much less) for implementing their marketing plans. In quasi-markets the production of goods and services is delegated to organizationally separate providers, usually by subcontracting as term 'purchaser' suggests. Of growing importance in quasi-markets, however, is the use of networks to implement policy and provide services (Kickert *et al.* 1997). Networks usually include voluntary and informal, besides public and commercial, providers. Members are linked, not by line management structures nor, usually, contracts but by ad hoc arrangements for mutual assistance and support-in-kind. For example, schools and health educators may arrange health education sessions for pupils, without any money changing hands, just because both sides have a common interest in doing so. Instead of exchanges of goods for money there may be returns of favours, assistance in kind or barter; and when services are exchanged for money, it is not necessarily for sums that reflect the cost of producing the service. Instead of 'contract', the term 'covenant' can be used for any nexus of these kinds. In quasi-markets, then, the 'make-or-buy' decision discussed in conventional marketing contexts turns into a 'make-or-buy-or-covenant' decision.

Tracking

In firms, tracking serves to make staff accountable to managers, and managers to shareholders for implementing the marketing plan and thereby helping realize the firm's wider objectives. In both markets and quasi-markets, one purpose of tracking data is to trigger rewards or penalties for those who actually provide services. But tracking systems in quasi-market organizations would differ in what substantive variables they tracked, because quasi-market organizations pursue such policy objectives as meeting users' needs for services rather than mainly financial objectives. In quasi-markets, tracking would therefore be directed towards 'real side' (non-financial) data about what impacts the service had on users' needs, demands and behaviour. The policy of letting users select their service provider, and the interests of public accountability more widely, create a presumption in favour of making all tracking data accessible to the public unless there is a compelling counter-argument (for example, users' wishes for confidentiality).

In firms, the practical use of tracking data is to enable corrective action when marketing objectives are not met, and to set more ambitious objectives when they are. Isolated implementation problems can be dealt with at individual user level (for example, by dealing with complaints, offering compensation or redress). Recurrent problems require a revision at organization level of how the marketing plan is implemented, of the plan itself or of the situation analysis on which it was based. The principle that tracking data should trigger this sort of 'error recognition' also applies in quasi-markets.

Figure 2.2 outlines the generic marketing model which results when we abstract from the commercial setting and transpose the principles into a quasi-market context.

From quasi-markets in general to quasi-markets in healthcare

Organizations pursuing different objectives through different organizational structures require different marketing models. Each of the next five chapters begins by outlining a theoretical model of the type of marketing that the healthcare organization would have to undertake, if its objectives

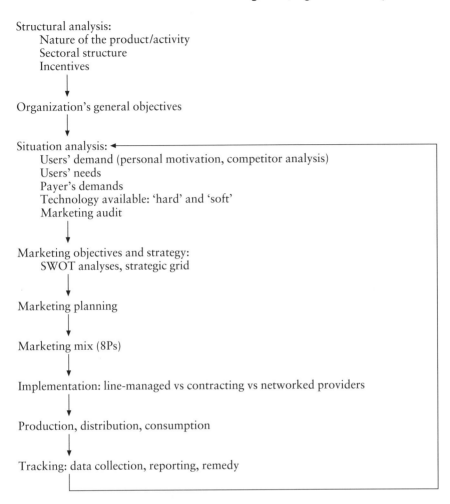

Structural analysis:
    Nature of the product/activity
    Sectoral structure
    Incentives

Organization's general objectives

Situation analysis:
    Users' demand (personal motivation, competitor analysis)
    Users' needs
    Payer's demands
    Technology available: 'hard' and 'soft'
    Marketing audit

Marketing objectives and strategy:
    SWOT analyses, strategic grid

Marketing planning

Marketing mix (8Ps)

Implementation: line-managed vs contracting vs networked providers

Production, distribution, consumption

Tracking: data collection, reporting, remedy

Figure 2.2   Marketing – general model for quasi-markets.

were really to maximize its ability to meet patients' needs for healthcare. In doing so we temporarily assume away all the real-life defects of health system structures and implementation deficits that prevent this happening in reality. We assume that the organizational objectives which a quasi-market produces are benign, not perverse. But having been critical and sceptical about commercial marketers' objectives, we cannot be so naïve as to assume that healthcare organizations' objectives will fortunately coincide automatically with their patients' needs at every turn, or that implementation and management failures never occur.

In the second section of each chapter we correct the deliberate naïvety of the theoretical model. We compare the theory with current NHS practice, showing how far NHS organizations apply the relevant parts of marketing theory and practice. In so far as NHS practice resembles the theory, it illustrates how far the relevant marketing model has been tried in practice, at least in one health system. If it has not been implemented to any great extent, we can then consider why not. In so far as the relevant marketing model has been implemented, we can then ask how far it has had the effects which the theory implicitly buried in any marketing model predicts.

In conclusion

The difference between objectionable marketing and its opposite is that the latter informs consumers but the former stupefies them. Both effects arise from the incentives with which markets confront firms. One purpose of providing public services through a quasi-market is expressly to meet users' needs. Consumers' needs are their rational demands, i.e. the demands they would have if they were well informed and consistent. By removing the specifically commercial assumptions and objectives from the commercial marketing model and replacing them with assumptions that apply to quasi-market services and prioritize users' needs, we can produce a general model of marketing for public services in quasi-markets.

Questions

1 What kinds of marketing promotion tend to be informative, and what kinds misinform consumers?
2 What factors have fuelled the rise of consumerism?
3 How do quasi-markets different from traditional 'command economy' public hierarchies such as the central civil service or an army?
4 How are quasi-markets made policy-responsive?

For discussion

What would a code for 'ethical marketing' stipulate?

Further reading

Douglas, M. and Isherwood, B. (1996) *The World of Goods*. London: Routledge.
Klein, N. (2000) *No Logo*. London: Flamingo.
Nader, R. (1965) *Unsafe at Any Speed: The Designed-in Dangers of the American Automobile*. New York: Grossman.
Packard, V. (1981) *The Hidden Persuaders*. Harmondsworth: Penguin.

3 Marketing for healthcare commissioners

Chapter overview

Healthcare in most developed countries is financed by healthcare purchasing organizations – health authorities, sick-funds and so on – rather than by patients themselves. Healthcare purchasers' role in the health system includes responding to the problems of:

- information asymmetry – patients are less well informed about healthcare than professionals and healthcare providers are;
- patients being, consequently, in a relatively weak position to influence professionals and healthcare providers.

The chief marketing role of healthcare purchasers is to act as a proxy for the patient to overcome these problems. This chapter explains the marketing model which this role requires, and then compares it with the practice of NHS healthcare purchasers.

Marketing theory for healthcare commissioners

Structure, objectives and incentives

Healthcare has three characteristics with marketing implications for its purchasers in a quasi-market. One is a market entry problem, whose solution is for a third party either to provide such services in kind (charities, voluntary organizations, employers, command-economy state systems) or to purchase them (employers, sick-funds, quasi-market state systems) on the users' behalf. These purchasers are the agents, at least ostensibly, of healthcare users. As explained in Chapter 2, there is in healthcare an information asymmetry between users and providers, which puts users in a weak bargaining position *vis-à-vis* healthcare providers. The objectives of the healthcare purchaser acting to meet users' needs would therefore be to act as the perfect agent of an imperfect principal, the user. 'Perfect agent' means that the purchaser would act as a competent, well-informed, assertive negotiator in buying users access to the healthcare they need. In descending order of impact upon individuals' health, the needed services are health promotion (through inter-sectoral anti-marketing campaigns), primary care services (both clinical pre-vention and treatment), and secondary care. The purchaser must also ensure that the services provided actually are effective and responsive to users, and secure redress for users in the event of mishap or provider's negligence.

The other side of healthcare purchasers' marketing activity is to obtain the necessary money. Sick-funds and charities, but not public bodies, re-quire methods which are closer to the marketing methods of a conventional firm. Studies are scarce (but see Wollnitz 1983), indeed there is a big gap in healthcare marketing literature here.

An obvious solution to the information asymmetry problem is for the purchasers to reward healthcare providers, and themselves be rewarded, according to the extent to which they achieve for their population such health benefits as are achievable. The principles and difficulties have already been outlined in Chapter 2. In healthcare, one main difficulty is that techniques for measuring health status and changes therein remain underdeveloped and extremely complex, as various texts explain (see, for example, Bowling 1991). Because health services process people, many of the relevant out-comes are inescapably ill defined (Harrison 1997). Estimating what health status the most technically competent healthcare organization could achieve, and even what health impact a provider actually achieved, is also complex (see Chapter 2). Nevertheless, as these difficulties are solved, it will become practical to pay healthcare organizations according to the health outcome they produce. However, the fallback method of paying healthcare organiza-tions according to how widely evidence-based methods of providing services are used applies more readily at provider level than to purchasers.

To remove the perverse incentives of a conventional market it is also neces-sary to separate these incentive payments from the other variable costs of service production (basic pay, consumables, energy, equipment, and so on), and both from the funding of investments. Purchasers, however, pass on the second and third of these to the actual service providers. This implies that the purchasers would receive an incentive payment with two elements:

- A payment for procuring the most effective healthcare they can on users' behalf, i.e. for successfully overcoming users' information asymmetry. This payment would be analogous to the incentive payments to providers for effective healthcare.
- A payment reflecting users' satisfaction ratings with the services the pur-chaser have obtained, or proxies for these ratings (for example, levels of complaints, waiting times, use of private healthcare), to reward purchasers for bargaining successfully on users' behalf.

To prevent these two payments' obstructing one another, they would have to be calculated and paid separately.

Situation analysis

A situation analysis assembles the evidence required for deciding what marketing objectives and mix a healthcare purchaser should get its providers to implement in order to meet users' healthcare needs. Because they delegate much healthcare marketing to providers, much of the detailed situation analysis is better made by the providers who do most of the marketing work intended to realize the purchaser's wider objectives. What remains is the truncated situation analysis itemized in Table 3.1.

Evidence about the *profile of user demands* can be discovered by consumer research (see Chapter 8), directly asking samples of users besides summarizing such sources as user complaints. The obvious research questions are: what services users think ought to be purchased, where they should be provided, which are the best and worst providers locally, sources of satisfaction

Table 3.1 Situation analysis for healthcare purchasers

Actions the purchaser depends on	*Factors determining these actions*
Users' demands	Health behaviours, patterns of service demand and utilization Factors promoting healthy and unhealthy health behaviours and conditions of life User mis/information about health and healthcare
Users' needs	Incidence and prevalence of illness, demography, health determinants 'Hard' and 'soft' technology available Criteria of appropriate referral and self-referral
Referrers	Referral patterns Criteria for appropriate referral
Paymasters	Whether paymasters have sufficient income to finance needed services Political/electoral and economic determinants of paymasters' income Competing purchasers (where relevant)
Providers	Profile of existing preventive, primary and secondary care services Each provider's effectiveness, volume, responsiveness to users' reasonable demands, transparency of information, prices Availability of alternative providers

and dissatisfaction with services, any omissions in the range of services purchased, and how able and willing patients are to change their patterns of service use. It is also necessary to ascertain how well informed patients are about the health services available, when and how to use them, and what sorts of health service patients demand. Secondly, utilization data showing patterns of service uptake are indirect evidence of users' 'revealed preference'. However, this evidence ignores the services which users do not reveal their desires for, either because desired services do not exist or because they are too difficult to use.

To manage these demands on the basis of needs, the healthcare purchaser also requires a health needs profile of the population served and an assessment of whatever relevant health technologies are available. The needs analysis within a situation analysis has to state which the main care groups are (i.e. the incidence and prevalence of main forms of illness). Various texts (Picken and St Leger 1993; Harris 1997) explain techniques for making a *needs profile* (or needs assessment), which is bound to reflect local demographic trends, especially in elderly people, numbers of children and women of reproductive age. This needs profile defines the scale of need for primary care. Within each group, the proportion satisfying the appropriateness criteria for referral to secondary care defines the scale of need for secondary care. All the population need intersectoral health promotion. The number of those in the relevant population categories (the level giving herd immunity for immunizations; heterosexually active people of reproductive age for contraception, and so on) defines the scale of need for clinical preventive care.

What types of service users need is shown by a technology assessment. 'Hard' technologies lie in the providers' domain, but to enable the purchaser to commission the needed technologies, services and providers, the situation analysis must state, for each care group, which forms of illness are preventable and/or treatable (either to cure or to palliate), given current techniques of prevention, diagnosis and treatment, and which are not. For those which are treatable, it must also state what treatment technologies are available for each disease group (drugs, surgery, therapeutic regimes, and so on) and, conversely, what technologies have become obsolete and should therefore be replaced. Needs which existing healthcare methods technically cannot meet (for example, effective treatments of many cancers) indicate R&D priorities.

Relevant 'soft' technologies include:

- Marketing techniques for countering behavioural and environmental threats to health (for example, new methods of tobacco promotion).
- Models of care, i.e. new organizational frameworks such as 'hospital at home' or outreach clinics.
- Knowledge-production, above all replacing individualized, craftworking practices with preplanned, evidence-based working clinical protocols, or, at one remove, methods for producing such protocols.

- 'Clever contracts', i.e. well-designed and targeted incentive systems for commissioning providers, or, in the case of networks, managerial techniques to strengthen relational and networked forms of influence over providers.
- Ways to monitor the impact which provider activity has on patients – partly, but not entirely, a matter of constructing formal, information technology systems.

The criterion for relevance and selection of technology is narrow. Not only must a technical innovation be no less effective than any alternative, but it must also offer additional benefits (or existing benefits with lower penalty to users or more cheaply to purchasers) – see Chapter 2. Evidence-based medicine (EBM) and health technology assessment are the relevant source of techniques and evidence. For costing purposes, it is necessary to estimate what the changes in technology imply for the unit cost of treating patients at the necessary volume.

Because healthcare purchasers subcontract much of the detailed work of healthcare marketing to providers, their marketing audit reduces to an evaluation of the providers they do, or could, commission (including providers of intersectoral health promotion). The audit compares each existing or potential provider's unique need satisfiers (UNSs) to users in terms of the following:

- Access to services, in terms of speed, distance, informational, financial or administrative barriers. Access also depends on the volume and range of services which local providers can offer.
- Clinical effectiveness – what use each provider makes of existing technologies (see above), compared with equivalent providers elsewhere, and of EBM protocols.
- How far providers satisfy users' other rational demands, including consumers' perception and experience of services and of particular providers, and how far the providers apply the results of consumer research.

An important part of the marketing audit is to review how strongly the purchaser can influence its providers' marketing activity, that is, what alternative providers are available, their capacity relative to healthcare needs, and therefore what bargaining power with providers the purchaser has.

Marketing objectives and strategy

It is quite simple to adapt SWOT analysis for healthcare purchasing in a quasi-market. If healthcare purchasers in a quasi-market are to be perfect agents meeting users' needs for access to healthcare (see above), the strengths and weaknesses of their marketing activities are defined in terms of the relationship between users' healthcare needs and the following:

- User's demands for healthcare. This comparison shows the strength (or weakness) of the healthcare purchasers' promotional efforts to inform their audience so that users' demands reflect users' needs.

• The health services which purchasers commission. This comparison shows the strength (or weakness) of the healthcare purchasers' 'product' strategy, i.e. their purchasing of access to healthcare for users.

A SWOT analysis for healthcare purchasers therefore proceeds as follows. *Step 1* is a situation analysis covering the topics outlined above.

Step 2 is a critical comparison of the demands and needs to identify any irrational demands. For some care groups it is possible that demand will more-or-less match needs. This implies the minimal promotional strategy which applies to all user groups (step 4, below). Otherwise, users' demands which fail to satisfy the criteria of rationality mentioned earlier (see Chapter 2) are demands for:

• adoption of health-damaging behaviours and (non-health-sector) goods or services. Those with the greatest health impacts indicate anti-marketing objectives for health promotion;
• too little healthcare, compared with the incidence and prevalence of disease. An 'iceberg' of unmet need implies a conventional promotional objective of stimulating demand and uptake for the relevant kinds of healthcare (for example, promoting uptake of ante-natal clinics, vaccination, genetic counselling);
• ineffective healthcare, for instance outdated services (incarceration of mildly mentally ill people), futile interventions (antibiotics for influenza) or for forms of medicine for whose effectiveness there is no evidence. Patients seeking needless healthcare are nevertheless seeking a benefit. Demarketing these services therefore necessitates offering alternatives sources of these benefits, for example advice lines, pharmacies;
• more healthcare than the incidence, prevalence and seriousness of illness implies users need, i.e. some relatively 'trivial' demand (patients using accident and emergency or ambulance services as a source of primary care are standard examples), or to substitute inpatient care for deficiencies in social care or the patient's home living conditions ('bed blocking').

The last two cases both imply a demarketing strategy. Demarketing is the use of marketing methods to reduce demand for one's own services. For certain user segments, the marketing mix is then designed to reduce demand rather than satisfy or create it. Healthcare demarketing is a primarily promotional strategy of informing users what healthcare providers and therapies can and cannot achieve, especially those promoted by drug companies and private hospitals. Gene therapy is also a likely future candidate for demarketing. In these domains, demarketing starts to involve anti-marketing, i.e. using marketing methods to reduce demands for other organizations' services (see Chapter 4).

Step 3 is to add demands which users would make if they were well informed about healthcare but do not actually voice. Neither consumer research nor consumer choice mechanisms (changing GP and so on) are very responsive to the demands of people whose health status is marginal or who are at certain life-cycle stages – young children, very frail people, people with severe mental health problems or physical disabilities, critically and terminally ill people. Methods for recognizing their demands include:

- Systematically consulting any user or pressure groups expressing their interests, being aware that informal carers' interests do not automatically coincide with those of the actual service user.
- Imputing to the group the same demands as others of their age, sex and social background normally express about the non-technical aspects of care (time, place and setting of services, rights to information and consent insofar as they are able to exercise these rights), and so on. Their needs for technical quality of care can then be discovered using EBM and HTA (health technology assessment) methods, as for any other care group.

Step 4 is to compare the profile of users' need with the profile of existing services. This suggests various possible product strategies and the corresponding promotional strategy. Service provision which more-or-less matches the level of need requires a fairly passive strategy of maintaining existing services, with the correspondingly modest promotional objective of informing patients that these services exist, and when and how to use them (see below). Should the comparison reveal that service provision exceeds the level of need indicated in the situation analysis (for example because certain diseases have receded), a product strategy of cutting provision is implied, accompanied, because reductions in healthcare provision tend to be controversial, by a promotional strategy explaining why this is occurring. In the opposite case, effective healthcare techniques are available but the quantity provided is insufficient. This implies a strategy of encouraging existing providers to expand and/or new providers to set up, especially if the situation analysis foresees an increasing scale of healthcare needs (for example, aging population, spread of obesity). Concomitantly, it will be necessary to promote uptake of the new services.

Whatever specific objectives the step 4 yields, the purchaser must ensure that patients who need healthcare have information about where and how they can obtain it, and how to use the services it buys or covenants to best effect. This requires promotional strategies for informing patients of what services are available, how to access them and what quality standards they are entitled to expect, including the maximum 'penalties' (waiting times, charges) they are liable to incur in using the services, and how to obtain redress for accidental or negligent harm that providers cause. In this way, the purchaser acts as the patient's informant and advocate, something particularly important in regard to such a basic need as the need for healthcare.

Marketing planning

Healthcare purchasers' first marketing planning task is to plan what healthcare marketing activities to undertake themselves and which ones to commission from outside providers; a 'make-or-buy-or-covenant' decision. Then they must plan how to select which providers will provide the externally commissioned marketing activities.

Some healthcare marketing activities are so closely tied, in practical terms, to service provision that it makes best sense for service providers to undertake them, integrating them with their other service-delivery activities. Such activities include:

- promoting and demarketing uptake of preventive, curative and caring clinical services;
- informing users how to access and use services;
- giving users redress for mishap or mistake;
- implementing the service quality ('product') specifications which providers have stipulated on users' behalf.

What a healthcare purchaser cannot delegate to the service providers are those marketing activities aimed at ensuring the providers meet the purchaser's marketing specification (informing patients what services are available, how to access them, what quality standards they are entitled to, their rights to consent (or veto); and obtaining redress for accidental or negligent harm that providers cause). Providers can hardly be commissioned either to undertake disinterested consumer research tracking their own performance or the relative merits of possible alternative providers. Lastly, purchasing organizations have public relations objectives of their own. However, the fact that service providers cannot be commissioned to do all this work does not preclude commissioning separate external agencies (universities, user groups, market research firms and so on) to do it.

All this implies that healthcare purchasers require only a deliberately truncated plan specifying just two aspects of the marketing mix of the services they intend to commission: what range and volume of services users will have access to, and the loci of competition between providers.

What range and volume of services users need access to could be read off from a situation analysis of the kind outlined above. However, lack of income may force the purchaser to ration access. Primary health services have open access, making it difficult to use administrative procedures or gatekeepers as barriers to services. All that a purchaser can do is to stop purchasing services for whole care groups (for example general practitioner dentistry). 'Implicit' rationing (by delay, service dilution, deterring uptake and displacing users to other services (cp. Hunter 1995)) then occurs at provider level. When access to secondary care is via a gatekeeping doctor (GP or equivalent), rationing can be imposed by raising appropriateness thresholds for referrals (i.e. not referring patients whose level of pain or loss of function or life expectancy without treatment is the least severe), by waiting list, or by using an ethical checklist defining what criteria or procedures to apply when prioritizing among patients or by care group. Our assumptions about needs and the purchasers' role as users' agent suggests as marketing activities:

- restricting the 'product mix' in ways which cause least harm to users, and making these decisions in ways that ensure transparency, 'equity', probity and accountability in rationing;
- promotions aimed at increasing the purchaser's income from government or other sources, and therefore exposing the political causes of scarcity and promoting policies to reverse it.

Next, the purchaser must plan how to recruit service providers, and therefore what marketing objectives shall be included in the criteria (loci of competition) for selecting providers. Scope for innovation and provider contestability are maximized by the purchaser limiting these loci of competition to those marketing requirements about which the user is ill-placed to choose (where information asymmetry is greatest) and which are most important for meeting its own marketing, and wider health, objectives. Generally these selection criteria concern clinical effectiveness.

Recent years have seen the emergence of 'evidence-based purchasing' as the main means of defining the planning criteria by which purchasers should select service providers. (Inviting multiple confusions, this method is also sometimes called 'evidence-based management'). Evidence-based purchasing extends the principles of evidence-based medicine from the choice of individual patients' treatment to the choice of what range of treatments should be publicly funded (on grounds of healthcare need) for each care group. The methods and results of these evidence-based studies are available in a burgeoning scientific and methodological literature. In essence, the method consists of discovering what range of treatments is available for each specific disease or care group, scrutinizing whatever evidence exists about the relative effectiveness (health outcomes) of each treatment, and selecting which treatment to commission on that basis.

For planning which treatments, and therefore which services and providers to commission, this method is valid, indeed indispensable. The only question is, what evidence counts as evidence of having satisfied users' needs for healthcare. The evidence-based approach concentrates on outcome indicators that range from high-level functions such as consciousness and mobility to biochemical-level indicators such as blood sugar or xenon clearance. They also include such outcomes as prognosis, survival rates, risks of recurrence or complications. The foregoing account of needs (Chapter 2) implies that these outcome indicators are important to users in so far as they cause, proxy or predict such outcomes as are perceptible and important benefits to them – pain, morale, self-image, tolerance of side-effects and so on. These are the types of evidence which are relevant to evidence-based purchasing. Indeed, much evidence-based medicine and purchasing work already uses such outcome indicators.

Health purchasers commission not only clinical treatments but also services which comprise the whole model of care in which clinical treatment is embedded. In respect of these other aspects of healthcare, there is no information asymmetry between purchasers and providers. The purchasers' role is

- Executive summary
- Situation analysis
- SWOT analysis (compares user needs with demands and with services)
- Marketing objectives:
  - those implemented by service providers vs those implemented by purchaser
  - marketing criteria for provider selection
- Marketing mix implemented by purchaser
- Monitoring arrangements

Figure 3.1   Quasi-market health purchasers – marketing plan headings.

only to enable users to choose, from among the range of acceptably effective providers, whichever one best satisfies the user's own preferences in regard to these ancillary needs.

Having stipulated these loci of competition, it falls to the contending providers to invent the rest of their concrete marketing mix. By planning only what the loci of provider competition will be, the purchaser is attempting to induce applicant providers to reveal what marketing (and other) standards can actually be achieved in practice (see Chapters 4–7).

The method of planning purchasers' other marketing activities – those not implemented through the service providers – is much more orthodox. What this residual marketing mix would contain, and thus the content of the corresponding marketing plan, is outlined below. All this gives health-care purchasers a rather different marketing plan to the standard models (Figure 3.1).

Marketing mix

As noted, much of the marketing mix for health services under the purchaser's aegis is planned and provided by the contracted or covenanted providers. Following the standard description of services' marketing mix (see Chapters 2 and 5), the purchasers' marketing mix contains a *product* consisting of access to healthcare. The healthcare purchaser decides this product by selecting its providers. This product subsumes the providers' marketing mix as a whole (see Chapters 4–6). Healthcare purchasers in a quasi-market therefore have a truncated marketing mix which excludes these items delegated to providers.

This leaves, firstly, promotions aimed at informing users of their rights to healthcare access and how to exercise them. An obvious way is to publish a patient directory of services. For example, Kaiser Permante Colorado provides patient directory outlining what services they provide, places, times and telephone numbers, also how to access their services outside one's home town and a list of local doctors and their clinical interests or specializations. HMO (Health Maintenance Organization) Colorado lists services covered, main hospitals used, doctors' addresses, pharmacies used (and how to get out-of-hours services) and what services the HMO provides, and so on.

To help users choose among these providers, one might expect the purchaser to publish data comparing the range and quality of alternative providers' services, covering the characteristics which consumer research shows that users want to choose by (for example, risks, survival and complication rates, waiting times, whether the providers practise evidence-based medicine). In some US states (for example, Philadelphia, New York) hospital 'league tables' have been published. Pennsylvania publishes league table data down to individual surgeon level. New York State is now proposing to post its doctors' professional profiles, including malpractice history and hospital dismissals resulting from harm to patients, on its website (Charatan 2000). US data suggest that consumers interpret such quality indicators in unexpected ways (Jewett and Hibbard 1996). Indeed, publishing the data seems to have little effect upon US patients' choices or upon clinical practice. The effects are more upon the providers themselves, for instance in withdrawing admitting rights from low-volume, high-mortality surgeons, provided they are in a competitive environment (Marshall *et al.* 2000). This suggests that referrers, as informed proxies for users, are a more suitable audience for such information than users themselves (which is not to gainsay users' need for access to the information too).

Publishing raw outcome figures also creates scope for press misrepresentation and public misunderstanding. The more specialized doctors and hospitals argue that their apparently worse figures reflect the fact that they receive the most complicated cases and most sick patients. To prevent such misinterpretations it would be necessary (but technically difficult – see above) to publish figures which have been standardized to allow for differences between the health status of different hospitals' patients at admission.

Implementation

In a quasi-market, the implementation of healthcare marketing mix (equivalent to the production, distribution, consumption stage on the generic marketing model – see Chapter 2) falls to providers, not purchasers. The main ways to make providers user-responsive are to:

- get the purchasers to operate a 'lateral re-entry' system whereby users choose between healthcare providers (Saltman and von Otter 1992) in respect of those aspects of marketing mix about which users are likely to be well informed (convenience, quality of interactions with staff, pleasant built environment and so on). Given these conditions, providers are paid according to how many users they attract. In order to get to the chance of being paid at all according to how effectively they treat users, the providers have to offer services which meet users' (other) reasonable demands. Because it depends on users' own choice and use of providers,

this is a self-adjusting system for rewarding provider responsiveness. Having installed it, the purchaser has only to monitor providers to ensure incentives are strong enough and have no perverse effects;
- let users choose their healthcare purchasers (Bassett 1993), applying the principle of contestability;
- let users choose who manages a single purchaser for each locality, for instance by electing the healthcare purchasers' board directly. A weaker variant is for users individually, or as representatives of user groups, to participate in managing the purchaser.

In the second and third cases, either the purchaser itself researches user needs and preferences and makes satisfying them a requirement of the service contracts, or the purchaser stipulates that the provider itself researches and meet users' reasonable demands. Then the purchaser's role is to monitor such mechanisms to ensure that they work. Either way, the contract has to link incentive payments to these requirements.

Implementation studies suggest that the strongest provider accountability (responsiveness) to users will result from the method which places fewest intermediaries between users and providers, which is least onerous for users to use (minimizes penalties) and which involves the most users. These criteria strongly favour lateral re-entry. But the other arrangements are necessary for when that mechanism works weakly or incompletely, or when it cannot be applied – for example, for purchasing services such as health promotion or involuntary healthcare, which users do not individually choose. The same implementation grounds commend direct election of healthcare purchasers as the most powerful fallback. There are also strong arguments for representatives of those users who are least well placed to choose or vote participating in marketing planning (see above).

To maximize the range of user choice, to make provision contestable and thereby help raise levels of effectiveness and user-responsiveness, implies opening the local health system to as diverse a range of providers as meets the technical standards for entry. To do this, purchasers can 'inspire' new providers and new models of care, whether by helping establish new providers or by inspiring outside providers to enter this part of the health sector. An extreme instance is the Finnish government's making contracts with private UK health services in order to demonstrate to Finnish providers the possibility of new entrants and the contestability of its contracts. To make the threat of contestability credible, there has to be slightly more provider capacity than users need. (The cost of the marginal excess capacity is the price paid for stimulating innovation.) Even in services with one dominant, long-established provider, users (or failing that, the purchaser) must be able to state credibly that it can and if necessary will shift work and income to other providers.

A public sector trend in parts of Europe since the 1990s has been to use non-commercial networking to commission services, as an alternative to contracting. Instead of being provided by a single, hierarchical organization, services are provided by networks of organizations and individuals, co-ordinated through 'covenants' amongst themselves and with healthcare purchasers. These arrangements emerged most conspicuously in health and social care systems (for example, in the Netherlands, UK) where voluntary organizations play a significant role. 'Covenants' are negotiated with and between members of networks, motivated not exclusively (or even mainly) by the sale of services but also by exchanges of other resources: information, legitimation, mutual assistance in kind, legal or regulatory obligations and informal links (including party, professional, trade union or pressure group links).

To implement its marketing objectives by this means, a healthcare purchaser has to:

- select which organizations will together provide the services. One way to identify who is involved is to map broadly the existing processes by which patients assemble packages for formal and informal healthcare, and related services, using the 'care pathway' or 'quality chain' technique (see Chapter 5);
- negotiate a division of labour between the partners;
- discover what resources it will be necessary for the purchaser to supply for the network to function;
- negotiate common objectives and standards for the service to be provided;
- construct coordinating systems to allow the services to operate, i.e. referral systems, patient record systems, ordering systems, information and monitoring systems. In particular, it is necessary to ensure robust systems for redressing patient grievances about the services provided, because networks are a setting in which responsibility and accountability are likely to be diffused.

Tracking

If tracking data are to reflect how far providers have met users' healthcare needs, data collection must focus on the following:

- The health impact of health promotion and clinical services, remembering the technical problems in devising and interpreting practice-sensitive health status indicators (see Chapter 2). To measure health impact, one must compare health status before and after the episode of care. An obvious way to mark the end of the secondary care quality chain is for the GP to sign off the patient as having received adequate treatment, and for the signing-off to trigger payment to the secondary provider. For primary care and health promotion, which are more continuous and 'longitudinal', it makes better sense to track health status periodically. It is practicable to track how far providers use evidence-based protocols even with care groups which are too small to analyse statistically to reveal outcome changes on so small as scale as the individual provider or so short a period as one year.

- Users' satisfaction with health services and the levels of penalty that providers exact from users. In health systems where users and referrers do not hesitate to switch providers, behavioural utilization data such as changes in GP registrations, waiting times and referral patterns are readily available proxy data for tracking user satisfaction. Utilization data also indicate the success or failure of purchasers' attempts at promoting and demarketing particular services.
- For health promotion, the gold-standard long-term tracking data are the incidence of preventable illnesses and deaths. But since these data take many years to respond to health promotions and are subject to many confounding influences, direct research into users' consumption patterns, health behaviours and living conditions is necessary short-term proxy tracking data.

The main mechanism of a quasi-market is provider contestation. Consequently the most important analysis of tracking data is to compare each provider (duly standardizing as explained for differences in case mix, patient's condition on first contact and other confounding factors): a 'benchmarking' approach. It requires all providers to use a common data set for tracking purposes. Thus UK private hospitals all use the Medax Patient Administration System as the industry standard, following BUPA's lead (as the largest purchaser).

Healthcare purchasers, we have assumed, are the agents of healthcare users not only in obtaining access to needed healthcare but also in obtaining redress for users who suffer medical mishap or mistake. This role requires access to and transparency of information about providers' work. Just as the availability of alternative providers ('contestability') is assumed sufficient threat to motivate providers to implement the purchasers' marketing plan even if providers seldom actually change, the possibility of open access to information is a safeguard for patients even if the right is exercised only occasionally. It is more than a hypothetical suggestion to say that purchasers and other agents of the patients should be able to exercise this right of access without warning where inpatient premises such as nursing homes are concerned (see Chapter 5). Where the provider is at fault, there is an obvious incentive value in the purchaser's ensuring that it is the provider who pays for whatever remedy can be made. But when the provider is not at fault (for accidents and non-culpable mistakes occur in healthcare as in any other activity), the purchaser as user's agent should itself ensure that the patient receives such remedies as are possible, through a no-fault compensation scheme such as the one used in New Zealand.

Because the purpose of tracking is to enable patients, referrers and purchasers to remedy any shortfalls in service delivery, the final task in the healthcare purchaser's marketing cycle is to feed the tracking results back into the provider audit section of the next situation analysis, as the marketing cycle repeats (Figure 3.2).

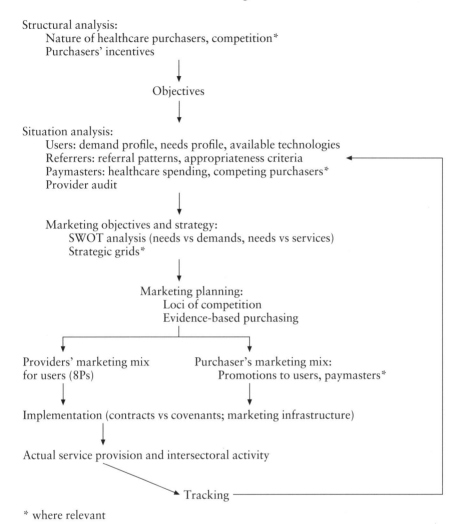

Structural analysis:
    Nature of healthcare purchasers, competition*
    Purchasers' incentives

Objectives

Situation analysis:
    Users: demand profile, needs profile, available technologies
    Referrers: referral patterns, appropriateness criteria
    Paymasters: healthcare spending, competing purchasers*
    Provider audit

Marketing objectives and strategy:
    SWOT analysis (needs vs demands, needs vs services)
    Strategic grids*

Marketing planning:
    Loci of competition
    Evidence-based purchasing

Providers' marketing mix   Purchaser's marketing mix:
for users (8Ps)   Promotions to users, paymasters*

Implementation (contracts vs covenants; marketing infrastructure)

Actual service provision and intersectoral activity

Tracking

* where relevant

Figure 3.2 Marketing model for healthcare purchasers in quasi-markets.

Quasi-marketing practice – NHS commissioning

Structure

British health policy rhetoric now suggests that competition and the NHS quasi-market are past: 'service agreements' have replaced contracts; commissioning or a 'partnership' have replaced 'purchasing'. Yet the fundamental structure of the NHS internal market remains: provider contestability and service contracts. *The New NHS* states:

The Government will retain the *separation between the planning of hospital care and its provision.* This is the best way to put into practice the new emphasis on improving health and on meeting the healthcare needs of the whole community.

(Department of Health 1997a: Section 2.6, original emphasis)

Consequently the marketing model for purchasers (see above) applies to health authorities (HAs), primary care groups (PCGs) and primary care trusts (PCTs). The purchasing of most hospital and community health services by PCGs, which will gradually evolve into PCTs, except for the commissioning of certain more specialized, low-volume services which regional specialist commissioning groups will purchase. As PCTs develop, they will manage NHS primary care in their locality more actively. General practices are starting to make personal medical services (PMS) contracts with their local HA or PCT. In so far as PCTs do subcontract general practices (under PMS contracts) and community health service, the foregoing purchaser marketing model and the following review of how far their marketing practice corresponds apply to them. Otherwise, a PCT functions as a provider, not a commissioner, of primary care, a role whose marketing aspects are considered in Chapter 5.

In any event, both HAs and PCG/Ts purchase secondary care, both acute and long-stay. Eventually, PCTs may combine with their local authorities at 'care trusts' to commission primary and social care services jointly (Department of Health 2000).

Health authorities and PCTs are line-managed by the National Health Service Executive (NHSE), an arm of the Department of Health. HAs line-manage the PCGs in their territory, summarizing the PCG or PCT's main objectives in an annual accountability agreement. With this structure goes the 'bedpan doctrine'. The Secretary of State for Health is formally accountable to Parliament for the last detail of NHS activity. NHS purchasers' managers' incentives are thus to implement whatever substantive objectives the Secretary of State passes down to them.

Until 1999, HAs' only statutory obligation was not to overspend their budgets. This had priority over providing services. A piece of guidance that deserves to be remembered for its perversity and indifference to patients' needs, told NHS managers:

Arrangements must be in place for working with clinicians and other professionals to manage activity 'back into line' if over-performance occurs. The later in the year that this is tackled, the more difficult the process is.

(NHSME 1992)

In 2000, however, the government decided to raise health spending to EU average levels, beginning with a 6.6 per cent planned increase in NHS spending in 2000–01. The 1999 Health Bill added two new, if less precise, obligations. One is for 'partnership' with local authorities; the other, more relevant to marketing, is to maintain and raise the quality of NHS services. This important addition is so recent that it is, as yet, too early to say what its incentive effects will be, and indeed whether it will be reinforced with powerful incentives or remain simply a token policy. NHS purchasers' income is allocated by formula, weighted to reflect the age and sex mix of the populations they serve.

Marketing thus has little relevance to how NHS purchasers obtain their income. Compared with the incentives to implement central policy and contain costs, incentives for NHS purchasers to act as 'perfect agents' for users' needs are weak. NHS purchasers rarely gain much reward for meeting users' reasonable demands conspicuously well, but only incur penalties when failures to do so are so conspicuous as to embarrass the government. The main incentives are a sustained pressure to maintain service activity, avoid breakdown or scandal, with a practical bias towards maintaining main local providers (Mulligan 1998).

Situation analysis

To record *user demands* many NHS purchasers have made user surveys. No recent NHS-wide study of patient surveys exists, but one in 1989 estimated then that all NHS organizations together had made about 300, mainly small once-off surveys (Dixon and Carr-Hill 1989). Only 18 per cent of PCGs attempted such surveys in their first year (1999). Occasionally these local studies reveal differences between users' and professionals' views about which services to prioritize (see, for example, Bowling 1993). Thus, anti-smoking activity appears to have been a higher priority for HA managers and doctors than for the general public (Mahon *et al.* 1994). The *Health Services Journal* commissions an annual public opinion poll about the NHS and the British Social Attitudes survey covers similar ground. Occasionally, commercial pollsters and market researchers are willing to release health-relevant data that they have collected for other reasons, but NHS purchasers rarely use it. The big exception to this pattern of under-using consumer research data is the NHS National Patient Survey, whose sample size (100,000 people) permits analysis down to HA although not PCG/T level.

NHS purchasers do have quite extensive service utilization data. On general practice, data about vacant lists and unregistered patients suggest where there is undersupply or other *prima facie* reasons to suspect patient discontent. These clues suggest, at least in urban areas, some problems with availability and access to primary care (cp. Chapter 5). Detailed referral data are collected and waiting lists reveal the most obvious bottlenecks in secondary care, usually general surgery, gynaecology, ophthalmology, orthopaedics. The extreme case is termination of pregnancy: about half are done by non-NHS providers. But NHS healthcare purchasers would have to undertake special research to find out how many GPs and patients use

---

Vignette 3.1   Anti-marketing the NHS

If you need one good reason to join the Universities and Colleges Personal Healthcare Scheme . . . NHS waiting lists exceed 1.2 million. How might this affect you or your family? 20% of people waiting for treatment under the NHS will have to wait in excess of 1 year.

Source: Burke Ford Healthcare and PPP healthcare mailshot PB16610a/10.98.

---

accident and emergency services either to obtain care which ought to be available from primary care providers or to bypass hospital waiting lists, or what appropriateness criteria GPs use for referrals to secondary care. Data for community health service utilization are more patchy, and like hospital data tend to focus on activity and cost rather than service effectiveness of responses to user demands.

Demand for private health insurance and non-NHS health services are indirect evidence of user dissatisfaction with the services that NHS purchasers obtain. Private medicine is concentrated in non-emergency, acute secondary care, although insurers have from time to time tried to expand into primary care and dentistry. These firms gain custom largely by anti-marketing NHS purchasers (Vignette 3.1).

Firms such as Laing and Buisson sell national data about the volumes and types of patient 'going private', but without breakdown to HA or PCT level. How many NHS purchasers use these data is another matter.

Users have no choice of NHS purchaser. The most powerful way in which users' voices reach NHS managers is indirectly, as government responds to adverse media coverage and potential electoral embarrassment. A circuitous, cumbersome circuit of control from users through elections to Parliament, government, civil service and then NHS managers gives ample scope for users' demands to be ignored, misrepresented or crowded out at each of the many intervening links. Users participate in PCG/Ts, but their voice is weak (see below) although over two hundred patient associations exist to represent specific medical conditions and pursue wider purposes than fund-raising alone (Wood 1999). Some networks also exist, for instance the Long-term Medical Conditions Alliance.

More data are available about needs than about users' demands (for example, in the General Household Survey, RCGP National Morbidity Survey, National Health Survey for England) although they cannot all be analysed at the level of the populations of approximately 500,000 which most health authorities serve nor, *a fortiori*, at PCG or PCT level. Censuses include quite detailed health data but occur only decennially. The Public Health Common Data Set combines and summarizes data from these sources. One effect of 'new public health' ideas is that HAs are taking a more active interest in health behaviours. Some now carry out health and lifestyle surveys, for example, three-yearly in Oxfordshire HA, covering health behaviours and self-reported health status (Griffiths and Bradlow 1998). Nevertheless, significant gaps remain in NHS purchasers' knowledge of the health and healthcare experiences of particular population groups such as black and ethnic minority women (Douglas 1998). However, the glaring omission is that NHS purchasers have, as yet, few means of summarizing the enormous information on patients' health status locked away in patient records. To be sure, these data would not give a comprehensive picture of healthcare needs because they are fragmented, do not cover the whole population, and cover only the period up to a patient's last NHS contact; but 81 per cent of people do contact their GP at least once a year (Airey and Erens 1999).

Methods of needs assessment have not changed much since the early 1990s, but the NHSE appears to be about to review them. PCTs' public health role is not yet clear. Each HA's director of public health makes an annual report about the health of their local population and is guaranteed immunity from disciplinary or legal action for reporting facts which do not reflect well on their employers or the government. From 1998, HAs have been obliged to produce Health Improvement Programmes (HImPs) in collaboration with PCG/Ts, local government, Health Action Zones (HAZs) and other interested local parties. The first round of HImPs have only recently (1999) been published and researchers are still analysing the contents. Recent NHS guidance documents say little about what HImPs' health needs analyses should contain. One's first impression is that HImPs contain some health needs information but concentrate much more on service provision (existing and planned). PCGs are undertaking or planning needs assessments mainly in respect of coronary heart disease, mental health, older people, cancer and accidents (Abbott and Gillam 2000).

Most NHS purchasers are thus in a position to produce a health needs profile for their population, although many of the data, especially about 'icebergs' of need, have to be collected specially since NHS information systems do not routinely produce them.

For assessing health technologies, NHS purchasers have growing resources to draw upon, including the Cochrane Centre, the National Electronic Library of Health, NICE and the NHS Health Technology Assessment Programme. The current National Institute for Clinical Excellence (NICE) programme contains a mixture of evaluations in response to product developments outside the NHS (for example, Relenza, taxanes) and studies of some widely used but not necessarily cutting edge techniques, such as the use of hip prostheses and wisdom tooth extraction. Since June 2000, NICE seems to have concentrated – reflecting national policy – on commissioning studies of cancer treatments. An important output of these bodies are National Service Frameworks (NSFs), evidence-based, national specifications for the broad content of NHS service contracts. Two for coronary heart disease and mental illness already exist, with others forthcoming (including services for elderly people, diabetes, respiratory tract infections).

NHS purchasers' (marketing) audits of their providers are limited mainly to scrutinizing routine managerial data collection (see below). Few data compare providers' effectiveness directly, although it is more feasible, through clinical audits, for NHS purchasers to compare different providers' willingness to use evidence-based guidelines and care pathways. Some islands of comparative information about providers' effectiveness exist (for example, unplanned readmissions to hospital within 28 days of discharge) amid large gaps, particularly about the effectiveness of general practices, community health and mental health services. NHS purchasers can audit GPs' clinical activity only if they collect the data specially. Data about how far GPs and hospitals satisfy users' reasonable demands for sufficient information, a pleasant surgery or hospital environment, for civil and agreeable staff, minimal disruption of patients' other daily activities and so on are scarce except for data on complaints.

For knowledge of what healthcare providers exist locally and what alternatives or additions are realistically available, most NHS purchasers rely on local, informal knowledge. Outside the massive London 'local health economy', that suffices.

Marketing objectives and strategy

Although NHS organizations do not much use marketing concepts, they do formulate objectives and strategies about how to manage their dealings with service users and other external interests. These equivalents of marketing objectives are scattered around formal decisions, policies and documents. There is little research available showing what NHS purchasers' equivalents to marketing objectives are or how they are decided.

Business grids have little relevance to NHS purchasers (see above), so it is to their credit that there is no evidence for their use in PCG/Ts' commissioning activities, and few instances in HAs. NHS purchasers have been enjoined to practise SWOT analysis since the early 1990s. Criteria of strength and weakness, and concomitantly opportunity and threat, were left for individual managers to intuit. The information available to them (see above) leaves NHS purchasers better able to compare needs and services than services with users' demands.

Formulating health promotion objectives falls largely to a special national body, the Health Development Agency. Other NHS purchasers implement these national objectives mainly by encouraging local NHS service providers to make use of the ready-made promotional material and campaigns (for example, National No-Smoking Day), and to supplement them locally by disseminating promotional materials from other specialist groups (Imperial Cancer Fund) and through local projects to promote preventive services (screening and so on) and health education (such as that to reduce risk of heart disease among Glaswegian women – see Laughlin 1998). A number of HAs where enthusiasts worked, such as Liverpool, have supported the World Health Organization's *Healthy Cities* objectives. Recently extending this approach, HAZs have been formed to ally HAs and PCG/Ts with other bodies who pursue health-related policies and provide health-related services. Research into HAZs' activities is still in progress.

In the situation facing most NHS purchasers (see Chapter 1) one would expect to see their adopting quite energetic demarketing objectives both for accident and emergency services and non-urgent hospital treatments. Long waiting lists for hospital care suggest a demarketing strategy of informing GPs where the bottlenecks lie, of alternative possible referral destinations and about appropriateness criteria for referrals. They also suggest giving patients information enabling them to decide whether to wait longer for a preferred or local provider, or (if available) how to obtain quicker treatment at an alternative provider. Yet a scrutiny of the English health management press for 1995 to 2000 shows practically no examples of such campaigns. Pressure for demarketing campaigns is nevertheless likely to increase. During 2000, HAs had to respond to intense public demand for NHS provision of beta-interferon for multiple sclerosis and Aricept for Alzheimer's disease. The UK government is also keen for NHS purchasers to buy secondary care from private hospitals, who can be expected to promote their services almost as actively as the pharmaceutical companies.

For obvious reasons, UK governments have wanted NHS purchasers to avoid explicit rationing altogether or, failing that, to distance the government from responsibility for it (Ham 1998; Locock 2000). What normally happen are public relations responses, in themselves usually competent enough (see Chapter 6), to particular service crises. Although many writers advocate 'explicit rationing' (see, for example, New and Le Grand 1996), the government has banned blanket exclusions of whole categories of patient from NHS care (Locock 2000). HAs' main approach to rationing pressures appears to have been to make modest adjustments at the margins of established budgetary allocations between providers (Redmayne *et al.* 1995).

In the circumstances, an obvious 'product' objective for some PCG/Ts and HAs is to promote additional forms of primary health care to relieve the gaps in current provision. Until 1997, however, the national GP contract gave NHS purchasers few means of influencing general practice. Few HAs therefore took much interest until the NHS (Primary Care) Act 1997 permitted them to make locally negotiated personal medical services (PMS) contracts with general practices. This enabled a number of HAs, and later PCG/Ts, to try to develop and promote the missing services. Nearly half the first wave of PMS contracts had objectives of increasing the supply of GPs, and about 30 per cent of extending primary care for hard-to-reach groups (teenagers, refugees, students, homeless). In general, PCGs' priorities for service development have followed national policy (Wilkin *et al.* 2000).

The formation of objectives in the NHS is more a negotiative process than one of situation analysis and SWOT analysis. Hitherto, the main negotiators have been the different NHS providers and the HA. Current policy emphasizes the addition of PCG/Ts and HAZs, and partnerships with local authorities and other local bodies are intended to increase users' role.

Marketing planning

Because the functions of a marketing plan are partly performed in these other ways, HA documents called 'marketing plans' are rare (although a few appeared during the 1990s). No PCG/T marketing plans are known.

Before 1990, NHS service planning and management tended to favour detailed intervention in provider-level decisions by HAs and to focus on acute hospital services, the most expensive and politically visible part of the NHS. These habits did not disappear with the internal market. HAs inclined to specify aspects of providers' marketing mix elements in some detail, particularly costs, staffing levels, service setting, the quality of inpatient 'hotel' services (cleaning and so on), complaints systems and, later, the more obvious penalties to users: waiting lists and times.

Now National Service Frameworks are being introduced as a standard contract framework within which NHS purchasers and providers can add detail and conditions to produce service contracts adjusted to local conditions. They concentrate on specifying forms of treatment (much more specifically in the case of coronary heart disease than mental health), leaving more open what standards are to be set for conveniences, times of access to service and users' other collateral (non-clinical) needs (see Chapter 4).

NHS purchasers tend to leave other aspects of services' marketing unplanned. Largely this is as marketing theory recommends (see above), but certain omissions are less benign. As a minimal requirement to prevent conflicts of interest at provider level (see Chapter 6), Light (1998) suggests that NHS purchasers stipulate the providers' managers, and not their consultants, manage their waiting lists and that NHS purchasers pool waiting lists across all their providers, to even out access. There is no known instance of any NHS purchaser doing so yet.

During the 1990s, NHS purchasers increasingly found themselves rationing services. By 1997–98 all HAs were carrying out some explicit rationing, mainly by placing volume or financial limits on provision but always presented with qualifications to allow exceptional cases on basis of clinical need, so as to side-step government's prohibition of blanket exclusions (Locock 2000). HAs have usually limited themselves to ad hoc marginal limitations of the range of services ('products') they pay for. Exceptionally, HAs have tried ad hoc to minimize authorizations of expensive treatments and then weather the following public relations storm; for instance, in the Child B case (Ham and Pickard 1998).

In open-access services, HAs have perforce left providers to ration implicitly, remedicalizing access decisions, placing them under the veil of clinical judgement (Klein *et al.* 1996). As ever more intense 'implicit rationing' measures are used (longer waits, less time with the doctor, earlier discharge home, and so on) they become increasingly obvious to all (see Chapter 1). Public and media awareness is making covert rationing harder (Locock 2000). Appropriateness thresholds for referral to secondary care have hitherto been a matter for individual GPs' discretion and rarely negotiated between GPs and consultants. In May 2000, however, NICE began piloting its first guide stating clinical indications and urgency indications for referrals for some common illnesses (NICE 2000). A few HAs have advocated ethical codes for rationing, partly in an attempt to make such decisions 'equitably', partly as a public defence for unpopular decisions (Locock 2000). Cambridge HA found its code cruelly tested in the Child B case. The content of its code is open to criticism (Pickard and Sheaff 1999) but at least it attempted transparent, systematic decision-making.

Evidence-based purchasing has appeared if not a solution then at least as a defensible response to the situation described above. The Welsh NHS can take the credit for innovating the application of evidence-based purchasing in publicly funded health systems in the 1980s, during which clinical protocols were drawn up jointly by clinical experts, users and voluntary group members, beginning with cancers and cardiovascular diseases (Welsh Office 1989). Since then various websites (for example, www.cochrane.org) and journals (*Bandolier*, *Effective Health Care Bulletin*) have appeared. When consumer survey data are available, there is little evidence of user survey findings being translated into practice through SWOT analysis and the marketing planning process. The usual NHS strategy for making its services user-responsive has, since 1974, been to involve users as members of the authorities and boards which decide service developments and through consultation about plans. PCGs boards and PCT executives include at least one lay member, but their influence on decisions appears to be modest compared with that of GPs and managers (Wilkin *et al.* 2000). Abolition of the community health councils weakens the lay voice further. A few HAs have held joint conferences and seminars with voluntary bodies and patient groups (for example, Stroke Association and RCP (Royal College of Physicians)). Service specifications are sometimes available from patient groups, for example on eating disorders, from the Eating Disorders Association (Wood 1999), but it is not clear how far HAs or PCG/Ts make use of them. Pickard *et al.* (1995) observe that even as a method of consultation it is inadequate for HAs to send a document such as a purchasing plan to interested parties and allow three weeks for response.

Marketing mix

Despite some retrenchments, most importantly GP dentistry, the NHS 'product' range remains wide. The main exclusions reflect rationing decisions (see above) or concern various alternative and complementary treatments and non-therapeutic cosmetic surgery.

The largest NHS promotion to help users exercise their rights to NHS services was the house-to-house distribution of leaflets, and supporting

---

Vignette 3.2   Patient advocacy and translation linkwork service: Maternity and Health Links, Bristol

Aims: Enable patients to make informed choice and benefit fully from available services. Bring Asian and other minority ethnic groups' needs to the attention of health professionals.

Services: Advocacy for patients at inner city health centre and GP surgery. Interpreting and advocacy in Bengali, Hindi, Punjabi, Sylheti, Urdu and some Chinese languages. Tuition at home on ante-natal, maternity and infant care (up to six months old). Video *Healthy Pregnancy, Safe Birth* in Bengali, Cantonese, English, Gujarati, Hindi, Punjabi, Urdu and Vietnamese (versions being prepared in Amharic, Farsi, Serbo-Croat and Somali). Keep-fit and parentcraft classes. Asian mother peer-counselling scheme. Training in cultural awareness (especially on health and welfare) to statutory and voluntary organizations. Will often attend or accompany patients to appointments, including emergencies outside normal working hours.

Resources: Eight employed linkworkers, 32 volunteers. Funding from HA and local authority. Service-level agreement with two local NHS trusts.

Source: Starkey (1998).

---

promotional materials in GP surgeries and other NHS premises, publicizing the *Patient's Charter*. Several NHS purchasers publish directories of services (for example, Oxfordshire HA's directory of counselling services for women (Griffiths and Bradlow 1998), *Glasgow Women's Health Directory* (Laughlin 1998)), commission outreach services to inform hard-to-reach groups how to access and use services (for example, Asian Mother and Baby Campaign (Starkey 1998)), or run patient advocacy schemes (Vignette 3.2).

At national level, a new project – Discern – has been established to help HAs develop better patient information materials. One purpose of the National Electronic Library for Health is as a channel to inform patients about their health and illness, partly with a view to promoting self-care, partly to enable them to make better use of NHS surgeries. Recently, NHS hospital 'league tables' appeared (Figure 3.3).

These tables are publicized quite extensively in the national media. In practice, much of the work of informing users of their rights and redress in NHS services has been left to community health councils, whilst they last.

A few HAs have also made more general promotions of their role as representatives of the NHS locally (for example, Mid-Staffordshire HA in the 1990s). Bradford HA's campaign in 1992 included a new corporate identity, press briefings on purchasing decisions, a mass distribution leaflet in six languages ('Health Matters For You') on patients' rights,

- Death rates/100,000 in hospital within 30 days of surgery after emergency admission.
- Death rates/100,000 in hospital within 30 days after non-emergency admission.
- Death rates/100,000 in hospital within 30 days of emergency admission with heart attack.
- Emergency readmissions/100,000 in hospital within 28 days of discharge.
- Percentage of patients waiting less than 2 hours for emergency admission, as percentage of all admissions through A&E.

Figure 3.3   Examples of NHS performance table indicators.
Source: http://www.doh.gov.uk/indicat (accessed 2000)

public consultation on its health plan and proposals for water fluoridation (slogan: 'Put a smile on Bradford's face – say yes to fluoridation'). A more common pattern, however, is for HAs (and in future perhaps, PCGs and PCTs) to limit themselves to ad hoc public relations responses to media coverage of particular instances of rationing or waiting list scandals, often jointly with NHS trusts (see Chapter 5). When it comes to responding to the media in such cases, the politicization of HAs and their lack of independence of government is a great inhibiting factor. At worst, it puts NHS managers in the position of defending the indefensible (such as rationing), in unfavourable contrast to the interests of patients, doctors and nurses whom the media tend to represent much more sympathetically. It remains to be seen whether, with their more medical voice, PCGs and PCTs can be any more outspoken.

Implementation

As noted, there is only limited contestation, let alone competition, amongst the providers of services to NHS purchasers, especially in suburban and rural areas. Current policy also plays down the idea of competition in favour of cooperation. Past policy of building one district general hospital per HA means that many rural and some suburban HA and PCG purchasers confront a single local NHS trust: a set of bilateral monopolies (Propper 1995b; Hamblin 1998). NHS trusts have been merging during 1997 to 1999, and the recent move from one-year to three-year contracts is likely to attenuate competition still further. Contractual relationships between purchaser and NHS hospital are also highly 'relational' (Ferlie 1994), conducted through many day-to-day interactions between managers and clinicians. Here PCG/Ts may find themselves in a stronger position than HAs. US commentators anticipate that it will be harder for providers to obfuscate problems in the clinical quality of services when they are dealing with PCG doctors rather than HA managers (Light 1998; Enthoven 1999). The large size of HA contracts means that moving them would cause financial collapse in NHS trusts: a counterproductive effect for purchasers already faced with a shortage of affordable provider capacity in secondary care. HAs rarely submit contracts to tender or undertake thorough service reviews or provider reviews

(Mulligan 1998). Generally, in the 1990s contracts were stable, 90–95 per cent hardly changing from year to year (Jones 1995). It is easier for purchasers to switch contracts where there is a high density of providers, meaning London (Mulligan 1998) and some large provincial cities.

The position in general practice is simpler still. There is almost no contestation of providers, despite the claim that GPs are independent contractors. Most GPs are on the national standard General Medical Services (GMS) contract which the NHS cannot terminate except in very constrained circumstances (see Chapter 5) which certainly do not include failure to meet the HA's requirements for user-responsiveness.

On occasions, NHS purchasers have encouraged new specialist voluntary and charitable providers, making innovative models of care originating outside the NHS, such as well woman clinics (for example, the London Black Women's Health Project (Douglas 1998), the Shanti women's mental health centre in Brixton (Payne 1998)) and hospices, among other innovative models of care, available to NHS patients (Benato *et al.* 1998). New NHS primary care services have also emerged (see Chapter 4).

The NHS plan also advocates that NHS purchasers buy private healthcare for NHS patients. A few HAs were already doing so: for example, east Cornish and Plymouth patients were being sent for heart bypass operations to private hospitals in London (De Bruxelles 2000). Although this measure would increase patient throughput, it also strengthens the perverse incentive of paying consultants who failed to treat these patients in NHS trusts a second time for treating them privately, reinforcing what is one of the apparent causes of long waiting lists in the first place (Yates 1995).

As for financial incentives, NHS organizations work within a general NHS policy that prices should equal costs, leaving the choice of pricing units open. The *NHS Plan* anticipates that, in future, NHS service providers will be graded, and rewarded, against the Performance Assessment Framework (Department of Health 2000). The 25 per cent who perform best will have direct access to investment capital. The others will have more controlled access to capital by a bidding and planning process. At present the GMS contract pays GPs by capitation (about 60 per cent of most GPs' income), fixed fee-for-service payments, and (for a small number of preventive services) target-related payments (for example, for vaccination and immunization – see Chapter 4). NHS purchasers cannot vary these payments, giving them few contractual means of influencing these aspects of general practice. Eventually, says the *NHS Plan*, most GPs will transfer to PMS contracts and, although there will be a right of appeal, HAs (not PCTs) will have the power to suspend GPs whose performance is unsatisfactory.

Networks of covenanted providers have been rarely used until recently. Until 1997 the main instance was cooperation between the NHS and local authorities in returning people with mental health problems to their local communities. In a few places (for example, Taunton) this approach led to the construction of joint social services and NHS provider organizations. A more usual practice was coordinated purchasing of 'packages of care' on a case-by-case basis from social services, the NHS, voluntary or commercial services. At present, HAs, PCGs and PCTs are being encouraged to construct strengthened NHS–local authority networks on a more localized scale, with PCGs rather than HAs as the main NHS partner; networked primary care providers (see Chapter 5) and, for health promotion, health action zones (HAZs). HAZs are networks of NHS and non-NHS organizations (which in Plymouth includes Royal Navy representation) which devise and implement intersectoral health promotion activities (for example, to reduce unplanned teenage pregnancies), besides experimental models of healthcare.

Tracking

From the account of their situation analysis resources it will be evident that NHS purchasers simply lack much of the information necessary for tracking the health impact of clinical services and how far they satisfy users' reasonable demands. They rely chiefly on financial data, NHS performance tables and a common data core which track some waiting times data, but predominantly activity and cost data. In recent years these tracking data have come to focus more on referrals and waits in the four specialties where waiting lists are worst and on delayed discharges from hospital. Nevertheless, the majority of items still mainly concern inputs and activities, especially outside the acute hospital sector. In addition, purchaser track ad hoc specific targets such as those in the *Patient's Charter*.

Data are available on complaints, both summaries and more detailed ad hoc data when the HA becomes involved in investigating the complaint, or when cases 'go public' via the community health council (CHC), media, courts or ombudsman. But complaints data present too optimistic a picture. The National Patient Survey (Airey and Erens 1999) suggests that for each patient who does complain, another eleven think they have grounds for complaint but to not actually make one. User involvement in service evaluation is rare, although as usual there are exceptions to this generalization. Some voluntary bodies also monitor NHS services of interest to them. For instance, the National Osteoporosis Society survey of HAs in 1996 indicated that half HAs have failed to implement the guidance of 1995 (Wood 1999). HAs themselves appear to underuse these tracking resources. The Commission for Health Improvement (CHI) has statutory powers of access to NHS bodies. Concealing data from it has been made a criminal offence. At the time of writing, the CHI is still being established and it remains to be seen how it will use these potentially stringent powers. It is allying with the Health Advisory Service in monitoring mental healthcare standards.

General practice data concern mainly GMS payments, largely irrelevant for marketing purposes. In general, NHS purchasers' systems for tracking primary care seem to be more fragmented, chaotic and ill-attuned to marketing purposes than those in secondary care.

Consequently NHS purchasers track providers' performance mainly by exception management. However, more systematic approaches are emerging

---

Vignette 3.3   A matrix for purchaser evaluation of services

Each main stage in the process of care is evaluated against Maxwell's criteria of healthcare quality (Maxwell 1984). Thus an 8-stage process of care produces a 48-cell (8 stages times 6 criteria) matrix. Each cell is filled by scoring the relevant aspect of service as one of:

A = Previous concern from report or visit by purchaser, provider or user agency
B = Previous omission
C = Key contractual issue
D = Media interest
E = Central issue (i.e. NHS Executive)
F = Untoward incidents
G = Complaints cluster

For each main standard in the contract, the provider also reports which of the following stages has been reached:

• Plan – i.e. specific plan for rectifying problems identified in monitoring process
• Do – i.e. implement the plan
• Check – collect new cycle of monitoring data to check the effect on services of implementing the plan
• Act – i.e. relaunch the cycle with a new plan to correct remaining or next service deficiency

Source: Squires (1999).

---

which focus on providers' normal rather than exceptional activities. As noted, public benchmarking of NHS providers through the performance tables began in 1999. Some HAs also invent their own tracking methods (Vignette 3.3).

Recent scandals of care in nursing homes indicate the importance of relatives' and purchasers' right of access to service providers and of inspection without warning. In a suspect nursing home, 'One nurse said bowls of fruit only appeared when inspectors were due' (Calvert and Johnston 1999).

From these rather partial tracking data, NHS purchasers make their equivalent of the next situation analysis and resume the rest of the marketing cycle.

In conclusion

Healthcare purchasers' main marketing role is to act as patient's proxy, correcting the problems of information asymmetry and the patient's weak bargaining power *vis-à-vis* healthcare providers. Because purchasers subcontract the provision of healthcare to other organizations, they require only a truncated marketing mix. Their main role is to ensure that the providers meet users' reasonable demands for effective and responsive health services. NHS purchasers have few incentives to find and satisfy users' reasonable demands. In so far as they perform the equivalents of situation analyses, the latter focus on user needs rather than demands. The whole process slants towards managing and developing services as professionals and managers see best. This places the emphasis more on objectives which concern clinical effectiveness and cost control than on marketing objectives to do with meeting users' demands.

Questions

1 By what criteria would you decide what items are relevant to healthcare purchaser's situation analysis?
2 How can healthcare purchasers act as a 'user's friend' in their dealings with healthcare providers?
3 How would marketing tasks of a healthcare purchaser which was also a primary health service provider differ from a purchaser which did not provide any services itself?
4 Why have governments allowed the NHS purchasers' role as a 'user's friend' to remain so limited?

For discussion

Should users be allowed to choose their healthcare purchaser?

Further reading

Harris, A. (ed.) (1997) *Needs Assessment for Primary Care*. Edinburgh: Churchill Livingstone.
Klein, R., Day, P. and Redmayne, S. (1996) *Managing Scarcity: Priority Setting and Rationing in the National Health Service*. Buckingham: Open University Press.
Picken, C. and St Leger, S. (1993) *Assessing Health Need using the Life Cycle Framework*. Buckingham: Open University Press.
Stevens, A. and Raftery, J. (eds) (1994) *Health Care Needs Assessment*. Oxford: Radcliffe Medical.

4 Anti-marketing for health promotion

Chapter overview

Health results more from individuals' living and working conditions, their consumption patterns and behaviour than from clinical care. This chapter outlines the principles of marketing communications. It then shows how they can be used for the purposes of anti-marketing for health promotion, to subvert the marketing of unhealthy goods and behaviours. How anti-marketing materials are used in practice, and how firms outside the health sector respond, is then demonstrated by the case of tobacco marketing and anti-marketing.

Principles of anti-marketing

The most powerful determinants of health and illness are not clinical services but the environment in which people live, their consumption patterns and health behaviours (McKeown 1979). Social marketing and anti-marketing methods can be used to take preventive healthcare beyond health education and clinical prevention to influence the causes of health and illness outside the health sector by:

- raising consumers' understanding (for example, of the benefits of exercise);
- promoting responses to illness (for example, immunization);
- changing public beliefs about health (ideas about 'shameful diseases', stigmatization of disabled people);
- changing consumer behaviour (eating habits, safe sex) (Kreitz n.d.).

The biggest contributions which marketing can make to health are in these domains.

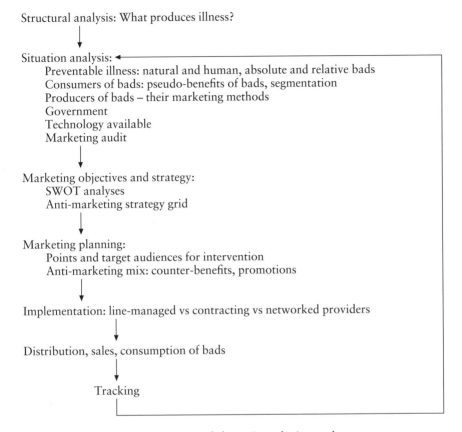

Structural analysis: What produces illness?

Situation analysis:
    Preventable illness: natural and human, absolute and relative bads
    Consumers of bads: pseudo-benefits of bads, segmentation
    Producers of bads – their marketing methods
    Government
    Technology available
    Marketing audit

Marketing objectives and strategy:
    SWOT analyses
    Anti-marketing strategy grid

Marketing planning:
    Points and target audiences for intervention
    Anti-marketing mix: counter-benefits, promotions

Implementation: line-managed vs contracting vs networked providers

Distribution, sales, consumption of bads

Tracking

Figure 4.1 Intersectoral activity and the anti-marketing cycle.

Figure 4.1 shows how the generic marketing process for quasi-markets has to be modified for health promoters undertaking intersectoral activities.

Structural analysis

Preventable illness and what produces it
There are two main kinds of cause of illness external to the individual. Some are natural, for example climate changes with their impact upon nutrition, the appearance of new microorganisms, epidemics, natural disasters, genetic mutations. Present aetiological knowledge is simply too primitive to give much idea of how to prevent the ill-effects of arthritis, cancers, other degenerative diseases, and the process of human development and aging. By contrast, other causes of illness are humanly preventable. It is possible to prevent people being involuntarily exposed to such causes of illness as workplace hazards, accidents and environmental pollution. It is also possible to mitigate the adverse health effect of the ways in which firms use the marketing of

consumer goods and manage the process of consumption. Many marketed products evidently improve health: relatively unprocessed foodstuffs, some pharmaceuticals, contraception, leisure activities involving physical exertion and so on. But many firms market health-damaging products. Ignoring errors (such as faults in production) or product misuse (for example glue-sniffing), certain products systematically damage health when produced and consumed exactly as the makers intend. Tobacco is the classic case. Some analysts (for example, Wolf 1979) call commodities which harm consumers not economic 'goods' but 'bads' – a conveniently brief label.

However, some bads are more bad than others. Some cause harm if people overconsume them but are not harmful, indeed are beneficial, when consumed in smaller amounts (for example, fatty and sweet foods, alcohol, cars). Others are harmful in any quantity (tobacco, some types of recreational drug). The latter may be called 'absolute bads'. An objective of health policy would be to eliminate their consumption. The former category can be labelled 'relative bads', for which health promoters aim only to limit consumption to health-maintaining levels.

Health promoters cannot rely upon policy-makers, business and consumers being hostile to causes of illness when the agent of illness itself is a profitable commodity (alcohol, dairy products, tobacco, some chemicals, cars, even some pharmaceutical products). Conventional markets give such firms strong incentives to increase the number of people consuming bads and the amount each person consumes. Public health policy therefore necessitates anti-marketing, that is the use of marketing methods to frustrate another organization's activities. Lest commercial marketers object to health promoters' anti-marketing, we should note that firms also anti-market their competitors (Vignette 4.1).

Vignette 4.1   Anti-marketing in the holiday trade

QVC, a holiday marketing company, selected its preferred customers (by using a competition, for which entry forms were given away at main railway stations) for stability of relationships, income and pattern of holiday consumption.

Customers who attended the sales presentation were then told how travel agents and their linked holiday companies operate, pointing out their main benefits but especially their disbenefits to consumers, illustrating with especially expensive or otherwise unsatisfactory holidays. (Pointing out the travel agent's advantages acknowledges that people who use them have reasons, and gives the appearance of balance.)

QVC then presented its own products as offering the same benefits but not the disbenefits of the high street travel agent, i.e. no need to go to the high street; choice of dates, destinations, accommodation and price; ABTA membership (reassuring – suggests redress is available if the customer is not satisfied), lower prices. Unlike time-share, the customer faced no long-term commitment to one holiday destination, and no liability for maintenance fees whether they used their holiday accommodation or not.

However, anti-marketing is rarely discussed in marketing literature. To devise an anti-marketing model, it is necessary to start from the principles of communication theory and the analysis of consumer behaviour, especially their application to health-related lifestyles and patterns of consumption. Then we reverse the application of these principles, to discover how health promoters can intervene to disrupt the promotion, consumption and production of bads. Usually, competition analysis barely applies to health promotion bodies. Not only are there few suppliers of health promotion in most developed capitalist countries, but even where alternative health promotion organizations do exist, health knowledge and health behaviour are non-rival goods. The main obstacle to health promoters' work are the firms which promote health-damaging goods. These firms are not so much competitors as antagonists of the health promoter.

Situation analysis

Health promotion depends on three main actors: consumers, antagonists and government. To start with consumers, a situation analysis for health promotion begins with the aetiology and epidemiology of personal consumption and health behaviours, enumerating the causes of illness, how many people are affected, the impacts on their functioning, pain (including distress) and survival. Public health literature describes the tasks and problems involved. Because of the different marketing implications, the situation analysis must distinguish bads whose consumption is involuntary (for example, water contamination) from those consumed voluntarily. To analyse voluntary consumption of bads, health promoters have to make much the same analyses of consumption patterns as would the sellers of these bads, namely:

- The 'market share' of each 'bad' compared with healthier substitute 'goods' (for example, what proportion of people eat five servings of fruit or vegetable daily) and the market penetration trends for the bad.
- Who makes the buying decisions and what processes of search, purchase and consumption they follow. The pivotal question is what apparent benefits consumers are seeking by consuming bads (relaxation, being 'adult', sophisticated or good company in the case of alcohol; being able to transport the children in the case of short journeys by car). The term 'pseudo-benefit' is apt for the apparent positive benefit of a bad whose consumption above a certain threshhold harms the consumer.
- Segmenting consumers of bads according to their propensity to adopt new consumption patterns. In order of adoption, the theory of product life cycle (see Chapter 1) distinguishes 'enthusiasts', 'opinion formers', 'later majority', 'laggards' and a 'resistant core'. The size of 'resistant core' indicates the maximum success that it is realistic to expect in health promotion. Nevertheless, many commodities which were strongly marketed in the past have been substantially anti-marketed away (for example the domestic coal fire).

Health promoters' main obstacles are obviously the sellers of bads, their suppliers (especially suppliers who depend heavily on the bad, such as advertisers in the case of alcohol), retailers and, in some cases, parts of the public sector (for example, state-owned tobacco firms in France, Sweden). To distinguish them from competitors, we can call them the health promoters' antagonists. An analysis of antagonists replaces competitor analysis, stating:

• the messages and pseudo-benefits used to promote bads (how McDonald's represents its foods as 'big', all-American (Ritzer 1996));
• antagonists' willingness and capacity to resist the health promoters. Partly this will depend upon how big an element of their income and profits bads represent;
• who the main producers of bads are, who controls them and benefits by the production of bads; and barriers to firms entering and leaving the market (whether the resources used to produce, say, cars or weapons, have other uses).

The core of the PEST analysis is a political analysis of the government's attitude to production of bads and what benefits the health promoters can offer that will appeal to policy-makers.

A health promoter's situation analysis would have also to note the emergence of new 'hard' technologies replacing bads with alternative products (for example, for building refrigerators without CFCs) that health organizations could promote as counter-benefits. 'Soft' technologies here consist of antagonists' new techniques for marketing bads. A recent example is high-sugar fruit-flavoured drinks. They need no refrigeration but manufacturers apparently insist that supermarkets display them in refrigerators, presumably so that consumers will associate or confuse them with fruit juice. Conversely, similar developments occur in the 'soft' technologies of health promotion (such as the invention of promotions designed to help ex-smokers through the discomforts of giving up tobacco).

Health promotion requires only a limited marketing audit, appraising the media and vehicles currently used for health promotion purposes, which audiences they reach, their credibility (authority) to these audiences, and their effectiveness at changing user knowledge, attitudes, consumption patterns and other behaviours compared with the antagonists' marketing of bads. As is shown later in the chapter, the soundness of the aetiological and epidemiological research on which health promotion messages and activity depends is a resource of the last importance.

Anti-marketing objectives and strategy

It would be naïve to expect businesses who depend upon selling health-damaging goods to collaborate voluntarily with health promoters unless non-compliance is made more inconvenient for them than compliance. Con-

Capacity to influence health behaviours
and health-related policy

		High	Low
Involuntary consumption		Social anti-marketing to change health-related policy	Secondary prevention, screening, contingency plans
Voluntary consumption		Consumer anti-marketing strategy	Harm reduction strategy

Nature of bads

Figure 4.2   Anti-marketing strategy grid.

sequently, the formation of health promotion strategies and objectives has to concentrate on influencing consumers not to use bads and persuading government to coerce the producers of bads out of doing so.

A SWOT analysis in health promotion therefore compares the prevalence of deficient health behaviours and patterns of consumption of bads in the health promoters' target audiences with the safe levels indicated by current aetiological and epidemiological research. Both sets of information would be contained in a situation analysis on the above lines. One would then target the bads where the contrast between actual consumer behaviour and the corresponding benchmark has greatest adverse health implications. Whilst the theoretically best level of consumption of absolute bads and involuntarily consumed bads is zero, product diffusion theory implies that zero consumption is seldom achievable for goods which individuals choose to consume. Instead, one should target an empirically best-achieved level, where there has been enough health promotion experience to indicate what that level is.

A next step is apply a marketing strategy grid, suitably modified (Figure 4.2).

For health promotion purposes, the 'attractiveness' of an activity consists of health promoters' capacity to influence consumers' health behaviours and health-related policy. Health promoters' capacity to influence consumer behaviour depends, at its most fundamental, on whether consumers consume bads voluntarily or involuntarily. The latter necessitates a social, indeed political, marketing strategy to change the law and government policy. A strategy aimed at changing individual behaviours is obviously of limited use (mainly, to minimize exposure) when bads are consumed involuntarily. The anti-marketing strategy focuses on the institutions and firms which produce involuntarily consumed bads or have an interest in doing so. For the voluntary consumption of bads, the balance reverses. The main focus becomes anti-marketing aimed at changing consumers' behaviour, supplemented with a social marketing strategy aimed at changing policy so as to make it easier for consumers to change their consumption patterns (for example, legislation on food labelling to help consumers to select low-fat or low-sugar foods). Young people, who are still forming their consumption and behavioural patterns, are the most important segment to influence. However, the existence of a 'resistant core' segment necessitates fallback strategies for harm reduction amongst them (for example, needle exchange, 'morning after' contraception).

Four market-compatible social marketing strategies can be applied when governments are loth to interfere with the free market:

- Raising taxes and ending subsidies on bads; but this can only work when the price elasticity of demand for the bad is substantially above 1.0.
- Full implementation of existing controls on the production and use of bads (for example, regulation of slaughterhouses).
- Controls or prohibitions on the promotion and use of bads (advertising bans, age limits).
- Compulsory use of informative labelling, health warnings and publishing full product information.

Planning anti-marketing

With relatively minor variations, texts on marketing communications (for example, Broadbent and Jacobs 1984; Kotler and Clarke 1987) enumerate the stages in planning and running a promotion as:

1 Producing the commodity
2 Deciding on messages and target audiences
3 Encoding the promotions
4 Transmitting the promotion
5 Consumers receive and decode the promotion
6 Consumers make a behavioural response
7 Sales and actual consumption of the commodity.

The first two stages take place within the walls of the firms which produce and market the bad, or those of its marketing or advertising agencies. Although they are almost entirely beyond the health promoter's reach to influence directly, the first two stages do determine how the health promoter can intervene later on.

Encoding consists of formulating and presenting the behaviour, knowledge or attitudes which the promoter wants to promote in a way that associates them with things that the audience regards as benefits (Leiss *et al.* 1986).

Where a commodity unequivocally benefits its consumers, encoding really is (as advertisers claim) a matter of informing consumers and presenting the benefit attractively; a 'needs-satisfying' approach (Berkowitz 1996). However one-sided, such encoding can at least be truthful so far as it goes. In the case of bads, though, it would be positively self-defeating to present the full effects of consuming the product. Promoters of bads face the problem of how to construct messages which will persuade consumers to consume something harmful to them. Paradoxically, more sophisticated marketing methods are necessary to sell bads than goods. Among them are:

- Outright misrepresentation of the product. However, false promotions are illegal in most countries and such crude methods are usually easily exposed to consumers.
- Associating the product with irrelevant, spurious pseudo-benefits. For example, images of attractive women are often used to advertise, say, chocolate. By present-day conventions about attractiveness, eating more chocolate is unlikely to make most people more attractive but such encoding is evidently intended to suggest that by eating chocolate one can somehow be like the person shown. The suggestion works by juxtaposition of images. No express statement of the putatively associated benefit is made, for obvious reasons.
- Emphasizing minor benefits to overshadow a greater disbenefit. Car adverts often show car and driver speeding along an exotic mountain road. Most drivers enjoy this benefit only for a couple of weeks a year. Their cars will spend most of the other fifty or so moving – or not – in dense suburban or motorway traffic. (Recent Volkswagen adverts bravely try to turn this snag into a selling point about the car's comfort, interior equipment and styling.)
- Being vague about the benefits ('new', 'improved', 'satisfying', 'traditional' and so on) or even attributing opposite characteristics to the same product (for example, Labour's health policies are presented as both defending and 'modernizing' the NHS).
- Keeping quiet about important disbenefits (such as those with endowment mortgages).

Similar criteria for selecting media and channels for *transmitting* messages apply to health promoters and the promoters of bads:

- Which media the target audiences use, and their preferred forms of presentation – whether scientific, humorous etc. The concept of 'reach' refers to how many of the target audience receive a given medium or vehicle. Media owners often provide data on what audiences their media coverage (Katz 1988) but commercial databases are an alternative to this obviously not disinterested source.
- Credibility to target audiences as authoritative or attractive role model. Thus doctors are more likely to be persuaded by a scientific paper than, say, a glove-puppet character on children's television.
- The choice of medium implies a choice of sensory channel. Visual and sound media are likely to suit messages with a high emotional weight (sales of cosmetics); print is more suitable for complex, factual material requiring longer or more active attention (presenting technical specifications).
- Cost-effectiveness, for example cost per 1000 persons reached or per point of television audience rating.

- Ability to manage the time of transmission. For instance, a firm wishing to advertise to workers might choice radio adverts because they can be heard by people driving to and from work (Helms *et al*. 1992).
- Whether the promoter or the audience manages the transmission. Television is promoter-paced whereas with print the reader chooses what to read and when. Promoter-paced material may therefore be more suitable for messages in which the audience is likely to have a low level of initial interest.

Decoding by the audience consists of the cognition and interpretation by which the promotional material produces whatever practical effects it may have on its recipients. Decoding is a multi-step process which different writers describe differently, although they agree in essence about the main sequence of events. The acronym AIDA is often cited to remind marketers that to be effective, a promotion must produce (in that order) attention, interest, desire (to act) and action in its audience, preferably 'adoption' (regular use). Only pilot testing can establish definitely how (or whether) an audience decodes promotional materials. An American soap-maker planned to use the slogan 'Dove makes soap obsolete', but on testing the advert discovered that 40 per cent of the US target audience did not know what 'obsolete' means (Albrecht and Zemke 1986). Besides misunderstanding and incomprehension, testing is also used to try to anticipate unintended audience abreactions.

For a person to receive and decode a message is one thing; for the message to produce the intended *behavioural response* is quite another. The main causes of consumer resistance, or simply apathy, are various forms of cognitive dissonance: the encoded message does not match the audience's preconceptions. This happens when the message mismatches the self-image which the audience has or would like to have. For instance, a person does not like to contemplate their own future heart attack. It also occurs when the practical difficulties in obtaining or using the good seem to outweigh the benefit; when the audience has tried the commodity but found it difficult to use or didn't like it; when the message is contradicted by counter-messages from friends, other promotions, the press; and when the audience distrusts the promoter's motives. An anti-marketing plan therefore has to specify:

- what change in consumer behaviour is to be produced;
- which stages of the promotion of bads to target – whether to disrupt production, disrupt the transmission of promotions, disseminate counter-messages, or disrupt the sale or use of the bads;
- what counter-benefit to promote (see below) – messages and target audiences; encoding; choice of transmission media and vehicles; and methods for tracking consumers' response and actual consumption of the bad.

Anti-marketing mix

Because anti-marketing concerns promotions rather than products, some components of the generic marketing mix disappear (price, place, people, physical signs, psychological interaction). Others take an unconventional form.

Counter-benefits are the anti-marketer's equivalent of a product. Consumers of bads have a reason to change their consumption patterns only if the alternative benefits are as good or better than the pseudo-benefit which the bad provides. The health promoter's marketing mix must therefore be built around inventing and promoting counter-benefits to the bad. For health promoters the obvious counter-benefits to promote are those associated with better health: morale, attractiveness, energy and so on. Conversely, the health promoter's counter-benefit must also have fewer *penalties to the consumer* than the competing bads. The health promoter therefore has to try to minimize the unpleasant or taxing physical and psychological effects of cutting down consumption of bads. Breaking an addiction is the extreme example; a mundane but common example is the practical inconvenience or greater cost of a healthier behaviour and consumption. Thus the health promoter's marketing mix has, if possible, to include ways of (say) making healthy foods available no further from home, no more expensive or difficult to prepare than junk food.

Health promotion will inevitably have failures. An ancillary health promotion 'product' is therefore the support which curative health services can offer by lending the social prestige attached to health professions in acute care to health promotion, inducing their staff to set examples of healthy behaviours and acting towards consumers as health 'opinion formers'; and by including secondary and tertiary prevention and health education in their own marketing mix.

The encoding of health promotion to consumers must, therefore, state the counter-benefits of healthy consumption patterns and, in *second* place, the bad effects of the bad. The foregoing account suggests encoding anti-marketing responses to bads by using:

- factual information about bads in order to break silences about disbenefits (for example, *Which* on banking 'rip-offs' in early 1999). The critical message content is the aetiological and epidemiological evidence of the benefits of the behavioural change advocated;
- counter-examples or, more effectively, caricature, mockery and parody of the most absurd promotions of bads (see Figure 4.3);
- a 'what have they got to hide?' message when advocating truthful description, packing and labelling of consumer goods;
- for relative bads, health promoters can disseminate their own instructions for use and how to avoid the hazards of overuse.

Many writers criticize moralizing and victim-blaming in health promotions (see, for example, Nettleton and Bunton 1995). Rightly so: victim-blaming is likely to stimulate cognitive dissonance and hence consumer resistance, and risks deflecting attention from the policies, firms or social conditions which produce or necessitate unhealthy lifestyles (poverty, ineffectual education, governments' half-heartedness about interfering with trade in bads). The

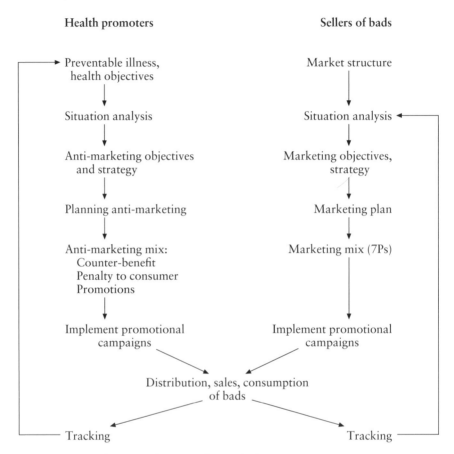

Health promoters   Sellers of bads

Figure 4.3 Marketing and anti-marketing bads.

health promoter will almost inevitably have to deal with the 'it won't happen to me' assumption in younger, healthier audiences (Helms *et al.* 1992). Moreira (1998) criticizes the majority of health promotion messages both of English health promoters and in magazines such as *Top-Santé* for encoding messages about health in a way that strongly associates them with medical treatment (not self-help) and thus with sickness (not health).

Different writers offer contradictory advice about how to encode messages destined for an ambivalent or hostile audience. Dubois (1981) advises encoders to begin by acknowledging the negative aspects of care (and, by implication, self-care such as healthy consumption patterns). Wolfe, however, enjoins against a ' "negative" sales approach – selling people something they would rather not have to buy by stressing the very attributes they find unattractive' (1994: 238).

The only solution to this dilemma is practical: to pilot-test anti-marketing materials as one would any other promotion. In Britain at least, governments and firms promoting bads tend to follow a characteristic sequence of responses to health promotions. As each response is exhausted they fall back on the next:

1 Ignore the message altogether.
2 Acknowledge the message but argue that more research is still needed to verify (or disprove) it.
3 When health promoters produce the evidence, try to find faults in it and/ or publicize counter-evidence.
4 When the evidence becomes irresistible, propose self-regulation by the firms producing the bad.
5 When self-regulation fails (as the odds are it will), substitute token regulation by an 'independent body' in which the producers of bads participate.
6 Legislate, but slowly and minimally, leaving loopholes and limiting the powers and resources of the bodies who enforce it.

Implementing anti-marketing

Because influencing health-related policy is a central objective of so much anti-marketing for health, participation in policy networks is often inescapable for health promoters. Depending on the case, such networks consist of alliances of individuals, interested pressure groups, official bodies, media, scientific, political and religious bodies, trade unions, and professional and consumer organizations.

Some bads attract near-consensual condemnation (environmental degradation, health effects of poverty, drug abuse). In these areas it is realistic to attempt to construct broad 'alliances for health' with substantial official support. But where substantial interests are vested in the production of bads (tobacco, cars) the conflict of interests limits the prospect for constructing broad, officially supported alliances for health. Then a narrower network faces the task of mobilizing support for more controversial and contested health promotion messages. Where stunts, protests or direct actions such as graffiti campaigns, boycotts etc. of doubtful legality or likely to embarrass the healthcare purchaser or government are to be used, it may be necessary to recruit network supporters to carry them out. That enables a publicly funded health promoter officially to distance itself from the outrage. Loud, eccentric, 'extreme' and unrepresentative pressure groups and enthusiasts are often among these potential allies. International experience on smoking control suggests that these bodies have contributed many innovations to anti-marketing for healthcare, often with much more style and boldness (essential to marketing) than their staid official counterparts.

Many advertising firms are unwilling or – ironically – consider it unethical to produce 'knocking copy' (material debunking or ridiculing other firms' promotions) about bads. If they have to choose which potential customer to antagonize, they are likelier to rebuff the one spending less money with them, i.e. the health promoter. Nevertheless, commercial advertisers have been used for health promotion purposes, with varying success. Another option is to subcontract organizations who have good knowledge, contacts and credibility with particular audiences (e.g. paying gay organizations to undertake health promotion on HIV). Helms *et al.* (1992) advises that it is better to use a few media well than to dissipate resources over too many.

Tracking

Similar principles apply to monitoring anti-marketing strategies as to conventional marketing campaigns. Promotional activities and materials are generally evaluated against the 4Rs:

- *Repetition* – how often the audience confronted the message. This is not the same as asking how often the message was published. What matters is how many instances of the published message(s) a typical member of the target audience actually saw (or heard, or downloaded).
- *Reach* – how many people were exposed to message (again, actually exposed, which is not the same as the number of copies published).
- *Reading* – what percentage of the audience reached paid attention to the message, and what their attitude to it was.
- *Recall* – the proportion of readers who can recall the message with or without prompting.

For anti-marketing in health promotion, the two critical tracking questions are: how much the anti-marketing strategies reduced the consumption of bads or changed other health behaviours, and, in so far as they did so, what effect that had upon consumers' health. Whilst answers to these questions are critical as the foundation for health promotion, the timescale for producing them is too long for the short-term monitoring of anti-marketing campaigns.

It would be unrealistic to expect the producers of bads to remain passive in the face of anti-marketing without taking remedial marketing action. When health promotion reduces consumption of a bad, firms selling the bad usually respond with new marketing activities of their own that attempt to reverse the effects of the health promotion campaign. This demands that the health promoters respond in turn, producing a second-generation anti-marketing strategy to neutralize the firms' response to the original health promotion strategy. Then the firms respond with a second-generation counter-strategy of their own, the health promoters with a third generation strategy, and so on. Figure 4.3 indicates how the two sides' marketing cycles interact. The next section illustrates how social marketing and anti-marketing developed as tobacco companies and health promoters responded to each other's promotional campaigns.

Anti-marketing in practice – tobacco

Some bads, for example traffic pollution, affect large populations. Others (such as asbestos) have severe effects even when their victims are few. On both criteria, tobacco is a deserving target for anti-marketing. About 120,000 premature deaths – around one-quarter of all premature deaths – in the UK each year are smoking-related (Department of Health 2000). Peto *et al.*'s (2000) re-study of the cohort of doctors he first studied in 1954 shows how much the adverse health effects of smoking continue through life. As one of the first domains for anti-marketing for health promotion (since the 1950s), smoking control is one in which anti-marketing experience is most developed, diverse and well researched.

As explained above, smoking control can be understood in terms of 'generations' of marketing and anti-marketing. Broadly, three generations of strategy have followed one another chronologically. But only broadly; the picture is complicated by the protagonists' inconsistencies, backtracking and reinvention of marketing strategies. For instance, when tobacco adverts disappeared from US television, anti-smoking adverts were also withdrawn. However, cigarette firms transferred their advertising to other media, leaving a nett gain of advertising cover for the tobacco businesses (Syme and Guralnik 1987). Today's health promotion and tobacco marketing methods used are an accretion of several such generations of antagonistic development.

Health promoters' first-generation strategy rested on conveying evidence (cp. Doll and Hill 1950, 1954; Hammond and Horn 1954, 1958) about the health effects of smoking to persuade consumers to reduce their smoking levels, and persuading government to control tobacco adverts, sales and use. This evidence and its implications were first publicized by public health and professional bodies (such as the RCP, from 1962), by individual researchers and pressure groups. The beginnings were, however, modest: the UK Ministry of Health spent just £200 on anti-smoking promotions in 1960. An obvious encoding for first-generation tobacco anti-marketing was to exploit doctors' status as experts and role models in health matters. In 1981 the RCP recommended that doctors not smoke, especially in the presence of patients. Action on Smoking and Health (ASH) advocated banning tobacco sales in hospitals and smoke-free hospitals, and from 1992 NHS policy was that NHS premises should be smoke-free. Progress was uneven, however. Eleven years later Tayside Health Board, for one, was reported still to hold substantial investments in tobacco firms. Canadian health promoters targeted retail pharmacists to establish no-smoking shops on the grounds that pharmacists are the health workers that the public most often meet and therefore the most often seen role model (Crofton and Wood 1985).

Tobacco market shares are heavily concentrated in the hands of international firms. In 1988, 38 per cent of sales by volume were in the hands of six such firms (Philip Morris, RJR Nabisco, British American Tobacco, Japan Tobacco Monopoly, Rothman, American Brands). The biggest European firm (the Rembrandt Group) then had between 15 and 51 per cent of market share in each of Eire, Germany, the Netherlands, UK, Belgium and Switzerland. To disseminate information about the epidemiology of smoking and health promotion internationally, ASH began in 1967 to hold annual world conferences, and the World Health Organization began to play a larger role in anti-marketing tobacco.

First-generation anti-marketing strategies necessitated getting the relevant health information to smokers themselves. Television documentaries appeared, most famously *Death in the West*, documenting the deaths from lung cancer of the original Marlboro cowboys. This archetypal marketing strategy is still routinely used, even in small ways such as anti-smoking slogans on health authority postmarks. Health promoters also secured legislation in the UK (and many other countries) requiring health warnings on cigarette packets. Many governments, including that of the UK, required cigarette packets to state whether, according to predefined bandings of milligrammes of tar per cigarette, the packet contents were high, medium or low tar. Legislation, however, requires a government and health minister who are sympathetic to smoking control and politically secure (Taylor 1984). One English and one Scottish health authority simultaneously devised a publicity campaign ('The Big Kill') which linked smoking-caused deaths, and the consequent use of hospital beds, to individual constituencies, local authorities and health authorities. They presented epidemiological data on smoking-related illness and death, and the costs thereof, to each MP for the country as a whole and constituency by constituency.

A converse strategy is to frustrate the dissemination of pro-smoking misinformation. The first-generation strategy form of this strategy was to advocate legal bans on cigarette advertising. Bans on tobacco adverts first came in the USA in 1971. By 1986, 20 countries had totally banned cigarette advertising, 15 had strong controls on it, and 20 had legal controls of some kind. (This was during the cold war; there was little advertising of tobacco or other consumer goods to ban in the communist countries.) Germany, Denmark, Greece, the Netherlands and the UK opposed an EU ban on tobacco adverts (1991) but the ban nevertheless became policy. In the UK, Tony Benn, then Postmaster General and responsible for television broadcasting, succeeded in banning tobacco advertising from television from 1967 by means of a regulatory decision without having to win legislation. The Advertising Standards Authority imposed voluntary restrictions on tobacco advertising from 1975, with the ulterior motives explained below. International evidence indicates that advertising bans produce a modest but definite reduction in tobacco consumption (Smee 1992).

Until the 1950s, many tobacco firms had promoted tobacco as a healthy product. Their first-generation response was to devalue or discredit the scientific evidence about the effects of smoking, for instance referring to it as controversy (not fact), describing the evidence as purely statistical and using a 'we're not doctors' message as a pretext to pretend not to understand the implications of the epidemiological evidence. In Britain, the Tobacco Advisory Council (see below) was still asserting that the effects of smoking were unsubstantiated as late as the 1993 parliamentary debates about banning tobacco adverts. Privately, however, the larger firms commissioned their own research into the health effects of smoking, publishing the results selectively and (US House of Representatives Committee investigations revealed in 1994) suppressing evidence of health harm.

Nevertheless, the tobacco firms also switched to promoting putative non-health benefits of smoking, advertising cigarettes as aids to style, poise and relaxation. Niche marketing aimed at women began around 1967 with Virginia Slims. Until they were banned in the UK, coupon and gift schemes to encourage brand loyalty and higher consumption were very successful during the 1970s (Taylor 1984). Advertisers now emphasized cigarettes' image and style, not the real effects of cigarettes themselves. Another strategy both conceded part of the epidemiological argument and (apparently) neutralized it by promoting filter and low-tar cigarettes as a 'safe' form. It was also impelled by a UK policy of reducing maximum tar yields from 29 mg to 18 mg per cigarette by 1986, and an EC policy of reduction from 15 mg to 12 mg during 1993–98 (Aitken and Eadie 1990). The tobacco firms' strategy even turned governments' fixed banding levels for tar content per cigarette into an apparent endorsement by enabling the firms to badge their latest products as low tar. Thus UK mean tar levels fell from 22.5 mg to 13 mg per cigarette by 1990, and 82 per cent of UK cigarettes sold were in low to middle tar bands by 1992.

As a lesser evil than legal regulation, the British tobacco and advertising firms have proposed various codes of self-regulation of tobacco advertisements since 1975, preferably with the regulations negotiated and monitored in secret. In Britain the tobacco business, central government (the Department of Health) and the advertising industry agreed the Cigarette Code of the British Code of Advertising Practice should stipulate that:

> Cigarette advertisements should not . . . appeal to the young or encourage them to smoke. They must not feature heroes of the young or anyone who appears to be under 25; they should not imply that smoking is an adult activity or that it confers adult qualities such as virility or femininity. They cannot suggest that smoking is healthy or aids concentration or relaxation; nor should sporting success be associated with smoking. Smokers should not be portrayed as glamorous, courageous, independent, or successful sexually, socially or materially.
>
> (Raw *et al.* 1990: 37)

Neither would tobacco firms sponsor sports events for or appealing to people under 18. Tobacco business negotiators offered controls and concessions on obsolete and ineffective advertising media, whilst demanding time for implementing other controls (Raw *et al.* 1990). There were also gaps in the resulting agreements. Those of 1986 to 1989, for instance, forbade tobacco adverts near schools, places of education and playgrounds but not in shops (ASH 1991). Tobacco firms advocated self-regulation because it is easy to abuse, evade or ignore in practice and there are no penalties for doing so. During the 1990s, British government ministers continued to argue for cigarette tax increases and tighter controls on adverts in women's magazines, on billboards and at points-of-sale instead of legal controls.

In response to the ban on television advertising, the tobacco businesses shifted their adverts to magazines and newspapers, leading those who depend on tobacco advertising revenue towards editorial self-censorship on smoking issues (Tye *et al.* 1988). It recruited influential new supporters for the freedom to advertise tobacco, including Saatchi and Saatchi, who besides holding the Silk Cut advertising account for Europe was also the British Conservative Party's advertising agent. Controls on tobacco promotion had the perverse side-effect of forcing advertisers to develop more indirect and subtle media and messages, leading some commentators to regard tobacco accounts as one of the more prestigious activities within the advertising world (Rawstorne and Hill 1991). Some firms' sales promotions began to exploit not the non-health benefits of cigarettes, but the style of the advert itself as the main means of attracting attention (for example, UK adverts for Benson and Hedges, Lambert and Butler, and Silk Cut).

Tobacco businesses can nevertheless obtain television coverage through sponsorship (although Philip Morris voluntarily stopped all sponsorship in 1994). Sport sponsorship was the main channel, especially rugby league, motor sport, snooker and cricket. This allowed tobacco advertisers to associate smoking with health, fashionability and manliness, proving much cheaper per minute of television coverage or per mention of a cigarette brand name than paid advertising. UK tobacco companies also sponsor cultural events – classical music, jazz, art, sculpture, opera – and have tried to sponsor health promotion research in England – provided it was unconnected with smoking (Taylor 1984). Portuguese tobacco companies have sponsored NMR and CT scanners (Antonanzas *et al.* 1992). Subsequently, tobacco businesses also began sponsoring music and fashion events in order to appeal to young smokers (Moore 1992), on whom tobacco firms appeared increasingly to target their promotions.

How much UK tobacco firms spend on sponsorship is contested. Industry organizations say tobacco firms spend £12 million annually, and ASH says £5 million annually, on non-sport sponsorships (Aitken and Eadie 1990). One tobacco industry publication has suggested that tobacco firms spend as much as £200 million annually on sports sponsorship (Tobacco Advisory Council n.d.(a)). Nevertheless, sponsorship actually provided a lower cost per minute of exposure or per mention than paid adverts, and one which is effective in reaching children and young people (Aitken and Eadie 1990). In 1990, 35 per cent of a sample of 7047 English 11–16-year-olds claimed to have seen cigarette adverts on television, and more could name the cigarette brand names promoted on television (Nelson and While 1992) although overt advertising had ceased 25 years before.

Health promoters' second-generation responses were partly to extend existing strategies, for instance extending advertising bans to cover sponsorship. From 1987 the independent British television companies ceased to broadcast tobacco-sponsored sports events, leaving only the BBC collaborating with tobacco firms. New second-generation health promotion strategies emphasized the social unacceptability of smoking, and confronted the tobacco business with both wider legal controls and extra-legal opposition. Although still small compared with budgets for curative services, extra funding was becoming available for health promoters, making it easier for them to match the greater presentational sophistication that tobacco promoters had meanwhile adopted. In response to tobacco business promotion of non-health consumer benefits of tobacco (see above), second-generation health promotion strategy also addressed these issues, challenging the advertisers' secondary claims and suggesting alternative routes to these consumer benefits (Crofton and Wood 1985). The new health promotion emphasized such messages as the social unacceptability of smoking, particularly to young people, rather than the direct health dangers. One UK cinema and television advert shows a young woman in a cinema pushing away her boyfriend: 'It's like kissing an old ashtray.' Another new medium was to copy the photo-montage comic-strips used in teenage magazines. Celebrity endorsement, for instance by footballers and the whole Northern Ireland World Cup team in 1982, and 'events' such as a national no-smoking day began to be used.

To these legal methods, second-generation health promotion added semi-legal and illegal methods. Satire and ridicule against fatuous advertising claims were the most potent (Vignette 4.2) and could be turned against promotions of the alleged social benefits of smoking as well as reinforce the health argument. For instance, London health volunteers performed their own street ballet to the queues for tobacco-sponsored ballet performances. Besides defacing and overspraying tobacco adverts, organizations like BUGAAUP and MOP-UP entered their own competitors for such tobacco promotional events as the 1981 Australian Marlboro Man contest. Marlboro had offered A$25,000 plus an advertising contract for the winner who would have a 'strong and distinctly individual masculinity – that unique difference that personifies the flavour of Marlboro'. MOP-UP produced posters supporting their entrant – a wheelchair-bound victim of peripheral vascular disease smoking, breathing through a tracheotomy. Their slogan was: 'The MarbleRow Man – Do You Think Frank Will Win?' (Raw *et al.* 1990).

Curative approaches to smoking also appeared in general practice and hospital services from 1980s, in the form of stop-smoking clinics. The NSF for cardiac heart disease cites a success rate of 20 per cent for the one in the Bethlem and Maudsley Hospital. From 1992, English GPs became eligible for special payments for providing health promotion clinics. However, this led to some GPs 'gaming' the payments system, claiming payments for the most token anti-smoking session advice. More directly curative developments have included prescribing nicotine-flavoured chewing gum, hypnotherapy, acupuncture and nicotine skin patches, in some cases through NHS prescribing and its equivalents in other countries. Stop-smoking counselling groups have appeared, although not on a large scale in the UK. In England, surveys on cigarette promotion began to be used for two purposes besides

Vignette 4.2   Cigarette anti-promotion

Source: The Guardian, 9 July 1992.

technical evaluation of methods. One was to demonstrate to tobacco retailers (amongst others) that health services were actively monitoring cigarette selling. Another was to generate data to persuade wavering politicians and to assist sympathetic ones.

Some second-generation tobacco firm responses were fallback strategies to reduce the impacts of bans on tobacco advertising and sponsorship. In the early 1990s British tobacco firms made detailed contingency plans to switch to junk mail lest the proposed ban on other forms of cigarette advertising materialized (Moore 1992). Another recourse was cross-branding, i.e. disseminating cigarette liveries, logos or brand names on non-tobacco products, for instance clothing (for example Martina Navratilova's Kim-motif costume at Wimbledon in 1982), clocks, signs and noticeboards. In Germany, Philip Morris painted bars, discos and taxis in Marlboro red (Fisher 1991; Moore 1992). After the fall of the Berlin wall, Bucharest and Moscow trams began to appear in tobacco company colours. Following marketers in other sectors, tobacco firms have used tobacco product placement, especially in films, soap operas, sports programmes and fashion magazines (Nelson and While 1992). Philip Morris allegedly paid US$42,500 to place Marlboro cigarettes in the film *Superman II* (Aitken and Eadie 1990).

Fallback defences of cigarette advertising were also used. One was to publicize such arguments as could be constructed against proposed bans. The main message was that adverts influence brand loyalty and brand switching not total tobacco consumption (Tobacco Advisory Council n.d.(b)). Early in 1992, adverts appeared in UK newspapers citing a Canadian court judgement in support of the brand-switching claim (although the court's judgement hinged on a legal technicality without endorsing the substantive brand-switching claim). Another message was that advertising bans have had little effect on tobacco consumption, although given the facts noted above, tobacco firms could only sustain this argument by selecting, trimming and defining data very creatively (Aitken and Eadie 1990; see also Vignette 4.3). Third, banning adverts would deprive consumers of information about, inter alia, the tar yields of each brand a feeble argument considering the content of most tobacco adverts and many others.

An alternative strategy was that tobacco firms tacitly conceded the futility of trying to dispute the epidemiological evidence and shifted their defence of tobacco promotions on to civil liberties grounds. In the UK and North America, smoking and cigarette advertising were now defended on grounds of freedom of expression (Raw *et al.* 1990). In 1992, MEPs reportedly received a barrage of tobacco industry lobbying and advertising against any further controls on tobacco use and advertising, some representing such figures as Aristotle and St Augustine as posthumous opponents of control, and Lenin as a supporter (Stern 1992). To give political substance to this strategy, tobacco marketers funded sympathetic pressure groups (for example FOREST in the UK) and in Canada orchestrated petitions and 'spontaneous' letter campaigns to politicians (Simon 1991). Some of these organizations were given official-sounding names ('Tobacco Advisory Council' in Britain,

Vignette 4.3   Why cigarette adverts do not make people smoke more

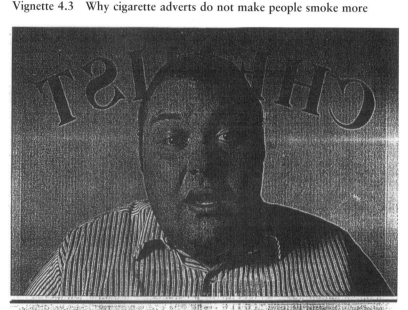

Source: Tobacco Advisory Council (1992).

'Tobacco Institute of Australia'), presumably to assimilate them (in readers' minds) with *bona fide* public health bodies. Their message to politicians now emphasized the economic (financial, regional, employment) benefits of tobacco production. In the UK their strategy was increasingly to try to recruit other ministries (the Departments of Trade and Industry, Employment, Sports and the Arts, the Treasury) against the Department of Health within government. The argument advanced against taxing tobacco was that such taxes are strongly regressive (Laurance 1991). During the 1992 UK general election, Imperial Tobacco allegedly donated 2000 advertising sites to the Conservative Party. In 1994, the government tried to filibuster the Tobacco Advertising Bill. In America during 1989, 420 out of 535 Congress representatives and 87 out of 100 senators accepted tobacco industry donations to their election campaigns. An extreme but minority strategy has been to represent frankly the health risks of cigarettes. Then the tobacco firm can hardly be accused of deceiving consumers, who have made an informed choice to risk illness and premature death. This was the marketing ploy of the short-lived Enlightened Tobacco Co., selling cigarettes under the brand name Death.

A three-fold product diversification strategy also developed. One component was to introduce new tobacco products, both as profit centres in their own rights and as an indirect means of leading consumers to take up smoking. The main products were synthetic tobacco substitutes, chewing tobacco (for example, Skoal Bandits), oral smokeless tobacco, snuff, sinus (oral snuff) in Sweden, and to divert cigarette sales to developing countries. Secondly, the tobacco firms diversified into non-tobacco products such as leisure products or foods (for example, Philip Morris bought Kraft and General Foods). These ventures, however, were not always financially successful nor, when they were, profitable enough to outweigh the firms' tobacco profits (Philip Morris for instance still made nearly half its profits from tobacco).

The third component was risk-spreading. Tobacco businesses have tried to replace reliance on US and EU markets with greater penetration of third world, eastern European and the Chinese markets (Lumsden 1992). Tobacco consumption was already increasing in eastern Europe before the 1991 (Anon (1989) but the collapse of the old regimes created an unexpected marketing opportunity for western tobacco companies, for instance to buy up the former Czechoslovak state tobacco firm Tabak and other potential eastern competitors at knock-down prices (Genillard 1992). Philip Morris hired Margaret Thatcher to advise them (for US$1 million) on how to penetrate eastern European, South African, Chinese and third world markets, and how to oppose tobacco taxation and proposed EC bans on tobacco advertising (Anon 1992). Recently it has become clear that many tobacco firms have not been overscrupulous in the methods employed to evade controls on the tobacco trade in developing countries. It is alleged, for instance, that British American Tobacco actively promoted cigarette smuggling into Asian and Latin American countries (Maguire 2000).

Third-generation health promotion responses included, as before, some which simply extended earlier strategies. Health promoters tried to extend advertising bans the new, non-cigarette tobacco products. They succeeded in banning oral tobacco in the UK, stressing, *inter alia*, the dangers of exploitation of children. Health promoters also tried to ban brand-stretching (legislation enabling such a ban was first passed in France in 1976, but not enforced), and to focus bans on the advertising of tobacco brands names *per se*. In Britain, ASH lobbied for effective implementation and enforcement of existing legislation, and increasing the size of health warnings to 50 per cent of the area of the front and 75 per cent of the back of cigarette packets, and for legislation requiring all cigarette packets to use a uniform size and typeface. The New Zealand government bought out tobacco firm sponsorship of sports events (Gulland 1997).

A newer health promotion strategy was to make use of the idea of product dissemination phases and product life cycle (see Chapter 1). From the mid-1970s the prevalence of smoking had been declining in the UK, but by the early 1990s the rate of decline was slowing, especially in children aged 10 and older (Raw *et al.* 1990: 18). The current problem is how to influence late adopters of anti-smoking messages, i.e. working-class women and adolescents (especially the pregnant women amongst them). The problem, in the UK, was not now one of information, because most of these groups know the risks of smoking, but rather a problem of deprivation. For many people, smoking is one of the few affordable and practicable self-indulgences in lives of hard work and poverty. The main objective of anti-marketing strategies for these groups was to reduce initiation rates, i.e. the proportion of 12–17 year olds who start smoking. Methods included Smoke Busters clubs for children, offering children discount cards to use in shops that do not sell tobacco, and publishing anti-smoking newsletters largely written by children. Health promoters have begun to campaign for tax increases to raise the price of tobacco faster than general inflation – in real terms the price of tobacco fell from the 1940s to the 1980s. It is known that, in the USA, the price elasticity of demand for cigarettes is −0.4 (a 10 per cent price increase leads to a 4 per cent fall in consumption).

European health promoters began to lobby against subsidies for tobacco production. In the early 1990s, the EU was subsidizing 225,000 tobacco farmers in Italy, Germany, Greece, France, Belgium and Spain to the tune of ECU 3.5 million per day (then £900 million annually) compared with an annual anti-smoking budget of ECU 1.5 million (Stern 1992). In respect of developing countries' producing tobacco, health promoters deployed more 'green' arguments stressing the deforestation and soil erosion caused by the wood-burning kilns used to cure tobacco, the comparatively high levels of pesticide and fertilizers that tobacco requires, and the consequent pollution of water supplies (Vidal 1992).

However, the most important third-generation health strategy has been to publicize the effects of passive smoking. This message directly undercuts 'civil liberty' defences of smoking and cigarette advertising. The World

Health Organization's 1988 Madrid conference 'A Smoke-free Europe' emphasized the consequent strategy of banning smoking in workplaces, except perhaps in designated areas (WHO 1990). Another formative event was a US Environmental Protection Agency publication which attributed 3000 US deaths annually to passive smoking (Rhein 1993). Over one-fifth of UK companies reportedly have no-smoking policies, including some major firms such as IBM, Marks and Spencer, and Midland Bank and some local authorities (Summers 1992). Test cases to establish rights to compensation for damage caused by passive smoking have been prosecuted in several countries. Ironically one of the first was against the New South Wales Health Department who had to compensate a health centre employee for illness caused by passive smoking (Zinn 1992). In France, smoking in public was banned – although these measures were not entirely enforced – under the Decrét Evin. The Metro operator RER introduced a FF300 fine for smoking on the Paris underground (*France-Soir*, 8 October 1992). Smoke-free aeroplanes (for example, Virgin and British Airways), hotel rooms (Trust House Forte) have become widely available.

As (third-generation) responses, tobacco firms have responded to demands for workplace smoking bans by promulgating their own workplace smoking policies which predictably advocated restricted but guaranteed rights to smoke rather than outright bans (see, for example, Tobacco Institute of Australia n.d.). Their response to attempts to raise the price of cigarettes has been discounting, which began almost accidentally as the result of price-switching competition within the industry. The US market share of discount brands rose from 10 per cent in 1987 to 36 per cent in 1993, and was found to stabilize the volume of cigarette consumption in the price-sensitive young and poor segments of the population. In Europe, tobacco firms have tried to exploit various loopholes in EU customs law to avoid paying duty.

Meantime, the health promoters respond by urging the authorities to plug the duty-free loopholes and recoup lost revenue from tobacco firms which have supported smuggling. A more sophisticated strategy takes the use of marketing theory, this time about the process of consumption, one step further by focusing on the difficulty of 'consuming' health promoters' advice to stop smoking. Latest UK health promotion materials focus on the difficulties of giving up smoking and concentrate on giving smokers practical advice about how to overcome the adverse effects of breaking the addiction and how to form new habits that are required. Marketing theory implies that reducing the prevalence of smoking, and initiation rates, will become harder the further one proceeds along the late adopter part of the dissemination curve. Indeed, there may be a practically 'irreducible minimum' number of smokers (Madeley *et al.* 1989).

Can these methods and successes be replicated to achieve health gains by changing the consumption levels and patterns for alcohol, fatty foods, sugar, salt, road traffic, exercise and so on? The evidence of anti-marketing tobacco suggests that three factors, which differ among bads, influence the answer.

First is the difference between absolute and relative bads. The consumption changes which health reasons indicate in respect of relative bads are more modest, hence more easily achievable, than those for tobacco consumption (i.e. zero consumption). Second, bads differ in how far attempts to anti-market them are contested. Some bads, for instance addictive drugs, are generally recognized as such (at least in Europe and North America). Efforts to anti-market them are unlikely to arouse much commercial or political opposition. By contrast, large commercial interests are vested in selling other bads, both relative bads (alcohol, sweet, fat and overprocessed foods, cars) and absolute bads (tobacco, weapons). US experience suggests that the meat, dairy and egg industries react much as the tobacco business does to health promotion (Levine and Lilienfeld 1987). The pharmaceutical industry is an especially deserving case for anti-marketing in those cases where it uses a 'pull' strategy which, should it succeed in getting users to demand medicines of marginal or no benefit (for example, branded medicines in place of generics), also increases pressure on healthcare spending. In contested sectors, anti-marketing for health promotion involves supplementing consumer anti-marketing strategies (promoting personal health behaviours, consumption patterns, knowledge to individuals) with social anti-marketing strategies (to alter the social and cultural status of smoking and tobacco promotions). The health gains produced by anti-marketing tobacco were, however, produced in the face of sustained contestation by well-resourced, unscrupulous firms who commanded active government support. Indeed, the health gains were achieved by organizations with far fewer marketing, informational, political and financial resources. That substantial anti-marketing successes can be achieved in such a heavily contested sphere as tobacco gives reason to think that health promoters can score similar successes in equally or less heavily contested domains.

A third critical factor in successfully anti-marketing tobacco was the strength, and continued accumulation, of epidemiological and then aetiological evidence about the health impacts of smoking. This provided the core content upon which all the anti-marketing messages depended for credibility, especially in the face of attempts to discredit them. The critical factor determining whether the anti-marketing methods developed in dealing with smoking can be (and on grounds of health needs, should be) extended successfully into other spheres is therefore the availability and strength of this evidence. At this point, we reach a new domain for evidence-based health policy.

In conclusion

Marketing communications theory and practice have a dual use in health promotion. They enable the health promoter to understand how health-damaging goods are promoted, and therefore where and how that process can be thwarted. They also enable the health promoter to design and implement their own promotional activities for that purpose. Successful anti-marketing for health promotion requires promotions aimed at both consumers and government, but the first requirement is a sound epidemiological basis for the messages. Wherever there are vested interests in the product and sale of health-damaging goods, promotional initiatives by the health promoters and the firms which they anti-market alternate in an open-ended sequence.

Questions

1 At what points in the marketing of a bad such as high-fat foods can health promoters intervene?
2 Under what conditions is social marketing (in addition to consumer anti-marketing) especially important for health promotion?
3 Which anti-marketing strategies have been the most successful against tobacco?
4 Which anti-marketing strategies should health organizations use against the marketing of pharmaceuticals?

For discussion

Which goods are a legitimate target for anti-marketing by health promoters, and what limits (if any) should be placed on anti-marketing for health?

Further reading

Broadbent, S. and Jacobs, B. (1984) *Spending Advertising Money*. London: Business Books.
Leiss, W., Kline, S. and Jhally, S. (1986) *Social Communication in Advertising*. London: Methuen.
Nettleton, S. and Burrows, R. (eds) (1995) *The Sociology of Health Promotion*. London: Routledge.
Taylor, P. (1984) *The Smoke Ring*. London: Sphere.

5 Marketing in primary healthcare

Chapter overview

Patients receive most of their healthcare from GPs and other forms of primary (direct-access) care. This chapter shows how concepts and practices from consumer marketing can be selected and adapted for use by primary care organizations. The resulting marketing model is then compared with NHS practice.

Principles of marketing for primary healthcare

Structures, objectives, incentives

With primary healthcare (PHC) we first encounter the marketing of health services for individual patients. In some health systems, PHC organizations not only provide primary healthcare but also purchase secondary care (Leningrad experiment, Dalarna experiment, English PCTs). This chapter considers not the healthcare purchasing role of such organizations (see Chapter 2) but the marketing aspects of the role they share with all primary care organizations, i.e. providing primary healthcare itself. As before, we adapt the generic model for marketing in quasi-market health systems to the specific circumstances of PHC, predicting how this marketing would be done maximally to meet the healthcare needs of PHC users (and relaxing the assumption in the interests of realism when, in the next section, we examine English NHS practice). We also focus on marketing to patients. Marketing to purchasers, where the structure of the quasi-market requires it, is considered in Chapter 6.

Primary healthcare can be defined as: interventions which individuals initiate for maintaining or restoring their health; which they can access directly and use whilst still living at home whilst continuing (so far as illness allows) their other everyday activities (Sheaff 1998). These 'other' (non-health-related) activities which preoccupy PHC users are self-care through domestic work, and work outside the home too for some people. For short, we call them the 'collateral needs' that PHC meets (or fails to meet). Users access PHC directly, much as they do other consumer services (but without price barriers, in a quasi-market). Primary healthcare has four main roles:

- *Preventive clinical care* delivered by healthworkers to individual users, for example anti-smoking 'clinics', immunization, counselling.
- *Diagnosis, treatment and care* of illness. Allowing open access, PHC providers have to be capable of identifying and dealing with any kind of illness that presents. Often the first-contact clinician diagnoses it and provides all necessary treatment immediately.
- *Longitudinal care*, i.e. continuous care over a period of months or years. The first-contact clinician may initiate further services: community health services, paramedical care, social services, education (for example for children with specific learning or psychological difficulties, sensory or severe physical impairments). Even when users can only access these services by a clinician's referral, they can receive them whilst still living at home, under the scrutiny of the referring clinician (whereas by referring to secondary care the lead clinician transfers clinical responsibility to a hospital doctor). Because of these benefits it makes sense in marketing terms to count these services as part of primary care.
- *Referral* to secondary care, when needed, and managing the survivors' return to 'ordinary' life and non-patient status afterwards. The 'gatekeeper's' role in referring patients to secondary care is discussed in Chapter 6.

Three types of organizational structure exist for providing primary care in quasi-markets:

- *Free professionals* – the majority of PHC providers are independent doctors (or partnerships or cooperatives of them) working under sub-contract to a healthcare purchaser.
- Conventional *hierarchical organizations* employing salaried doctors and other staff, and sometimes serving quite large populations (for the larger Russian polyclinics, up to 50,000).
- *Networks* – in many primary health systems the small scale of providers means that PHC has to be given by a network of providers. A 'focal' or 'nodal' network-level body (a PCG or HMO, say) coordinates and manages a constellation of constituent PHC providers, which, depending on the case, may include free professionals, local government, social services, voluntary bodies, firms, charities, patient groups and informal carers (Vignette 5.1).

Vignette 5.1   Tipton Primary Care Organization

Tipton Primary Care Organization operates in an urban setting with some deprived populations. It is attempting to establish durable close working relationships amongst a number of bodies that cannot be combined into a single formal organization: several general practices, a community health service (CHS) trust, a voluntary body, a publicly funded urban regeneration body and social services. The project was initiated by a few local GPs. Two members elected by the GP Association (an association of the member practices) and representatives of the voluntary body, social services, the NHS trust and a practice health visitor make up a board controlling the project. It employs a manager and all the non-GP staff in its constituent general practices, for whom it has standardized and updated employment practices. CHS trust staff are subcontracted to the 'virtual organization'. It plans to recruit a salaried GP. The project's contract with its health authority provides for establishing common clinical standards across the member practices. The project is also establishing GP cross-referral systems and standard practices for referrals outside the network. However, the level of involvement required of the leading GPs has placed some financial and workload pressures on their own practices.

In some countries, PHC providers compete for purchaser contracts, sometimes (as in France) by way of competing for patients whose registration or treatment generates a capitation or fee-for-service payment.

Our assumed objective of meeting patients' healthcare needs requires incentives to be so structured as to reward effective healthcare, i.e. successful preventive care and evidence-based medicine. We have also assumed that the incentives should reward providers who best satisfy users' collateral needs, i.e. which suit users' travel patterns, working hours, domestic circumstances and so on. One way to do both is to let users choose amongst effective providers on the grounds of convenience and so on, and then reward the chosen providers according to how far they achieve such health impacts as the circumstances allow. To remove known perverse incentives, these payments should be separated from the other direct variable costs of services and from capital investments (see Chapter 2).

Situation analysis

In primary healthcare, the key actors are patients and their proxies (relatives, friends and other informal carers who obtain PHC for them). A situation analysis would begin by profiling their demands (see Chapter 2), starting with an analysis of who currently uses PHC services, how and why. Because PHC users access it directly like other consumer services, fairly conventional consumer research methods are required. The patient's illness 'career' from awareness of a symptom to entering formal care has been researched from marketing, sociological and psychological standpoints (see, for example,

Rogers *et al.* 1999; Sarafino 1999). We can analyse the process by synthesizing Berkowitz's (1996) general marketing account of how consumers select products or services with Rogers *et al.*'s (1999) account of how people enter primary care:

- *Problem recognition ('awareness').* First the prospective patient becomes aware of bodily symptoms, but symptoms only trigger help-seeking when certain 'psycho-social' stimuli also operate.
- The prospective patient undertakes an *'internal search'* for responses, i.e. recalls their own knowledge of available remedies. Users frequently consider using social networks and informal care as substitutes for formal primary care.
- If necessary, the user supplements their internal search with an *'external search'*, gathering carers' and friends' advice and publicly available information about what remedies are available and likely to be useful.
- Next the user evaluates the options so discovered. This *'evaluation stage'* frequently mobilizes further advice, for instance discussions with family or a friend whether to call out-of-hours service before actually doing so.
- As a 'purchase', or rather, *'use decision'*, the user may decide to seek formal PHC.
- Having had the service, they decide whether to repeat the experience should the occasion recur (in marketing jargon they make a post-use evaluation to decide whether, on the basis of this trial, to *adopt* the service for regular use). The experience may 'teach' a patient to self-refer less; for instance, more experienced patients with chronic disease may self-refer less as they learn the technical limitations of currently available services.

Chisnall (1975) gives the standard criteria for segmenting consumer populations as income, life-cycle stage and psychological characteristics. Life-cycle stage relates the biological life cycle (child development, adolescence, child-rearing, aging) to the corresponding healthcare needs (Picken and St Leger 1993). Economic status is known to be correlated with health status and use of primary care services (Jarman 1983). An important form of benefit segmentation differentiates proxy users and those who seek healthcare for themselves; the former appear to seek formal care more readily. A tenable segmentation criterion has to yield segments large enough to be worth marketing to separately, and sufficiently different to need a different marketing mix. How far the above criteria satisfy these two conditions will depend on local conditions facing the particular PHC provider.

In particular it is necessary to know when and why the process of seeking healthcare breaks down, resulting in 'icebergs' of non-trivial and treatable asymptomatic and presymptomatic illness. These icebergs of unexpressed needs (or, in marketing terms, 'latent demand') for primary care are known to be largest for illnesses with less severe symptoms (which do not necessarily reflect the importance of the disease or the complexity of treatment it needs) (Rogers *et al.* 1999), for people with poorer socio-economic status (the 'inverse care law'; Hart 1971) and for particular hard-to-reach groups such as ethnic minorities, homeless people, refugees, drug misusers and students. To understand and influence the process of care-seeking one must know what benefits patients are actually seeking from PHC. This information can only be found empirically on a case-by-case basis using consumer research, as the next section illustrates.

The same principles apply to producing a user *needs profile* in primary care as in healthcare purchasing. The principles were explained earlier (in Chapter 3). In a quasi-market, indeed, one might expect the healthcare purchaser to produce the detailed needs analysis and incorporate its main points into its service contracts with its primary care providers. Normally a situation analysis contains a scan of technological development at this point. PHC, however, relies little on 'hard' technology although there are some exceptions (for example, pharmaceuticals, diagnostic equipment) which enable primary to substitute for hospital care, and self-care to substitute for formal services (self-testing kits for patients). Soft technologies apply to service organization as much as to clinical work, for example new forms of service contract and new models of care (such as 'hospice at home'). In primary care, the practicability of new models of care often depends heavily on the background economic and cultural conditions. For example, the feasibility of community care as an alternative to long-stay hospital depends partly on the availability of informal carers and their attitudes to providing informal care to friends and relatives. A situation analysis would note the emergence of both kinds of technology and their implications for service redesign including, where relevant, the redesign of competing or substitute services.

Marketing strategy and objectives

The strengths and weaknesses of needs-oriented PHC are its success or failures in meeting users' needs and informing their demands. The way in which a SWOT analysis leads to marketing objectives is therefore straightforward.

Where users' demands are ill-informed (for example, demanding antibiotics for non-bacterial illness) or inconsistent, the PHC provider requires an essentially promotional demarketing strategy of re-educating the users and explaining why unnecessary services are not being provided. However, even users whose demands are ill-informed are still seeking healthcare benefits, so a demarketing strategy has to be complemented by a 'product' and 'promotional' strategy offering less wasteful (and possibly more effective) alternative ways for users to get these benefits. For some care groups, for instance, it will be possible to promote self-care as the alternative (for example, for 'flu patients who have no other health problems).

Where users' demands are rational but the PHC provider is not meeting them, the implied marketing strategy is of expanding service provision with a concomitant promotional objective of informing users what services have become available, why and how to use them. In particular this strategy applies to health 'icebergs'. The corresponding promotional objective is to inform consumers what benefits they get from the service, how to access and use it, and to help them create their own referral routes and information networks to recruit other patients.

A more modest marketing strategy is implied where users' demands are rational and the PHC provider is meeting them. It is to maintain existing services and 'operational promotions'. Operational promotions are those which are used during everyday service delivery to explain to patients how to access and use services, what standards to expect and how to obtain redress for any problems (practice leaflets, instruction sheets and so on).

A customer-service grid is one way to summarize a SWOT analysis. For PHC, such a grid would show user segments horizontally and the main services vertically. Each cell contains comments on the strengths and weaknesses of each service, its centrality to the PHC provider and current trends.

Whether marketing grids are also relevant depends on the PHC provider's size and role. In so far as small to medium-sized PHC providers really do compete for patients, they require a competitive strategy. Larger organizations or networks who are sole providers of PHC for a given population do not. Small providers are at greater liberty to specialize, pursuing 'niche marketing' or 'positioning' strategies. Larger PHC providers responsible for all PHC for a given population have, contrariwise, to be generalists providing for all patients. Strategy grids thus apply to some primary care providers and not others, but to nearly all secondary care providers in a quasi-market. The use and adaptation of strategy grids is therefore discussed in Chapter 6.

Marketing planning

In one respect, services are like physical products. Many writers (Levitt 1976; Sasser *et al.* 1978; Normann 1984; Sheaff 1991; Grönroos 2000) note that they produce both a practical benefit (in this case, health gain) and various ancillary psychological and symbolic benefits (in this case what we have called collateral benefits). But services differ from physical goods in that production and consumption are the same process. Consequently the marketing of services involves managing the way in which they are produced (Grönroos 2000). Quality management has mainly to occur during service production itself (see Chapter 7), as does tracking. Not least, a service is 'inseparable'. The user participates in production, in PHC through self-care and 'compliance'. Services' marketing mix has therefore to be planned by means of analysing and redesigning the process of production itself, including the processes by which users refer themselves (see above) and eventually leave formal care. Different writers label the core approach differently; as a 'care pathway', 'quality chain', 'critical path' and so on. Berkowitz shows its use in other services, in his case car rental (Berkowitz 1996: 201/figure 7.2). The method is as follows.

Step 1: Articulate the PHC provider's objectives, here assumed to be meeting patients' needs for healthcare.

Step 2: Map the production process itself, following the user's progress through each stage from the earliest to the latest events which the provider can influence and that contribute to achieving objectives of PHC. In theory, the chain for preventive care begins shortly before the patient's birth and ends at their death. But since almost all patients change PHC provider during their lifetime, the chain for preventive care has to cover the whole period in which the patient is served by the particular PHC provider. For episode-based care, the chain starts with the onset of symptoms and ends when the user returns to their 'normal' daily life, or dies. It thus covers the whole episode of treatment, which may be as long as the natural history of disease. As necessary it crosses the boundaries between different providers, including the boundaries between formal and informal care. In particular, the map also shows points at which patients or referrers can choose between alternative routes. (Diagrammatically, these are where alternative possible paths diverge.) Amongst the alternative paths are those which lead to the PHC provider's competitors and substitutes, as identified during the situation analysis. A worked example for an inpatient service is shown in Chapter 6 (Figure 6.4).

Step 3: Identify critical events on the chain which determine whether the process of care meets the provider's objectives – what Normann (1984) calls its 'moments of truth'. These critical events are usually decisions or actions taken by an actor (the patient, informal carer, clinician, receptionist or other healthworker). Forks in the chain (such as where referral decisions are made or triage) are especially likely to be critical events because they decide what sort of treatment a patient receives, and how soon. Given the objectives, which events are critical to achieving them is an empirically researchable question. Two types of evidence are required.

- For users' and informal carers' decisions, consumer research and social research evidence is necessary to disclose these actors' reasons for their decisions and the resulting patterns of service use.
- For clinical decisions, the technical evaluations of evidence-based medicine which reveal which treatment decisions critically influence health outcome.

Unlike the approach taken in some quality monitoring packages (especially in nursing) developed during the 1990s, the method outlined here is not to produce an exhaustive account, leading to exhaustive standard-setting, for every event in the chain, but to focus on identifying and managing only the most influential, critical events.

Step 4: Redesign the chain. 'Re-engineering' the chain is in part an act of imagination and invention, an opportunity to incorporate unique need satisfiers. One option is to insert new decision points to increase the range of user choices (for example by offering evening or weekend appointments), to give a more precisely tailored clinical service (by routing some patients to a nurse practitioner) or to offer additional services (such as referral to on-site physiotherapy). For instance, telephone access to Danish NHS primary healthcare – which is organized rather similarly to English general practice – incorporates triage run by GPs. The triager decides whether the patient calling receives telephone advice, a clinical consultation or home visit, although the patient's own GP retains final medical responsibility and can in principle overrule the triager's decision (Hallam *et al.* 1996). One can also build in real-time safety checks. For instance, Boots' till system warns the operator to check with the pharmacist if a customer buys more than two items with Paracetamol.

Taken as a whole, the PHC system must be generalist in the sense of being able to receive all forms of illness and (individual) preventive health-care requirement, both episodic and long-term. To triage and refer patients on to services they need, the care pathway must be integrated, including scope for provision of (or referral to) complementary and supplementary clinical services, for example electronic links between pharmacy and GP (as in Denmark), referral routes between community nursing, diurnal general practice and out-of-hours services (Hallam *et al.* 1996). Conversely, one can eliminate unnecessary steps such as doctor and nurse both measuring blood pressure within minutes of each other.

Revising the chain as an evidence-based care pathway to make it more clinically effective is necessary rather than optional. However, in PHC, evidence-basing has limitations. Clinical protocols are not yet available for a large number of common illnesses seen in primary care and the caseload is varied. In respect of nursing homes, and still more the informal home care of patients, it is difficult to specify treatment or care pathways as accurately as in hospitals (cp. Maturen and Zander 1993).

Another point of revising the chain is to meet users' rational collateral demands. Our theory of user demands and needs (see Chapter 2) suggests that users know better than anyone else how satisfactorily the service meets their needs for convenience, intelligibility of information, quality of built environment, ease of access, social relationship with healthworkers and so on. In these matters, service specifications can therefore be read off directly from the results of consumer research. In doing so, the objective is not necessarily to maximize specifications (for example, reduce waiting time to zero) but to 'satisfice', i.e. to achieve a specification which is sufficient to meet users' own demands in these areas. The simplest way is to allow individual patients to choose as much of their own service specification as possible (such as their appointment time, what printed information they take, which healthworker they see).

Redesigning the chain thus involves integrating user-led with provider-led standards; what Crosby and Deming call 'designing in quality' (Crosby 1979; Deming 1986).

Step 5: Identify the main actors in the redesigned chain. These are the actors whose behaviour achieves the provider's objectives. They are especially liable to be found at forks in the pathway. In PHC contexts they are likely to include informal carers, volunteers and non-health organizations (social services, schools, employers, pharmacies). This step reveals who the target audiences are for the promotional activity and materials required to help implement the new form of service.

Step 6: Specify behavioural objectives for each audience, i.e. what actions, decisions each agent must take to meet the provider's objectives. A situation analysis carried out as outlined above will show what decision criteria each actor uses in making these decisions and what benefits they seek. This information enables one to specify what benefits one has to offer them in return. Thus in one district in northern England, mothers-to-be attended ante-natal class partly in order to get information about how to claim child and maternity benefits. An unpublished survey of mothers attending child health clinics gave, surprisingly, weighing the baby as a main reason for attendance, followed at a large gap by getting advice and purchasing modified milk or vitamin drops cheaply (Biswas and Sands 1987).

Step 7: Specify a marketing mix to realize these behavioural objectives. A different marketing mix can be devised for each audience provided there are no inconsistencies such as contradictory messages to different audiences.

Marketing mix

Services have a wider marketing mix than manufactured consumer goods: Product, place, physical resources, people, psychological interaction, penalty to consumer, promotions and price to purchaser. A marketing mix combines these items into a coherent service design. In primary care, 'physical resources' are much less important than in secondary care (see Chapter 6), and the principles of price-setting in a healthcare quasi-market have already been outlined (see Chapter 3). Rather, the purpose of the primary care 'product' is to provide clinically effective, direct-access healthcare which a patient can use whilst still living at home, with minimum *'penalty'* to their non-healthcare needs. This objective and the foregoing situation analysis suggest a marketing mix which combines the following:

- Initial access to a generalist clinician, i.e. one who can recognize a wide range of illnesses, treat some and refer the rest to someone else who can. Typically, doctors make this initial generalist triage, but nurse practitioners, *Feldschers*, physician assistants and paramedical staff also can (and do, in different health systems). Because of the importance of initial triage in primary care, receptionists or telephonists play a critical role, which should be to assist, not hinder, access to the initial triage. Indeed, *Which* advises patients choosing a new GP to 'visit your short-listed practices – the receptionist's attitude will tell you a lot' (Anon 1999a: 21). One can decide skill mix (*'people'* element of marketing mix) by using the care pathway to determine what clinical and non-clinical staff each point on the pathway actually requires (Gilligan and Lowe 1995; Berkowitz 1996).

- Opening hours which, besides the ordinary working week, include primary care services being open at evenings and weekends for those who cannot easily access them during working hours (remembering that different religions use different weekly and holiday calendars (Baum and Henkel 1992)). Long opening hours minimize such penalties to users as time off work. Emergencies require that some form of primary care be immediately available all day every day.
- 'One-stop' PHC, integrating the full range of primary care skills and services at a single 'place' and into a single, coherent care pathway. Relevant services include nursing and paramedical besides medical care, and diagnostics, besides access to relevant voluntary services. Access to pharmacies is especially important in primary care. Access to services provided by other public bodies (for example social work, housing, education) is likelier to be harder to provide on-site, but in this case the care pathway can be designed to include the option of referral from the PHC provider. One-stop provision is a reason for moving services such as diagnostics and paramedical services from secondary into primary healthcare providers as far as possible (and a way to reduce the over-load pressures which many hospitals face in publicly funded systems; see Chapter 6).
- Places of PHC provision which are accessible by foot, especially for disabled people, or people with a pram or wheelchair – for example in housing estates, workplaces, places of leisure, shopping centres – or in places well served by public transport. In England, Arndale centre or market sites have different symbolic connotations and attract different types of patient than would, say, a Harley Street site (cp. Contreras *et al.* 1994). Nevertheless, an Arndale site would be the better choice for accessing, say, young unregistered patients. Inevitably, patients who cannot travel need the option of call-out to home. HMO Colorado includes pharmacies willing to deliver to patient's home or workplace. Patients can also get information or reassurance at home by telephone, letter, Internet, video conferencing, or from automated points in public places.
- Walk-in access to services without prior appointment, at the user's risk of having to wait their turn, using appointments for longer, more complex tasks, or to guarantee a time and place of treatment.

For many patients the most important psychological benefit lies in the quality and continuity of their social relationship with the doctor and other healthworkers.

Primary care includes much self-care and informal care. Consequently, it is also necessary to recruit and practically support informal carers. In Germany, for instance, a family can receive payments for giving nursing care at home instead of admitting their relative to institutional care. It is also possible to support informal carers in kind with training, respite care, house modifications, hoists and so on. This also involves a promotional task of legitimating self-care, providing information both about how to undertake it, and when to stop and seek formal healthcare. On US evidence, self-care manuals seem to be acceptable and bring low clinical risk, although the evidence that they reduce demand is equivocal (Rogers *et al.* 1999). A situation analysis on the foregoing lines would indicate each audience's preferred media and presentation, for example printed materials for people who may have difficulty remembering appointment times or complex instructions. For printed materials a reading age test can be applied, and a Fog Test of clarity. However, there is no substitute for pilot-testing new promotional materials on users themselves.

Implementation

A primary care marketing mix on these lines would appear to be most easily provided through a single organization supplying primary care for, say, 10,000 or more residents; in short, a polyclinic. UK experience suggests that this scale of provision would suffice to sustain the less frequently required services such as those of a counsellor. An entity at least this large, and probably larger, would be necessary to accumulate the information for a situation analysis, to plan and manage the care pathway as a whole.

Even when no single provider provides the whole care pathway, it remains necessary to plan and manage the pathway as a whole. Viewing the care pathway as a whole indicates which providers it is necessary to recruit to the network, and any gaps. When PHC provision remains fragmented, the foregoing marketing planning method is a way of combining separate providers' working arrangement into a network (see Vignette 5.1). Taken as a whole, the resulting network of providers can in principle provide a similar range and volume of services to a polyclinic. In effect, the network operates as a virtual polyclinic. Networked provision is also one way to deal with the tension between obtaining the advantages of a polyclinic-sized provider and trying to minimize travel penalties to users by opting for smaller, geographically dispersed (hence small-scale) providers, especially in rural areas.

One implementation task especially deserves mention. The importance of initial triage in primary care makes the training of the first people whom patients contact particularly important. Methods suggested by Baum and Henkel (1992), Gilligan and Lowe (1995) and Lee *et al.* (1998) for training receptionists and telephonists include:

- Making receptionists exercise what it might be like to be old, for example by trying to use the surgery, especially its reception area, with a splint on one or both legs (to mimic mobility restrictions such as those which arthritis causes) and wearing thick gloves, earplugs and thick glasses (to mimic lost sensory acuity).
- Agreeing explicit criteria for screening incoming telephone calls to the clinician(s), especially when receptionists or telephonists feel tempted to make diagnoses.

- Training and rehearsing common reception tasks.
- Training to deal with distressed, mentally disturbed patients entering the surgery. This also builds the receptionists' self-confidence.

Tracking

Because production and consumption are combined in services, much tracking of service quality is concurrent with the process of care and can therefore also be designed into the care pathway. An obvious requirement for tracking the effectiveness of primary care is a shared, standardized patient record which follows the patient along the care pathway, healthworkers reading and writing it in the course of their work. However, there are two important exceptions. Some monitoring data, especially health outcome data, can be collected only once treatment is completed, which may be after – indeed long after – the episode ends. Assuming patients are prudently cautious about criticizing providers face-to-face before their treatment is finished, tracking data are likely to be more critical and valid if collected on neutral territory by third parties after the end of the episode of care. These are further arguments for an information-gathering infrastructure which is semi-detached from the immediate service providers (see above).

The characteristics of PHC mean that tracking data resist analyses showing PHC's impacts on patients' health (small populations, slow effects, many brief episodes, strong confounding factors, ill-defined outcomes). These characteristics often make it necessary, as a proxy, to track how far evidence-based medicine is being practised. Objective data can be collected on some penalties of treatment (time, cost to patients, distance travelled) but data on user satisfaction have to be collected by consumer research (survey, interview and so on; see Chapter 7).

To interpret such data one must first know what quality of service patients were expecting; a relatively poor quality service that exceeds users' low expectations is, paradoxically, likely to produce higher satisfaction ratings than a better service which still falls short of very high expectations (Albrecht and Zemke 1986). One must also understand users' behaviour. Amongst English GPs, for instance, competition for patients is limited and most of the relatively few patients who change GP each year do so as a result of removals (theirs or the doctor's). In these conditions, low rates of patient transfer between general practices is not necessarily a sign of satisfaction; inertia is not proof of loyalty (Gilligan and Lowe 1995). Women with access to several GPs may 'save' the better doctor for their children's use (Rogers *et al.* 1999), so their own use of another doctor is not necessarily a vote of confidence.

These results form part of the input to the next situation analysis, from which the marketing cycle starts (see Figure 5.1).

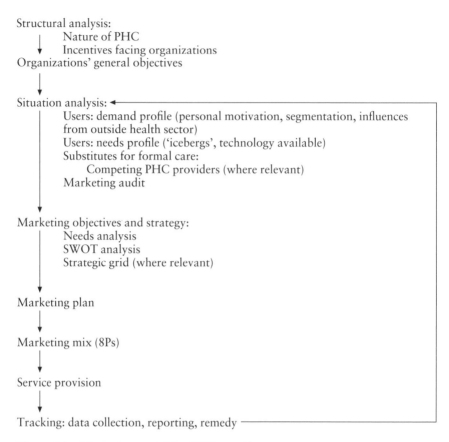

Structural analysis:
    Nature of PHC
    Incentives facing organizations
Organizations' general objectives

Situation analysis:
    Users: demand profile (personal motivation, segmentation, influences
    from outside health sector)
    Users: needs profile ('icebergs', technology available)
    Substitutes for formal care:
        Competing PHC providers (where relevant)
    Marketing audit

Marketing objectives and strategy:
    Needs analysis
    SWOT analysis
    Strategic grid (where relevant)

Marketing plan

Marketing mix (8Ps)

Service provision

Tracking: data collection, reporting, remedy

Figure 5.1   Marketing model for PHC providers.

Practice – primary care in the NHS

Structure, incentives, objectives

The main source of NHS primary care are general practices and community health services (CHSs). Nearly all GPs are independent contractors, working mostly for the NHS under general medical service (GMS) contracts (see below). General practices usually subcontract their out-of-hours services to commercial deputizing agencies or GP cooperatives. Many employ nursing and paramedical staff. Community health services employ nursing and paramedical staff, often outposting them to general practices. Patients reach these services by referral from their GP. Community health services are generally organized as NHS trusts (see below), sometimes freestanding, occasionally combined with hospital and/or mental health services. They are financed through contracts (recently relabelled Service Level Agreements (SLAs) or

Service Agreements and Financial Frameworks (SAFFs)). Health authorities are gradually handing these contracts over to primary care groups (PCGs) and trusts (PCTs), and CHSs are likely to merge with PCTs in future.

Other sources of primary care include hospital accident and emergency services and ambulance services, frequently organized as separate NHS trusts. Patients have open, direct telephone (or Internet) access to NHS Direct, which may then refer them on to GP or ambulance services. NHS Direct's telephone helplines, websites and publications are directly managed by NHS Executive (NHSE) regional offices, except in a few cases where GP cooperatives manage them under contract from NHSE. Community pharmacists are private businesses who receive nationally standard payments for dispensing NHS prescriptions. They are often the first point of contact for many people looking to self-treat their minor – or seemingly minor – ailments with over-the-counter (non-prescription) medicines, as well as for some preventive materials (such as dental hygiene and chiropody supplies, contraception). Local authorities' school health services and social services are important complements to NHS primary care. Reports sporadically appear of attempts to establish private general practice, followed at an interval by reports of their demise (see, for example, Hinde 1998; O'Dowd 1998).

Patients apply to join a GP's list, and the GP may accept or refuse. Most people find a GP. Where GP vacancies are hard to fill, the list may be reallocated or simply held without a GP until one is recruited. HAs allocate the handful of unpopular individual patients (very demanding, violent, prone to call at night and so on) amongst GPs for fixed periods in turn.

PCGs and PCTs have the task of coordinating all these providers into a coherent system of primary care provision for populations of (typically) about 100,000. They are also becoming the main purchaser of secondary services (see Chapter 3), but here we concentrate on their primary care role. In that respect, most PCG/Ts constitute a network. As the network's centre (its 'focal body'), the PCG/T's board, managers and support staff coordinate the constituent providers of clinical primary care, above all general practices. A PCT may also employ clinicians itself. In what follows, PCG and PCT are taken to refer to the whole network.

PCG/Ts do not compete. Each has only one source of income (the HA) and there is only one PCG/T in each locality. Neither do the constituent providers below PCG/T board level compete much in reality, although general practices are independent small businesses and sensitive to charges of 'poaching' each others' patients. Alternative PHC services do, however, partly substitute for each other, as many GPs perceive in regard to NHS Direct. But this substitutability does not necessarily harm GPs: it eases their personal workload. The relationship between a PCG/T and its HA is an attenuated line-management relationship (see Chapter 3). The 'bedpan doctrine' results in PCG/Ts' pursuing a mixture of HA, national and local GPs' priorities, and those of the PCG/T board itself. PCG/Ts' objectives have initially emphasized improving quality (including that of premises), increasing practice staff and various services developments such as improving diabetes, ophthalmology and out-of-hours services, walk-in centres and personal medical services (PMS) schemes (Leese and Gillam 2000).

PCG/T budgets are set by a weighted capitation formula. Yet PCG/Ts' material incentives for marketing to patients are similar to those for CHS trusts, i.e. weak. They have no incentives either to 'skim' or to 'dump' patients. If one practice 'dumped' a patient, that patient would only transfer to another practice in the same PCG/T (Mays and Goodwin 1998). A capitation formula is well adapted to reflect likely cost differences reflecting population profile and case mix. In theory, it creates an incentive for preventive care, but it does not directly reward achieving the best currently attainable health outcome gain (cp. Chapter 2).

Most GPs face incentives that are determined independently of the PCG/T board. GMS capitation fees, and in some cases PMS contracts too, give GPs an incentive to recruit and retain enough patients to ensure sufficient practice income, to carry out a range of activities and claim the corresponding expenses. GMS payments are complex, fragmented and rigid in respect of payments for activity and expenses, but vague about clinical practice and quality or how GPs are to make their practice responsive to user demands. A perverse incentive in the GMS system is that the better quality the service, the lower the GP's nett income is likely to be, assuming that higher quality service is more expensive to provide. But the GMS target payments for vaccination and immunization match quite closely the patterns of incentive which marketing theory would indicate (see Chapter 3 and earlier, this chapter).

At general practice level, a gradual shift to PMS contracts is occurring (see Chapter 3). Provided that the range of services is not less than under the GMS regime, PMS contracts allow the parties to agree a wide variety of incentives, terms and conditions. Many of the first PMS contracts consolidated former GMS payments into a single block payment (often retaining the separate target payments for preventive healthcare), creating an incentive to maintain open access to services and contain costs (Sheaff and Lloyd-Kendall 2000). Exemplary incentives have been added in the form of Bevin awards which are intended to reward 'high quality of recent improvement in service. They must have objective measures of success and be of such a standard as to arouse considerable interest from colleagues in the NHS' (www.doh.gov.uk/nhsinfo/pages/quality/beacon.htm, accessed 2000). Many GPs gain supplementary income by providing health certificates and other health-related documentation privately, selling occupational health service to local firms and so on.

The NHS trust-based providers listed above are generally paid on an historical basis reflecting the cost and volume, rather than the quality or, still less, the health impacts of their activities.

Situation analysis

PCG/Ts are better able to assess users' healthcare needs than their demands when it comes to making a situation analysis. In order to assess the user-responsiveness of NHS primary care it is necessary to note briefly what a situation analysis would currently show in most PCG/Ts.

Nearly all Britons suffer symptoms of some kind in the course of a year, and over 80 per cent use some form of PHC. Overall, the level of demand for PHC has remained stable. Its composition is what is changing. Besides an aging population, who are heavy users of PHC (Office of Health Economics 1998) demand for services for young children is also increasing (Rogers *et al.* 1999), as are night visits, 'with commensurate increases in evening and weekend visiting' (Hallam *et al.* 1996). At the onset of symptoms, about 24 per cent of people take no action, 54 per cent rely on self-care, 17 per cent on combined professional (formal health service) and self-care, and 5 per cent on professional only (Rogers and Nicholaas 1998; Rogers *et al.* 1999).

Little is known about contemporary patterns of self-care in England (Nicholaas *et al.* 1997). Informal support networks appear to be of more use for patients suffering from physical than for psychological and personal problems. But informal and self-help networks are gradually decaying (Hallam *et al.* 1996; Rogers *et al.* 1999). To a very limited extent, supermarkets are becoming more active retailers of self-care. Self-test pregnancy kits have been available for many years (despite doctors' apprehension of the 'dangers' when they first appeared), and now blood sugar and cholesterol tests.

Patients most commonly decide to consult their GPs when their symptoms become so severe as to start disrupting their daily functioning, seeking help if symptoms have not abated by an arbitrary, self-imposed deadline. When their symptoms seem serious or patients are uncertain what to do, they turn to out-of-hours (OOH) and emergency services: in descending order of likelihood, their GP (42 per cent), one-third call ambulance and one-fifth go to accident and emergency (Anon 1999b). Figure 5.2 compares the advantages and disadvantages, in English patients' eyes, of three main alternative sources of primary care.

Applying our basic segmentation (see Chapter 2) to primary care starting with underusers, one marker of how far using NHS primary care does exact penalties from consumers is that for each GP, a mean of 260 patients miss their surgery appointments each year (Department of Health Press Release, 17 February 1998). For instance, some mothers are too busy on account of childcare to use follow-up treatments such as physiotherapy, screening or progress monitoring. For people with mental problems, the main disbenefit is the embarrassment and potential stigma of reporting them.

Overusers or misusers include the 'trivia' or 'heartsink' patients of whom GPs often complain, especially in regard to out-of-hours services. One large survey reported that GPs thought 40 per cent of OOH contacts were unnecessary or could have waited until the following morning (Robertson-Steel 1998). Overusers infer that GPs are there to treat trivial illnesses from:

Community pharmacist
- Convenient
- Easier to use outside working hours than GPs
- No wait for appointment
- Prescription charges make some OTC products as good or better value than prescription medicines
- Pharmacists better informed on medicines, especially OTC medicines, than GP
- May provide more effective treatment for minor conditions than an unsatisfactory GP
- Source of medications for self-diagnosis and treatment
- Easy for user to act as proxy for someone else
- No obligation to accept advice (may be important to marginal groups of patients, for example drug users exchanging needles)
- Approachable about relatively minor ailments when GP 'should not be bothered'
- Can confirm patient's self-diagnosis that GP treatment is not needed – or correct it
- Longer, more informal contact with staff.

GP doctor
- Knows patient's medical history
- Most legitimate, 'right' source of advice (important in proxy consultations, especially for children)
- Can authorize sick-leave
- Can prescribe a wide range of medicines
- Can circumvent charges for medicines
- Privacy for consultation
- Able to influence the outcome, or failing that, symptoms and emotional effects of disease
- Suitable person with whom to discuss symptoms of disease, especially familiar and understandable symptoms
- Can detect masked serious disease
- More competent for dealing with serious illness
- Better quality advice than pharmacist
- Will visit patient at home
- Referral to further sources of NHS care.

A&E departments
- Quicker response than GP often provides
- An alternative to an unsatisfactory GP
- Seems suitable for trauma or frightening symptoms (for example severe pain, blood loss)
- Appears clinically specialized
- Meets patient's need to act promptly when child is ill or patient finds it hard to predict outcome of illness
- Dental care sometimes available, especially in cities with dental hospitals.

Figure 5.2   Relative merits of PHC providers – English patients' views.
Sources: Calnan (1983); Salisbury (1989); Green and Dale (1992); Roberts (1992); Hallam (1994); Khayat and Slater (1994); Anon (1995); Black *et al.* (1996); Boersma (1996); Cantrill *et al.* (1996); Hallam *et al.* (1996); Hassell *et al.* (1996); Anon (1999b); Corney (1999); Rogers *et al.* (1999).

- short consultations (below 5 minutes);
- non-hospital place of consultation;
- infrequent physical examination of the patient;
- routine recourse to prescription-writing;
- apparent lack of specialist equipment;
- some GPs' habit of encouraging patients to present and discuss just one problem at a time. (Cartwright 1979; Rogers *et al.* 1999)

Normal users apparently sub-segment into self-users and proxy users. Around half of calls to OOH services are proxy calls, mainly on behalf of children. Patients appear more ready to call the doctor when acting as proxy or adviser. Thus adults with an infection are more likely to seek treatment for themselves when they wish to prevent their infecting their children or grandchildren (Rogers *et al.* 1999).

Despite the publications and Internet sites now available, patients' informal knowledge on how to manage illness appears to be based largely on their own, friends' or relatives' experience of how they managed past illnesses (Rogers *et al.* 1999). Otherwise, users and non-users of NHS primary care taken together rely on three main sources of information about health. For women (over 15 years old), the most used sources of information are magazines and newspapers (44 per cent of respondents mentioned), GP (39 per cent) and television (29 per cent). Men use the same three sources but relied more on the GP (37 per cent) than television (34 per cent) or magazines and newspapers (33 per cent). However, the GP was the most credible source for 48 per cent of people, the second most important source, magazines or newspapers, scoring only 16 per cent. Generally, women are better informed about health matters than men (Griffin 1994). Since the 1990s, computer-based self-diagnosis in CD form and online has become available, not least NHS Direct (see below). Whilst this results in some patients' becoming better informed about their illnesses, many American websites are in essence sales promotion channels, with the potential for misinformation which that implies.

In *marketing audit* terms, NHS primary care services are fairly successful in providing the volume of care needed. Across the UK as a whole, registration levels are 99 per cent (Airey and Erens 1999). Nevertheless there are places, especially poorer urban areas, where some GPs' lists are closed to new patients (no figures are kept nationally). There remain deficits in the provision of psychiatric services, especially out of hours (Hallam *et al.* 1996) and for patients of intermediate severity between primary and secondary services' present admission thresholds. The Department of Health increased payments to NHS dentists in 1995 but then tried to claw some of the payments back, with calamitous results for GP dentists' willingness to do NHS work. Occupational health services are another gap. The Health and Safety at Work Executive fulfils a preventive and investigatory role, but diagnosing and treating individual workers falls to GPs. The existence of commercial providers suggests that even employers regard NHS coverage as deficient here.

Until the first National Patient Survey (Airey and Erens 1999), the only data on user satisfaction available came from various ad hoc surveys. They tend to report high general levels of user satisfaction with GP services (80 per cent very or fairly satisfied), although this level represents a fall over the previous decade (Royal Commission on the NHS 1979; Williams and Calnan 1991; Khayat and Salter 1994). Under 45s are more likely to be dissatisfied (Khayat and Salter 1994), especially women aged 25–34. However, a recent MORI survey for Age Concern suggested that 1 in 20 over-50s believes their GPs have refused them treatment and regard them as lower-priority patients than younger people (Laurance 1999). Patient dissatisfaction appears more to concern information the GP gives them about their illness than other aspects of care. Other dissatisfiers are: not having enough time with GP, not having what the patient regards as a requisitely thorough examination when necessary, the obtainability of appointments, and waiting and arrangements times (Anon 1995). Patients appear to like on-site outreach consultant clinics (Corney 1999).

Marketing objectives and strategy

Because PCG/Ts have difficulty making the necessary situation analysis, their scope for basing their objectives and strategies on a SWOT is correspondingly restricted. Instead, PCG/Ts have as their nearest equivalent to marketing objectives the objectives for user responsiveness, service development and service quality embedded in other documents (national policy guidance, accountability agreements, HImPs, Primary Care Investment Plans and so on). Until these are researched one can only infer from their marketing mix (see below) what service objectives PCG/Ts are pursuing; but those do correspond fairly closely with what the foregoing situation analysis would suggest. For instance, about half of PCG/Ts have plans to prevent or relieve shortages of GPs in under-doctored areas (Leese and Gillam 2000). In the absence of situation analysis, SWOT analyses and marketing planning (see below), these objectives are formulated from a synthesis of national guidance and initiatives by leading local GPs.

Marketing plan

By now it will be little surprise to learn that some of the relevant activity does occur in NHS primary care, but under different names. Care-pathway-based planning is gradually becoming familiar, although more at the level of planning the clinical elements and procedures nested within it than the whole care pathway. But there are some exceptions, such as the planning of discharge arrangements from secondary care: about 43 per cent of GP fundholders have agreed guidelines for discharge arrangements (Audit Commission 1994). Planning in NHS primary care tends to focus service development with a view to achieving more effective outcomes and cost control. At PCG/T level the main planning channels are Health Improvement Programmes (HImPs), National Service Frameworks (see Chapter 3) and Primary Care Investment Plans (PCIPs). The first PCIPs prioritized resource development: in descending order of frequency, prescribing support, information hardware and software, nursing staff, clinical governance support and other practice staff (Leese and Gillam 2000). These forms of planning are better at profiling services and user needs than they are of identifying user demands.

Use of data on user preferences is rarer. PCG/T boards all have one or more lay members but their influence on board decisions is slight compared with that of other members, especially GPs and the chief executive. Patient representative bodies or their active members do not necessarily react to promotions as other members of the public will, and are already sensitized to health issues and campaigns in ways that non-members are not (Consumers Association 1998). In future, *The NHS Plan* says, all NHS trusts (primary and secondary) will have a patients' forum, half selected from local voluntary bodies and half randomly chosen from respondents to patients' surveys. The forum will both advise the trust board and elect a lay member of it.

Consumer surveys are used, but only by 18 per cent of PCGs in 1999. Fifty-six per cent of first wave PMS contracts (i.e. 40 sites) specify that the providers should promote user involvement, although without really specifying how (Sheaff and Lloyd-Kendall 2000). Otherwise, general practices have undertaken such consumer research and involvement as has occurred in PHC. There are isolated reports of such activities as patient consultation groups on waiting times and clinical protocols (New and Le Grand 1996), the appointment of a researcher who interviewed over fifty community groups in Newcastle (Freake *et al.* 1997) and (more widely) use of locality groups, patients' forums. Some marketing-related skills (IT, personnel) are found in CHS trusts rather than general practice (Hudson 1999). Their small scale means that general practices' managerial and planning capacity tends to be limited.

Consequently, users' demands are little recognized in the planning of NHS primary care. Any analysis of which of these demands it is reasonable to meet, and which to try to re-educate, can therefore occur only in an intuitive, informal way.

Marketing mix

How does the NHS marketing mix for primary care compare with the mix which the previous section outlined?

For most NHS patients, initial access to a generalist primary care clinician still means seeing a GP doctor. *The NHS Plan* proposes a national standard of a wait of one working day to see a 'primary care professional' (who might be a nurse or paramedic) or two days to see a doctor (Department of Health 2000: 102). However, there are experiments with making nurse practitioners the first point of patient contact. Some general practices make a nurse practitioner the first point of contact during normal surgery hours, either triaging patients or providing primary care in their own right (Chambers 1998). A protocol indicates which patients the nurse will diagnose and treat (for example those with chronic diseases); all others see the doctor (Mulligan 1998). Provided the criteria defining when nurses decide the patient's treatment and when doctors do are clearly worked out, these arrangements appear not to compromise the quality of healthcare and are, if anything, somewhat more satisfactory to patients because of the nurses' communications skills (Chambers 1998; Venning *et al.* 2000). Although nurses are paid less, there is little cost difference because they give longer and more frequent consultations than doctors do.

In two nurse-led general practices, a nurse practitioner fills the role hitherto played by a GP doctor (Vignette 5.2). However the most extensive use of nurses as a first point of contact is in NHS Direct, whose telephone advice services are rapidly being extended throughout England.

Diversified points of entry accentuate the problem of how to coordinate the various care pathways. 'A single point of access to all services, staffed

---

Vignette 5.2   A nurse-led practice

This PMS pilot scheme originated from attempts to fill a vacant GP practice in a particularly deprived inner-urban part of Salford. A nurse who has trained as a health visitor and nurse practitioner duly took over the practice.

Clinical activity apart, the lead nurse fills the role of a single-handed independent practitioner GP. Using protocols, he provides both first-contact primary medical care, referring patients whom the protocol does not cover, to a part-time GP employed by the practice. The practice has now arranged with a nearby general practice (itself a PMS pilot) to supply it with a half-time GP. The lead nurse receives clinical mentorship jointly from a senior nurse manager and a GP, formerly chair of the local medical committee.

The practice has a PMS contract with Salford HA, buying in managerial services (human resource management support for the other nurses, building maintenance and clinical mentorship) from a local CHS trust. The lead nurse employs all the practice staff except the (other) nurses, whom he strongly preferred not to line-manage. They are therefore employed by the local CHS trust.

Some local GPs have argued that special circumstances made this project viable: the drive and personality of the lead nurse; the minister's personal support for this project; and that in a poor, under-doctored area, almost any service would be an improvement. All true; nevertheless, the practice has recruited patients, extended its hours of opening, and supported various community activities (such as questioning the extension of the Manchester metro system).

by well-trained professionals able to provide triage would remove much confusion and duplication' (Hallam *et al.* 1996: 2–3). *The NHS Plan* says that, in future, NHS Direct will be the point of first contact, at least for all OOH services, referring patients on to GP, ambulance or other providers – or advising self-care – as needed.

As for opening hours, NHS general practices typically hold surgeries in the early morning and late afternoon (making home visits in between). The GMS contract pays GPs a fee for all face-to-face consultations made between 22.00 and 08.00, encouraging the use of cooperative or sub-contracted commercial OOH deputizing services (Hallam *et al.* 1996). Full integration of OOH with diurnal services is rare (Hallam *et al.* 1996).

One-stop PHC integrating the full range of primary care services on a single site and into a coherent care pathway is slowly becoming a reality in the NHS, but it remains the exception rather than the rule because of the organizational independence of general practices from NHS community health services, and the organizational separation of both from community pharmacies. Before 1997, many practices (mainly, but not only, fundholders) had introduced counselling services. A few general practices have received bursaries to provide Relate (relationship counselling) or Cruise (bereavement counselling) services (Lee *et al.* 1998). From 1998 about one-third of first-wave PMS pilots introduced new services for hard-to-reach, underusing patient groups. A handful of PMS sites have attempted to stem the loss of NHS GP dentistry. During the 1990s, some fundholding general practices also established outreach clinics, bringing hospital specialists to PHC premises. How far this reduced waiting times for first appointments with a specialist or offered easier physical access appeared to depend on local circumstances such as the speciality and how the consultants managed their workload overall (Bailey *et al.* 1994; Black *et al.* 1996; Kerrison and Corney 1998). Primary care resource centres are a recent move towards one-stop provision, typically accommodating general practices, CHSs, outposted local authority social services, a base for voluntary bodies (for example Citizens' Advice Bureaux) and outposted hospital services (Glendinning *et al.* 1996; see also Vignette 5.2).

An obstacle to one-stop primary care is that many practice premises are too small for many more treatment rooms (Glendinning 1999). The Birth Control Trust has cited lack of suitable premises as one reason for the sluggish replacement of surgical with pharmaceutical (RU486) termination of pregnancy which could be provided in primary care.

It has been NHS policy since 1947 that patients should have locally accessible primary care services, preferably within a pram-journey from home. As independent contractors, GPs usually own their surgeries and sell them on leaving the practice. This is an incentive not only to invest in the surgery, but also to buy premises only in areas where property prices are at least stable in real terms. There are still pockets of population (especially, but not only, newer housing estates) without a GP surgery. Few NHS primary care organizations have tackled the gap in occupational health services, although NHS trusts in Cambridge, Walsall, Reading, Sandwell and Salisbury are attempting to sell occupational health services (Stirling 2000). *The NHS Plan* announces that a national service for this purpose – NHSplus – will be created and operate 'at no cost to the taxpayer' (Department of Health 2000: 100).

Around twenty NHS convenience clinics started in 1999, giving walk-in access to services without prior appointment. Some, such as one recently opened in Glasgow, are sited in shopping centres. Their siting (in town centres) and opening hours (0700–2200 weekdays and weekends) (NHSE 1999a) are evidently intended to attract people who tend to underuse GP services and might otherwise use accident and emergency services for minor conditions. It is still too early for there to be much evidence as to their successes and failures. Additionally, a few deputizing services and GP cooperatives run Primary Care Emergency Centres constructed and equipped much as GP surgeries are. The largest also provide convenience clinics open to patients 24 hours a day without prior appointment.

Little research exists about the *psychological impact* of an episode of NHS primary care taken as a whole. As for educating patients about how to access and use primary care services, NHS managers have hitherto concentrated on encouraging general practices to produce practice leaflets. These leaflets often have a rather uneven, 'home-made' quality. A 'fog index' analysis of practice leaflets in Avon in 1992 indicated that 30 per cent were written in the style of tabloid papers, 45 per cent in a style 'comparable to papers such as the *Daily Mail*', and 13 per cent 'had a score similar to the *BMJ*'. Only 10 per cent met Royal National Institute for the Blind guidelines for the use of clear typefaces (Albert and Chadwick 1992). Such findings suggest that few leaflets are pilot tested. Many voluntary bodies also 'campaign' to encourage people to take up services such as breast screening (Wood 1999), but it largely remains left to general practices' discretion which ones to support and how actively. NHS promotions aimed at marketing primary care to underusers have had mixed success. The Doctor–Patient Partnership promotional campaign (jointly promoted by the British Medical Association and Department of Health) was intended to influence patients' decisions about whether and when to see a GP, but with mixed success, according to the Consumers Association, with some inconsistent, unclear, overdramatized and poorly targeted messages (Rogers *et al.* 1999: 186–8).

Until NHS Direct's web service began (www.nhsdirect.nhs.uk), promotional materials enabling patients to decide whether or when to call the doctor existed more often as an adjunct to managing established disease rather than as an 'instruction for appropriate use' of NHS services at the onset of symptoms. Now an *NHS Home Healthcare Guide* has appeared, and the first guides for patients on how diseases are managed (Kennedy and Robinson 1999). These, incidentally, won the Plain English Campaign's Crystal Mark. *The NHS Plan* announces a digital NHS-TV service for this purpose.

Implementation

Notwithstanding the arguments in favour of integrated primary care (see earlier this chapter), only about 16 per cent of general practices are based in large health centres (Bailey *et al.* 1997). Since 1970, the proportion of GPs working in groups of four or more has risen to about a half (Hallam *et al.* 1996: 13), but most general medical and dental practices are still small, rarely above ten partners. One consequence is that receptionist recruitment and training is often neglected. Complaints about receptionists acting more as a barrier than as a route to the doctor recur in informal surveys of general practice such as those published in women's and consumers' magazines. Even at PCG/T level, NHS primary care management resources in general, let alone for marketing management, are too modest for a PCG/T to form even a situation analysis drawing mainly on secondary data (cp. Chapter 3). PCGs' average support staff was just under five people in 1999. This problem may be palliated over the next few years by the transfer of HA and CHS staff (in particular those with planning and research skills) to the PCTs. In future, PCTs will be able to employ their own staff, including GPs, which appears a powerful way of implementing its marketing (or any other) objectives.

Meantime though, PCG/Ts provide few, if any, clinical services themselves and rely on two governance structures to implement their (nearest equivalents to) marketing objectives and plans. Whilst GMS-based independent contractor GPs remain, PCG/Ts will rely on a network structure to implement their marketing (or any other) policy. The PCG/T can only influence them financially through budgets for support services, indicative prescribing budget and the use of commissioning budgets. These are not inconsequential to a GP but are not their main source of income either. Otherwise, PCG/Ts' main means of influence are through clinical governance: discussing data about the profile and quality of the GPs' clinical work, retraining, the exchange of protocols and other technical advice. Community health service contracts tend to be formulated in terms of cost and volume of activity. In so far as is known – the area is under-researched – quality and marketing objectives are rarely elaborated in any detail beyond standard requirements that medical audit should occur and staff be properly qualified.

Since 1997, a gradual shift towards personal medical service (PMS) contracts has begun (see above). PMS contracts are locally negotiated between, on the purchaser side, health authorities or, in future, PCTs. However, the experience of GP fundholding suggests it is easier to use contracts to improve the process and organization than it is to use the clinical aspects of quality of care (Glennerster *et al.* 1994). One danger signal is that PMS contracts extend cash limiting, and therefore scope for 'rationing', into NHS primary care. It remains to be seen how far this process will go and its effects.

Nevertheless, a handful of NHS entrepreneurs have provided a wide range of PHC services on a single site. The Peckham experiment was a notable

Vignette 5.3   Anticipations of polyclinics?

Peckham Health Centre	Leisure, community centre, educational services
Bromley by Bow Centre	GP practices, CHS, nurseries, community café, complementary therapists
West End Health Resource Centre (Newcastle)	GP practices, CHS, nurseries, community café, complementary therapists, fitness centre
Brockenhurst Health Village Project (Southampton)	Exercise, yoga, dancing classes rehabilitation programmes
Looking Well Centre (High Bentham)	Arts and crafts activities, children's play area, meeting rooms, women's self-help group, Alzheimer's Disease Society's carer support group, young people's health project, local 'exchange trading' (skills barter), facilities for people with learning difficulties
Kath Locke Community Health Resource Centre (Manchester)	Community nurses, health visitors, community mental health team, social workers, crèche, café, yoga, massage, counselling, physiotherapy, 'youth shop'. Salaried GP outreach surgery planned; PCG offices on-site
Neptune Health Park (Sandwell)	GP practice, OOH centre, outreach OPD (outpatients' clinic) and minor surgery clinics (run by acute NHS trust), community services, X-ray, pharmacy, optician, Citizens' Advice Bureau and advocacy service, exercise classes, healthy eating café, health support groups. Health promotion information, diabetes clinics, dietician and chiropody to come
St Matthews Health and Community Centre (Leicester)	PHC, welfare and legal rights, police, Benefits Agency, mental health services, social services, services for victims of domestic violence

Sources: Ashton and Seymour (1988); Davies (1998).

achievement of this kind (Ashton and Seymour 1988; see also Vignette 5.3). Its neglect and demise in the 1950s shames the NHS administration of the period.

Tracking

Tracking is perhaps the weakest part of the management of NHS primary care. The health impact of PHC is practically unmeasurable in present NHS systems. They collect data mainly about GP income and activity and about

CHS activity, prescribing patterns (percent generics, availability of protocols and so on) and about referrals to secondary care. These data are used to monitor PHC because they are available rather than for their relevance to clinical effectiveness or user satisfaction. Data about user demands, experience, satisfaction and behaviour are collected only occasionally and ad hoc. In default, systems for tracking the quality of NHS primary care depend heavily on use of exception management (for example, complaints) or patterns of re-registration to detect underperforming practices or GPs (Hallam 1994). Until recently, the only means of redress for users who suffered a poor quality of general practice were, at one extreme, to take legal action, complain to the General Medical Council or try to get an ombudsman's investigation: extreme measures, rarely invoked. The alternative was to make a disciplinary charge under the Service Committee procedure. But Service Committees could only investigate failures to comply with the GMS contract. Its requirements about service quality were so vague as to make it nearly impossible to demonstrate that a GP had breached it. Recently, though, complaints systems of the types used in NHS trusts (see Chapters 6 and 7) have been extended from CHSs and NHS Direct into NHS general practice. Whatever their limitations, these systems provide fuller redress than was previously available in general practice.

Prescribing data are the exception to this disorganized picture, because those data are absolutely standardized, collected through relatively simple channels, and serve useful clinical purposes (monitoring prescribing practice) when they return to PCG/Ts and GPs.

It remains to be seen how long these problems will continue, however. PCG/Ts are new organizations, still developing their information systems and governance structures. In any event, NHS general practices are so small that their data sets would still be too small and unstable to reveal patterns for tracking purposes. Analysis inequality measured at practice level is about ten times that measured at health authority level. Both technical and cost-saving reasons thus suggest that tracking is best carried out no lower than PCG/T level.

Prescribing apart, so few tracking data are analysed as to make it almost otiose to ask how tracking data are used to detect marketing problems for later remedy. In NHS primary care, this feedback is a meagre indeed.

In conclusion

Users have direct access to PHC and continue to use it whilst living at home. Primary care services therefore require suitably adapted consumer marketing methods, based on a good empirical understanding of how and why patients use primary care, and a realistically wide view of what users' sources of primary care are. One difference with conventional consumer marketing, however, is that primary care is often delivered through networks of small providers and informal carers. A care pathway approach can be used to coordinate this pathway and the marketing mix which it requires, but that requires a network coordinating body and strong information systems. The range of NHS primary care providers has widened considerably, owing both to government interventions and local initiatives by GPs, nurse practitioners and others. They have a broad marketing mix. But consumer research information and marketing activities are fragmentary in NHS primary care, and network coordinating bodies (PCTs) are only starting to develop.

Questions

1 What forms of primary health care, and what substitutes, are available to people in a developed industrial society?
2 How do networks differ from quasi-markets, in primary care settings?
3 What incentives and constraints do NHS general practices face in making their services user-responsive?
4 What are the marketing implications of the proliferation of forms of NHS primary care?

For discussion

What are the marketing pros and cons of all GPs' becoming salaried public employees (for example, of PCTs)?

Further reading

Anon (1995) 'What makes a good GP?', *Which*, June, 18–19.
Baum, N. and Henkel, G. (1992) *Marketing your Clinical Practice*. Gaithersburg: Aspen.
Katz, B. (1988) *How to Market Professional Services*. Aldershot: Gower.
Rogers, A., Hassell, K. and Nicolaas, G. (1999) *Demanding Patients? Analysing the Use of Primary Care*. Buckingham: Open University Press.

6 Marketing for secondary healthcare providers

Chapter overview

Hospitals provide relatively specialized healthcare to patients who enter hospital mostly by way of a referral from a GP or similar. In a quasi-market they therefore confront three audiences: patients, GPs and commissioners. Being relatively large organizations, hospitals can develop the more diverse and specialized marketing activities which this more complex role requires. This chapter examines the relevant marketing methods, concepts and practices, and compares the activities of NHS trusts with the resulting marketing model.

Principles of marketing for secondary healthcare providers

Structures, incentives, objectives

Our account of primary care implies a corresponding marketing definition of secondary care as healthcare provided without the patient's living at home, at inpatient settings such as acute hospitals and long-term residential care entered by clinician's referral. Secondary care providers in quasi-markets therefore market to three main audiences: purchasers, patients and referrers. Since referral from primary care is the main 'distribution' channel for hospitals (Anderson and Near 1983) this chapter concentrates on hospital marketing to purchasers and referrers. In 'primary-care-led' quasi-markets (such as British PCG/Ts, various experiments in Germany, Sweden and Russia) these are the same body. Nevertheless, the two activities require different marketing activities. To prevent repetition, hospital marketing to patients is discussed only in so far as it differs from the methods discussed in Chapter 5.

Despite an increasing volume of day-cases, secondary care providers remain substantially inpatient institutions. Both the two main exceptions allow (most) patients to remain at home but have historically been provided on hospital sites. In terms of access and benefits, both accident and emergency services, and outpatient clinics are a form of primary care to most of their users (see Chapter 5). Consequently both are similar to primary care in many aspects of their marketing mix (place, physical signs, psychological impact).

In making their referral decision, the referring doctor (or other clinician) acts as the patient's proxy, compensating for the patient's information disadvantage in doing so. In accepting the referral, the hospital acts as the GP's agent and therefore as a proxy-for-a-proxy for the patient. However, the GP's demand is in turn corrigible by secondary provider staff who have knowledge not available to the GP about the more narrowly specialized aspects of the patient's diagnosis and treatment. Fatal emergencies apart, secondary care is nested within wider primary healthcare as a fallback resource providing care which primary care cannot, with the objective of eventually returning the patient to resume primary care. A needs-oriented secondary care provider's fundamental objective would be to satisfy referrers' reasonable demands for a suitable range of accessible, timely, effective treatments for their patients. When they are not misinformed or underinformed, the patient's own demands do express their healthcare needs. Subject to the requirement of effectiveness, a needs-oriented secondary care provider's second main objective would be to satisfy patients' reasonable demands about the social aspects of treatment, 'hotel' services, and minimizing disruption to the patient's normal activities (for example by minimizing the length of stay). Such a provider also would have to correct patients' (and referrers') demands where they are misinformed or inconsistent.

In marketing to purchasers, the provider's immediate practical aim is to attract the necessary income to meet the above objectives. In some quasi-markets, secondary providers' incomes depend on the volume of referrals they attract. Then a concomitant objective for secondary providers is to attract the requisite referrals. The concomitant incentives were outlined earlier (see Chapter 3).

Situation analysis

Having three marketing audiences trifurcates the situation analysis into analyses covering users, purchasers and referrers.

Hospitals usually have a geographically defined catchment area. Its 'served market share' is its percentage of referrals from that catchment (Berkowitz 1996). Amongst the residue, volume and distribution of referrals to other hospitals indicate which ones local referrers regard as substitutes for this hospital.

Referrers decide, on the patients' behalf, which secondary services their patients need. One would expect the process by which primary care clinicians select a provider to resemble the process by which the consumers themselves would do so (see Chapter 5), but with different selection criteria. The main differences between this decision and the process by which a patient decides to seek primary care are that for the gatekeeper:

- 'problem recognition' consists of making a diagnosis indicating treatments which PHC cannot provide, i.e. confirming that the patient satisfies the appropriateness criteria for referral;
- the 'internal search' for a provider relies on their own technical knowledge, experience of secondary services and, increasingly, published evidence about the relative merits of possible secondary care providers;
- evaluations of possible providers are made by different criteria and data from those that the patient could use. The critical criteria are clinical effectiveness, and what different providers could contribute to the GP's wider treatment plan for the patient (for example, whether they can provide physiotherapy or other rehabilitative services). As (at best) proxies for effectiveness, further criteria might include: location of 'star' clinicians (for example, being a university, regional or national speciality centre or a research institute); location of equipment or other facilities; trust in institutions or clinicians with whom they previously trained or worked;
- the foregoing criteria are also the criteria for 'post-purchase' evaluation of secondary providers.

The hospital's situation analysis has therefore to state which appropriateness and selection criteria referrers use and how they trade off conflicting criteria (such as when a patient can be admitted sooner in a hospital of slightly poorer clinical quality). Neither, in real-life situation analysis, can one assume that referrers always refer according to criteria which reflect patients' needs. The first requirement is to find what criteria referrers actually apply.

Referrers can therefore be segmented according to:

- what benefit (specific treatment, resource or expertise) different referrers seek (Miaoulis and Corson 1994);
- loyalty, separating habitual referrers from those who switch between hospitals;
- their propensity to refer appropriately, or the opposite (i.e. to refer patients who do not really need secondary rather than primary care).

The test of whether the resulting segments are accessible to the provider's marketing efforts and imply differences in marketing mix (see Chapter 1) recommends segmentation by appropriateness and then, within the category of appropriate referrals, benefit segmentation.

Where gatekeepers have freedom of referral, a secondary care provider requires an analysis of competition for referrals showing whom the gatekeepers tacitly regard as the main competitors and substitutes and what the loci of competition are. Whether or not private hospitals are important competitors in terms of volume or effectiveness, they are a symbolically important alternative to public provision, especially if they appear to be of higher status or quality than public provision. Primary care substitution for hospital care is likely to occur at the 'low' end of the technology spectrum – diagnostics, rehabilitation, outpatient consultation but also some inpatient services such as 'hospital at home' and 'hospice at home'.

The situation analysis also requires a needs profile, i.e. a profile of the prevalence and incidence of conditions requiring hospital care (given current technologies; cp. Chapter 2). The relevant figures are for this provider's share of its catchment population, not the whole population. For marketing purposes they must be apportioned to each primary care referrer, just as referral data are in many health systems.

For operational purposes, a more concrete situation analysis is required for each specific patient group within the trust. Vignette 6.1 is an example.

Vignette 6.1   Situation analysis – elderly people

Demand

Increasing numbers – UK projections:

	2001	2011
65–74 yr:	4.8m	5.2m
Over 75:	4.4m	4.5m
Over 85:	1.2m	1.3m

Sex-mix varies with age:

65–74 yr:	45% male: 55% female
75–84	37% male: 63% female
Over 85	25% male: 75% female

Approximately 5% of 65-year-olds institutionalized, approximately 35% of over-85s. Falling family size and marriage rates, and rising geographical mobility are raising numbers of old-elderly without spouse or children's support.

Cognitive age approximately 10–15 years less than chronological age. 'Life satisfactions' sought:

- Pleasure in everyday activity
- Feeling that life is meaningful
- Positive self-image
- Happy, optimistic outlook
- Feeling success in achieving goals
- Interpersonal relations, friendships
- 'Philosophical introspection'
- 'Little' experiences
- Learning
- Doing for others.

Unwelcome messages and self-image:

- Unable to function
- Need to be directed
- Sick
- Poor
- Dependent
- Cannot think for themselves
- Wish they were young
- Conservatively minded
- 'Crumblies'/'wrinklies'.

Prefer to be 'senior citizens' or 'retired', not 'elderly', 'old person', 'old age pensioner'.

Healthcare needs

Tendency to chronic and slowly degenerative conditions, multiple pathologies and complications, rapid deterioration if untreated: arteriosclerosis, arthritis, diabetes, sinusitis, hypertension, hearing loss, incontinence (males), dementia, reduced mobility. Risks of falls (trips or accidental falls account for one-third of these). Social isolation can lead to self-neglect, hence malnutrition, hypothermia. Main causes of death, UK, in decreasing order:

65–74 yr: ischaemic heart disease; cerebro-vascular disease; lung cancer
Over 75s: ischaemic heart disease, cerebro-vascular disease; lung cancer (men)/pneumonia (women), circulatory diseases

Function:

- Vision: 80% loss of acuity from ages 50 to 85; slower processing of visual information
- Hearing: loss after age 60, especially ability to hear high pitches and low-intensity sounds; greater susceptibility to distraction by background noise
- Memory: loss of short-term (processing) but not long-term memory. Slower processing of information using memory, partially compensated by use of schemata. Possibly less efficient use of encoding and mnemonics

Segmentation:

- Young elderly: physically able, more-or-less stable health, limited income, able to be active consumers. Household head retired, no children still at home, live at home, couple able to care for each other to significant extent. Active independent life beyond work and parenting
- Old elderly: partly or increasingly physically unable, more house- or institution-bound. Often a 'sole survivor' – widowed spouse, living alone, increasingly dependent

Sources: Cooper and Maioulis (1994); Office of Health Economics (1998).

Hard technologies are continually developing in secondary care, leading, in the extreme, to 'medical arms races' between hospitals (Wohl 1984). For marketing purposes, important technologies are those which enable the following:

- Substitutions of daycare and outpatient for inpatient treatment: for example, substitution of keyhole for radical surgery, of pharmaceutical for surgical treatments and of home for hospital obstetrics. Around 75 per cent of US surgery is already done on an outpatient basis (Berkowitz 1996). A corollary is the development of hospital hotels to replace wards for low-dependency, short-stay inpatients.
- Substitutions of primary for secondary care, in the forms of community care (for elderly people, people with mental health problems), intermediate care (for people recuperating from hospital inpatient treatment), 'telemedicine' and other remote diagnostics and primary care alternatives to A&E treatment for minor complaints (see Chapter 5).
- Longer term, the Human Genome Project holds out prospects of gene therapies, ectogenesis and phylogenesis.

Conversely, note also which treatments have become obsolete, or exposed as iatrogenic, unproven or second best practice.

Of soft technologies, by far the most important are the emergence of evidence-based medicine (EBM) protocols, in particular the emergence of evidence-based criteria for appropriate referral. Technological changes may shift these thresholds either upwards (if new treatments can be given in primary care settings, as some genetic treatments probably will (Wigzell 2000)) or downward (if previously untreatable conditions become susceptible to hospital treatment; for instance if techniques for remedying spinal cord injuries improve in future). In general, the effect of technological changes on general hospitals in recent years seems to have been towards upwards respecialization, i.e. to withdraw from services where new technology allows day case, outpatient clinic, PHC provision to be substituted, and at the other end of the spectrum of complexity, a strategy of substituting for tertiary care. The converse of primary care substitution for hospital care at the 'low' end of the technology spectrum is to encroach 'up' the technology spectrum by taking on work formerly limited to tertiary providers. (For instance, hip replacement was once limited to tertiary provision.) The behavioural, social and economic background also influences what technologies emerge and can be implemented. For example, the spread of daycare as an alternative to hospital inpatient treatment depends in part on the availability of informal carers, high level of telephone ownership and a reliable telephone network.

A marketing audit of a secondary care provider compares its own benefits with those of substitute providers:

- Unique benefits for gatekeepers, patients and purchasers.
- Access to services, in terms of waiting time and distance especially, and ratio of demand to capacity.

- 'Volume concentration', i.e. sufficient throughput for each care group to maintain quality, safety and effectiveness.
- Reputation with referrers, patients and purchasers.

Where purchasers and gatekeepers are different bodies, the secondary provider has to repeat the analysis to report the purchasers' situation. In theory, purchasers should reflect referrers' and therefore patients' needs (see Chapter 3). In practice, however, one cannot assume that they do and must analyse separately the following:

- What benefits the purchasers are seeking, the selection criteria (loci of competition) which they set and how they evaluate alternative providers' services. Purchasers have to consider the volume and costs of referrals as a whole besides clinical effectiveness and satisfactoriness to patients (see Chapter 3). If so, purchasers' selection criteria will include the volume and costs ('efficiency') which alternative providers can offer. Public purchasers also seek opportunity to implement other aspects of health policy or public policy (regional policy, labour market policy, equal opportunities) more widely.
- Segments of payers, in terms of size, benefits sought and mobility between providers.
- The share of potential purchasers' spending obtained by this provider, and how the rest is distributed amongst other providers, i.e. which other providers are the main competitors and substitutes in the purchasers' eyes.

For hospitals in a quasi-market, a critical question is how vigorously the purchasers intend to 'play the market', i.e. whether they intend to stimulate competition (for example, inspire new providers to enter the local quasi-market), use the contestability of service to pressurize hospitals, benchmark only or none of these (see Chapter 2). The lower down this continuum, the less relevant competition analysis is to the provider. Exit barriers for secondary care providers are usually political. Even in such dire conditions as the Russian economic collapse in the 1990s it proved politically difficult to close whole hospitals.

What hard and soft technologies are available will be the same as before. However, purchasers are likely to be interested in new technologies' potential not only for cost reduction but also for greater effectiveness. In dealing with purchasers, critical review of the provider's cost base and internal information systems is more necessary than in the case of gatekeepers.

Marketing objectives and strategies

Both SWOT analysis and marketing strategy grids have to be adapted for use by secondary healthcare providers in a quasi-market (see Chapter 2). SWOT analysis is relatively easy to adapt, but separate analysis is required for each main audience:

- *SWOT analysis – referrers.* This analysis compares the profile (case mix and volume) of referrals with the prevalence and incidence of conditions in the catchment population needing secondary care. This comparison reveals both care groups and referrers where there is inappropriate referral (greater than need) and 'icebergs' (under-referral). Depending on the case, icebergs may indicate under-referrals of patients who do present to primary care needing secondary care, or an iceberg within primary care because such people are not even going to their GP (or equivalent) to begin with. This comparison shows which services it is necessary to promote to GPs and which to demarket.
- *SWOT analysis – purchasers.* This SWOT analysis compares the providers' volume, cost, patient profile (case mix) and effectiveness with the purchaser's own demands, and with any health policy requirements it is required to implement.
- *SWOT analysis – users.* This analysis focuses on patients' willingness to accept referral to the hospital.

Firms in conventional markets use strategy grids (business grids, portfolio analyses) to decide which marketing strategy will enable them best to reach firm's objectives (profit maximization, ROI, market share and so on) in the face of competition. Not having to be generalists, secondary care providers can pursue clinical specialization and niche marketing to a much greater extent than their PHC counterparts. They also face competition. To that extent, marketing grids are relevant to them. But public hospitals in quasi-markets face different incentives from commercial bodies, pursue different objectives and have to deal separately with purchasers, gatekeepers and consumers. For them, the standard marketing grids must be modified.

Table 6.1 summarizes the criteria of 'market attractiveness' in the better-known marketing strategy grids (see Chapter 1) and in some proposed specifically for health services (Dubois 1981; MacStravic 1989; Gilligan and Lowe 1995; McDonald and Miles 1995). These grids also differentiate markets according to a firm's capacity to exploit them successfully (Table 6.2).

To reconstruct a marketing strategy grid for quasi-market providers whose objective is (we assume) to meet users' needs for healthcare, we firstly replace references to markets with references to care groups. Then we replace commercial criteria of market 'attractiveness' with more relevant criteria, i.e. how far the work contributes to meeting users' healthcare needs. This criterion ('level of need in patient segment') summarizes the seriousness of the effects of non-treatment compared with treatment in terms of mortality, disability, pain, and the numbers of patients affected. A third revision is to redefine 'capacity' as the provider's capacity to effect the health improvement which users need. Adapting the idea of triage, we can distinguish patient segments where:

- the provider cannot significantly improve patients' health status compared to non-treatment;

Table 6.1   Criteria of 'market attractiveness' in marketing grids

Marketing strategy grid	Criteria of market attractiveness
Boston (1968)	Market growth (cash value, annual rate)
Gilligan and Lowe (1995)	Growth and revenue potential
McDonald and Miles (1995)	Little competition, not price-sensitive, high procedure success rate, few complications, low inpatient content, growth
Porter (1981)	Breadth of target segments or market
General Electric (cp. Kotler 1991)	Market size, growth, profitability, competition, technological requirements, inflation, energy requirements, environmental impact, socio/political/ legal context
Ansoff (1957)	New market
Dubois (1987)	Profitability, risk of competition
Kotler and Clarke (1987)	'Un/wholesome' demand
MacStravic (1989)	Size, own market share, customer loyalty

Table 6.2   Criteria of firms' capacity to exploit markets

Marketing strategy grid	Criteria of the firm's capacity
Boston (1968)	Market share (percentage of cash value)
Gilligan and Lowe (1995)	Ability to service areas of need
McDonald and Miles (1995)	Competence, compatible with existing resources, good relations with purchasers, good reputation, quality, staff calibre
Porter (1981)	Competitive scope
General Electric (cp. Kotler 1991)	Market share and growth, product quality, brand reputation, distribution, promotional effectiveness, production capacity and efficiency, costs, R&D, managerial talent
Ansoff (1957)	Existing vs new products
Dubois (1981)	Product life cycle stage, resources

- the provider has the capacity to restore health completely (for example, appendicectomy or cataract extraction in otherwise healthy patients) or to maintain health during such events as childbirth. This absolute criterion is labelled 'complete capacity' in Figure 6.1;

Provider's capacity for health impact

		Complete	High	Low	None
Level of need in patient segment	High	Service development		R&D, and maintain palliative services	
	Low	Maintain service		Withdraw, demarket	

Figure 6.1 Strategy grid for healthcare providers in quasi-markets.

- existing healthcare technologies enable a provider to restore the patient's health partially but not fully. Then the provider's capacity is defined relative to that of other providers (who may perform better or worse than it does).

In marketing to referrers, a secondary care provider should, we assume, concentrate on those segments of patients which it is capable of benefiting. Figure 6.1 shows the resulting marketing strategy grid.

Where levels of need are high, service development means a maximal strategy of devising new unique need satisfiers (UNSs) and promoting services as the best available for a specific care group, which implies a long-term strategy of investment. However, when existing services are insufficient to accommodate the volume and range of reasonable demands (needs) which the provider faces, the provider needs not so much to promote its services as to undertake demarketing and service redesign (see below). Longer term, the 'service development' strategy especially also implies investment to increase capacity. 'Maintain service' denotes a threshold strategy of ensuring the service is of sufficient quality to satisfy accreditors and licensers.

A last revision to conventional business grids is necessary in those healthcare quasi-markets where the referrers and the purchasers are separate bodies. Having limited its fields of activity to user segments that will benefit in health terms (see Figure 6.1), the hospital has next to get purchasers to finance its work. A second-order, tie-breaking criterion for selecting which patient segments to concentrate on is, therefore, according to which of those segments purchasers are likeliest to finance. Conducted as outlined above, the situation analysis will indicate what benefits purchasers seek (low cost, health policy implementation, volume concentration, informational transparency, redress; see Chapter 2). The marketing audit will indicate the hospital's relative strength in providing these benefits.

Marketing planning

Now the focus shifts to the concrete marketing mix to be provided at operational level. In hospitals as in primary care, marketing planning can be undertaken by using the 'care pathway' or 'quality chain' method to redesign (re-engineer) the process of care (see Figure 6.4). Chapter 5 explains how this is done. Here we briefly illustrate how these methods might be used to plan the marketing mix of a service which is already oversubscribed, since that is a common and politically important scenario in healthcare quasi-markets.

In essence the method is as described in Chapter 5, but the context which we are now supposing also necessitates meeting reasonable demands of the GP besides those of the patient and commissioner. For patients who survive it, secondary care is nested within a longer episode of primary care. In quasi-markets with gate-kept access to secondary care, the hospital acts as a resource supplementing and supporting primary care (and especially the GP). The GP acts as patient's proxy in selecting the secondary care treatment, in selecting the provider and in evaluating those aspects of the secondary care received which the patient cannot readily assess for themselves. For such a secondary care provider, Step 1 (Articulate the provider's objectives) and Step 3 (Identify critical events) of the marketing planning process have to be extended to include the GP's reasonable demands on the patient's behalf and to enable the GP to provide whatever further primary care ensues. A situation analysis on the lines indicated above would supply the necessary evidence as to what benefits the GP (besides the patient and the payer) seeks from secondary care. Step 4 has also to be extended to ensure that redesign of the care pathway (see below) provides these benefits too.

To minimize lengths of stay and thus increase service capacity, critical path analysis and process flow analyses can additionally be applied at Steps 2 (Map the production process) and 4 (Redesign the chain). In essence, a critical path analysis itemizes the events in the care pathway and the sequence in which they must be performed ('dependencies' – for example the patient must recover from anaesthesia before they can return to the ward). Knowing the minimum time each event requires makes it possible to calculate the quickest overall time in which a patient can traverse the pathway and, when activities are performed in parallel (the patient recuperates on the ward whilst tissue obtained during surgery is tested), which events have to be completed punctually to enable earliest discharge (Figure 6.2 illustrates).

Software is available to automate the analysis, and various textbooks explain the technique and the (fairly simple) mathematics involved. However, there are limits to routinizing clinical care. Although a hospital department is likely to take a narrower variety of patients than a PHC provider, non-standard cases still occur. For those patients it is necessary to design a generic path, probably quite loosely defined and leaving scope for clinical discretion. However, the main problem facing hospitals in some health quasi-markets (as in the Netherlands and UK) is not so much length of stay as shortage of capacity.

Minimizing lengths of stay palliates the problem of undercapacity in an existing hospital infrastructure, but to solve the problem at root requires redesigning the infrastructure itself. Here, too, the quality chain method provides a framework. A process flow analysis identifies bottlenecks in the care pathway. Having divided the care pathway into its constituent stages, one can observe how many patients can be treated in parallel at each stage and

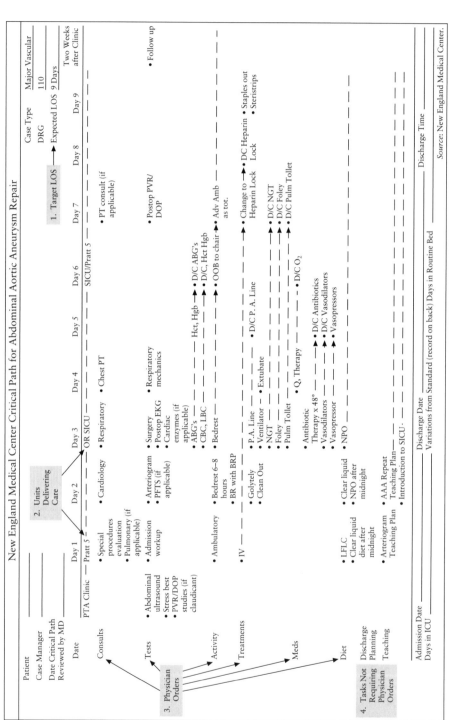

Figure 6.2 Critical path analysis – a surgical example.
Source: Health Care Advisory Board (1992).

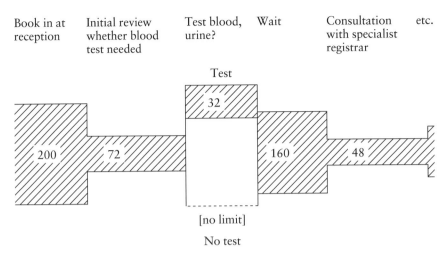

| Book in at reception | Initial review whether blood test needed | Test blood, urine? | Wait | Consultation with specialist registrar | etc. |

Figure 6.3 Process flow analysis – an outpatient's example. Width of bar shows maximum number of patients per working day (0900–1700).

how long each stage takes. These factors constrain the possible throughput at each stage. Thus a 20-bed ward whose average length of stay is 6 days could, in a 30-day month, treat $(30 \times 20)/6 = 100$ patients. However, one must subtract a percentage to allow time for routine planned maintenance, a percentage (ordinarily around 5 per cent) which can also be found by observation. A further percentage may be subtracted to allow for haphazard fluctuations in need. How much to subtract for these fluctuations is an arbitrary decision depending on how averse to risk one is. But even here it is possible to observe past fluctuations and calculate how often each year the ward will run out of beds if (in our example) one takes, say, 85 planned admissions per month. The throughput of the whole pathway depends on the capacity of its narrowest bottleneck. Calculating maximum throughput for each stage in the pathway shows where its bottlenecks are (Figure 6.3 illustrates).

It might appear that one could plan how far these bottlenecks have to be opened up simply by extrapolating past referral trends. But since, in England at least, GP referrals respond to the sheer availability of secondary services (Gravelle *et al.* 2000), an obvious way to avoid the problem of increased service supply's stimulating its own demand is to decide clinical criteria for appropriateness of referral, and then match secondary service capacity to the incidence of conditions for which referral is appropriate.

Planning 'hotel' services is more important in secondary than primary care. We assume that in secondary as in primary care, patients' 'collateral needs' are to continue caring for themselves in their preferred ways, so far as their health status allows, that is to decide for themselves what clothes to wear, meal times and menu, waking and sleeping times, temperature, exposure to fellow residents, choice of reading, radio or television programme or other diversions. For long-stay patients the obvious point of comparison is their own home; for short-stay patients, it is the hotels or other places they stay in on holiday or whilst travelling. In short, the aim of planning the hotel services is to normalize, not institutionalize, users' experience as inpatients: an aim having therapeutic value in itself.

Marketing mix

Having applied the sorts of planning technique outlined above, what sort of marketing mix would the foregoing marketing principles suggest for a quasi-market hospital attempting to raise the quality and capacity of an over-subscribed service? Vignette 6.2 shows a deservedly celebrated example.

Vignette 6.2   MNTK ophthalmological hospitals

During the late 1980s, Svyatoslav Fyodorov was able, through his Central Committee connections, to finance a number of ophthalmological hospitals organized as an 'intersectoral scientific–technical combine' (MNTK) independently of the (then) USSR health ministry. Their distinctive characteristics were:

- Concentration on a limited number of procedures (radial keratotomy, cataract extraction etc.), performed on a large scale.
- 'Production line' methods, based on a standard care pathway. The production line was a large turntable with patients on trolleys positioned with their heads at the circumference. Each part-turn of the turntable brought the patient to the next doctor, who performed one specific stage of the surgical procedure. The operation was completed during one revolution of the turntable.
- Before-and-after outcome measures (vision tests).
- Outcome-based contracts with industrial enterprises; an agreed price of treatment paid only if the patient's vision was sufficiently restored for them to resume work.
- Hard currency generation by selling capacity to western individuals and organizations.
- A guaranteed share of capacity reserved for Soviet health ministry patients.
- Patient hotels for patients and carers who made long journeys, and for patients to use if overnight observation or follow-up treatment were needed.
- Latterly, a ship-borne clinic brought these services to Mediterranean and Black Sea ports.
- Equipment and accommodation to world standards.

Short of comprehensive rebuilding, the hospital 'product' might be designed to minimize 'penalties' to users (by reducing length of stay) and increase throughput in the following ways:

- On-site but separate primary care provision, reserving access to a fully equipped trauma department for patients requiring complex diagnosis and treatment as an emergency.
- Permitting GPs' patients to use paramedical and diagnostic services relevant to primary care without requiring prior consultation as a hospital outpatient.

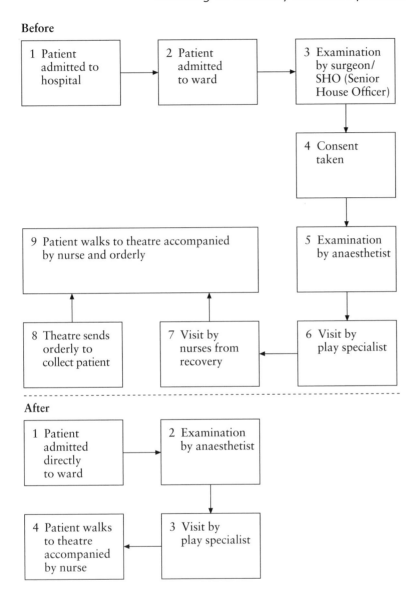

Figure 6.4 Part of a care pathway before and after redesign.
Source: Brooks (1998).

- Substituting day-case and outpatient diagnosis and treatment for inpatient care where possible.
- Using the aforementioned planning methods to simplify the process of in-patient care so as to increase the throughput capacity of the existing infrastructure. Figure 6.4 illustrates part of a hospital pathway before and

after redesign. (A play specialist helps prepare children psychologically for surgery; and afterwards provides physical and psychological rehabilitation and, when necessary, education.)

- Hospital 'hotels' offering cheaper, less institutionalized accommodation for low-dependency patients (for example those having cataract or wisdom tooth extraction under general anaesthetic). They can be used to substitute for inpatient beds, which are over-resourced for those purposes. Similarly, accommodation at the patient's home, community hospital or nursing home can be used at the later stages of recuperation.
- Minimizing the number of follow-up examinations by ensuring that they are performed by senior rather than trainee clinicians (who tend, justifiably, to be more cautious about discharging patients).

The principles are to eliminate redundant steps in the care pathway and to substitute other providers where feasible.

Hospital 'hotel' services comprise the physical infrastructure and the routines of the patient's daily life within them. Normalizing inpatients' daily life as far as possible involves the following:

- Making their daily routines predictable to allow inpatients a greater level of control.
- Providing patient space which staff symbolically treat as private (for example, by knocking before entering) (Williamson 1992).
- Designing visiting hours and rules to maximize social contact with family, friends, informal carers, voluntary workers and PHC staff, subject only to a patient's own rights to refuse visitors.
- Staff dress codes, which on wards and operating theatres have an ostensibly hygienic function, also signify different staff groups' role, self-image and status (for example when senior doctors ignore the rules) (Fox 1992). These symbols are not lost on patients.
- Giving the patient information about their illness and its treatment, so they know what to expect in terms of events, sensations, side-effects. This allows the patient at least a 'cognitive control' over what happens in hospital. Using the correct technical names for diseases enables the patients who can and want to, to find out more (Williamson 1992). Video can be used to explain complex medical subjects (Baum and Henkel 1992).
- Hospital building design can also produce therapeutic effects (or the opposite) (Williamson 1992). Accommodation can be graduated to allow for patients' changing needs. For instance, some US providers combine different types of housing ranging from community care (near-independence) to assisted living (patient has a few limitations) to nursing home to hospice (De Friese and Hogue 1999). The Fyodorov hospitals were among the inventors of the 'hospital hotel'. The Arts for Health movement also attempts to improve the quality of the patient's physical environment in more subtle ways (Vignette 6.3). Another example of what can be done was shown when one NHS trust invited the 'Changing Rooms' television programme to redesign and redecorate the play and relatives' stay areas

---

Vignette 6.3 Arts for Health

The Arts for Health holds that the arts:

- improve the quality of all healthcare environments, linking art, architecture and interior design;
- enrich the lives of patients, visitors and staff;
- may assist recovery, alleviate stress and encourage a feeling of well-being;
- can improve wayfinding systems and provide landmarks.

Among many Arts for Health projects are:

- Hospital corridor murals
- Stained glass ceilings
- Mosaic maps
- Design and decoration of playrooms
- Humorous posters (for example giving the otherwise awkward instruction 'Please do not empty your bladder until after your scan')
- Concerts
- Music-hall shows
- Etched and sandblasted windows
- Reminiscence projects, including handicraft work, for elderly people to stimulate mental activity and rebuild self-confidence
- Textile works
- Lifts designed as a spaceship or submarine
- Stone cleaning and gardening

Source: Arts for Health (n.d.).

---

for neo-natal ICU. Granted, television companies have access to more fashionable designers than most hospitals do, but the timescale and cost of the work would be within most hospitals' reach.

These items cover the 'people' and much of the 'psychological interaction' and 'physical resources' aspects of marketing mix. 'Place' considerations are much the same in secondary as in primary care (see Chapter 5).

Meeting the reasonable demands of GPs and payer is a mainly promotional activity. Daily contacts between primary and secondary care doctors constitute, in marketing terms, the mainstay of secondary providers' 'relational marketing' (Gilligan and Lowe (1995) call it 'personal selling') to referrers. Because referrers use secondary care as input to a wider episode of primary care, communications between hospital and primary care services are important benefits to them. These communications (referral letters, test reports and so on) occur mainly when patients are diagnosed, admitted and discharged. For the GP's purposes they have to be designed to yield the necessary information for any ongoing care and arrive before the patient does. Baum and Henkel (1992) make many practical suggestions, the most relevant here being:

- Meet all primary care doctors who are new to the area.
- Do not do tasks which the referring doctor can.
- Keep referring doctors informed of major developments in your specialty.
- Maintain good relationships with the referring doctor's staff.
- Be easy for the referring doctor to contact.
- Sending discharge letters promptly.
- Make the referring doctor look good to the patient.

Two other elements of hospitals' promotional mix can only be mentioned. Although hospitals' health promotion role is limited, they can still 'model the behaviours' required for health maintenance, for instance by discouraging smoking (see Chapter 4) and offering 'healthy' choices of food. Hospital mishaps are newsworthy. Various works discuss public relations in health-care (Silver 1985; Karpf 1988; Mitchell and Tayler 1988; Lewton 1995). For publicly funded hospitals, two main principles of transparency are: not to deny obvious problems, and, so far as the facts allow, to demonstrate what has been done to remedy them.

As explained in Chapter 3, prices of hospital services in a quasi-market should be structured so as to separate payments for the variable costs of services (basic pay, consumables, energy, equipment and so on), 'investment', and incentive payments for realizing the best achievable health outcomes. In a healthcare quasi-market, a provider's prices face not only downwards pressure to equal or undercut competitors' prices, given equal or better clinical effectiveness, but also an upwards pressure to cover the provider's costs. Together these imply designing the care pathway to a cost limit. Obviously, the lower the price, the easier to offer the purchaser the benefit of side-stepping rationing decisions.

Implementation

The foregoing implies a 'product-line' organizational structure, with a dis-crete, integrated managerial sub-structure for each quality chain. Just as secondary care is a nested pathway within a primary care pathway, so purely clinical pathways are nested within the larger pathway of the whole secondary care episode. This suggests a division of labour based on expertise: the relevant clinicians design and manage their nested part of the pathway, managers design and oversee the whole. Alternatively, standard clinical path-ways can be developed at national or profession level for 'slotting into' care pathways which (otherwise) vary from provider to provider – an approach which the US Agency for Health Care Policy and Research reportedly favours (Robinson and Steiner 1997). A large organization such as a hospital also allows the creation of a specialist marketing department (or equivalent under another name), for the purposes of making regular situation analyses; formu-lating marketing objectives, plan and mix; jointly designing care pathways with clinical experts; liaising with referrers and purchasers; and undertaking the concomitant consumer research.

Tracking

In services, the combined process of service distribution, production and consumption is also the occasion for much (not all) tracking activity. An integrated organizational structure such as those found in hospitals makes it easier than in networks to construct single tracking system following the care pathway. The marketing activities outlined above already define the service objectives and critical events on the care pathway. To construct a tracking system it is next necessary to decide which data would operationalize achievement (or not) of the critical events and the organization's objectives (or, which proxy data would have to be used). It saves cost and makes for more reliable data collection to reuse, where possible, data which are already collected for other purposes. Then it is necessary to establish data collection routines at the start, critical events and end-points of the quality chain (Sheaff and Peel 1995).

In a quasi-market the purchaser's main data requirements will ordinarily be stipulated in a service contract. An important benefit which the provider can provide for purchasers is access to the information which the purchaser requires for contract monitoring, for public accountability, and in the purchaser's capacity as patient's proxy. However, it follows from the objectives which we have assumed that the main data sets to collect for tracking purposes concern the following:

- Health impact – as a minimum, this requires that comparable data on the patient's health status be recorded on admission and at discharge. How easy this is varies by speciality: relatively easy in ophthalmology (Vignette 6.2), harder in such domains as mental health.
- User satisfaction and related objective standards such as length of stay, bed-blocking and waiting times.
- Referrer satisfaction.

These data have to be contextualized by comparing them with the benchmarks of local, national or international competitors or substitutes, as relevant. For the provider, it is only prudent to ensure reports note any extenuating circumstance or confounding factors making it especially hard (or easy) to make a good showing. Tracking data can also be used to check the assumptions on which the situation analysis and marketing plan rested.

Meantime, it is also necessary to redress for whatever failures of service provision occur. For individual patients, the necessary systems as essentially the same as in primary care (see Chapter 5). At organizational level the critical task is to distinguish isolated errors, faults or accidents from recurrent cases which indicate systematic defects in the design or operation of a care pathway (Deming 1986). The resulting diagnoses have then to be fed back into the situation analysis for the next marketing cycle (see Figure 6.5).

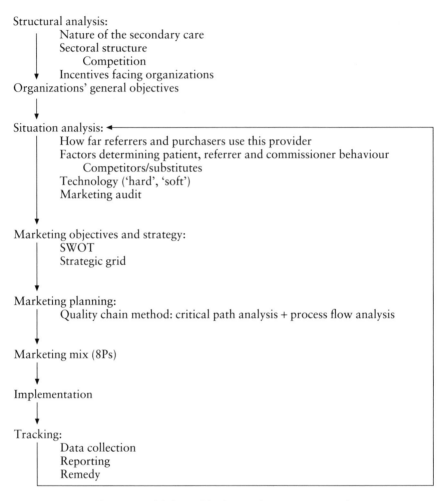

Structural analysis:
    Nature of the secondary care
    Sectoral structure
      Competition
    Incentives facing organizations
Organizations' general objectives

Situation analysis:
    How far referrers and purchasers use this provider
    Factors determining patient, referrer and commissioner behaviour
      Competitors/substitutes
    Technology ('hard', 'soft')
    Marketing audit

Marketing objectives and strategy:
    SWOT
    Strategic grid

Marketing planning:
    Quality chain method: critical path analysis + process flow analysis

Marketing mix (8Ps)

Implementation

Tracking:
    Data collection
    Reporting
    Remedy

Figure 6.5   Marketing model for public hospitals in a quasi-market.

Marketing secondary care in practice – NHS trusts

Structure, incentives, objectives

NHS trusts are in an ambivalent position. They continue to be financed predominantly through Service Level Agreements (contracts) with primary care groups (PCGs), health authorities and, in future, primary care trusts (see Chapter 3). NHS trusts are large, hierarchical organizations (indeed, many have become larger through recent mergers). Emergencies apart, access to their services occurs only through a general practice's referral. Whilst GPs are expected normally to refer patients to trusts with whom their local HA had a service agreement, the volume of 'extra-contractual referrals' in the internal market suggests that GPs were continuing to refer rather freely. In principle, HAs, PCGs and PCTs can shift contracts to alternative providers. Thus the marketing model outlined in the previous section applies.

In practice, though, the contestability of contracts is somewhat limited and the UK Labour government is unsympathetic to the idea of competition anyway (see Chapter 3). NHS trusts have a relationship more like attenuated line-management with their HA and NHSE cp. Enthoven 1999. In reality, NHS contracting is heavily 'relational', supplemented by frequent routine contacts between trust and HA managers, who tend to work both at trust and HA levels during their careers (cp. Ferlie 1994). NHS trusts are accountable to NHSE regional offices for implementing their statutory obligations and a mass of policy guidance. The Health Act 1999 gives NHS trusts two new but amorphous duties: a duty of partnership (i.e. to collaborate with local authorities, especially social services, voluntary organizations and other NHS bodies), and to maintain the quality of NHS services. Quality is measured, implicitly, by the criteria of the NHS performance tables (see Chapter 2). Weak performance against the NHS performance criteria can precipitate a 'management support team' visit. A deluge of central guidance concerns some routine matters (such as the names of struck-off doctors) but also dozens of 'top priorities' – waiting lists, winter overload crises, cost controls, use of new healthcare technologies and so on. A minimum political requirement is that NHS trusts avoid politically embarrassing the government, and preferably generate a flow of 'good news' stories about new services, falling waiting lists and so on. Their public image is no less closely monitored by central government than during the years of Conservative government in the 1980s.

The prime incentives facing the medical and managerial coalition in charge of NHS trusts are to maintain trust income and to contain growth of range of services, service development and quality and therefore costs within that 'envelope' – until 1999, their only statutory obligation. It is not the same as profit maximization: the four conditions which create structural pressures to maximize profits do not all apply. NHS trusts do derive their income from sales, but competition for sales is not strong (see below). Investment gives competitive advantage only in some services (see Chapter 5). Ten per cent of the additional £600 million allocation for NHS growth in 1999–2000 was allocated by NHS performance table criteria. A 6 per cent return on assets is automatically costed into contracts and NHS trusts cannot vary it. When they do make surplus, HAs may attempt to claw the surplus back. Incentives to make a surplus are therefore weak (Bartlett and Le Grand 1994).

Tight cash limits increase the pressure on NHS trusts for supplementary 'income generation'. Some offer private services in competition with commercial hospitals. The Health and Medicines Act 1988 allowed NHS trusts to keep the proceeds of these sales.

The main incentives facing NHS trusts are therefore to implement central policy guidance, attract contracts and avoid adverse publicity. Whilst the payments for their service contracts are volume-sensitive, they are not usually so volume-sensitive as to be much incentive to attract referrals and satisfy patients and GPs, especially since most trusts already face more referrals than they can absorb (hence waiting lists). *The NHS Plan* proposes to rectify this by linking trusts' income to the results of the National Patient Survey. Trusts will also be graded as green, yellow or red according to their performance by National Performance Framework standards (see Chapter 3). Those who rate 'green' will be given greater management discretion, easier access to capital and, in principle, the right to take over those who rate 'red'.

Situation analysis

In order to state concretely what marketing objectives and mix an NHS trust might develop if it followed the marketing model outlined earlier in the chapter, we have next to outline what points a typical NHS trust situation analysis would have to cover early in 2001.

'Market size' for an NHS trust is its geographical catchment, which NHSE guidance takes as the area within 30 minutes' travelling time. Table 6.3 summarizes the GPs' reasons for referring surgical patients, in descending order of frequency of mention (cutting off at 50 per cent).

Another study (of Yorkshire GP fundholders) mentions the same referral criteria but in a slightly different order (Miller 1997). Note that the consultant's, not the hospital's, reputation is what influenced these GPs. Surprisingly, GPs' referral patterns appear even more geographically constrained than patients' willingness to travel (see below). Patients' preferences influenced GPs' referrals, but not decisively (Mahon *et al.* 1994). GPs seem not to be particularly price-sensitive, but more bed-supply-sensitive, with an elasticity of referral demand with relation to beddage of approximately 0.25 (Gravelle *et al.* 2000). They are also sensitive to service quality and maintaining local providers (Goodwin 1998). Many GPs took up fundholding as a way to deal with one or two NHS trust specialities

Table 6.3 GPs' reasons for choice of referral, ranked by number of GPs mentioning

Reason	%
Local (i.e. within 16 km) and convenient	95.2
GP knows consultant	84.8
Good clinical care	78.2
Patient prefers	70.9
GP familiar with hospital	69.1
Patient has attended previously	68.5
Consultant has good manner	64.2
Short waiting time for appointment	57.0
Short waiting time for surgery	52.7
Good overall service	52.1

Source: Mahon *et al.* (1994).

Vignette 6.4   GP segments

'Good' GPs

- Understand problems about hospital being busy.
- High admission rate for their referrals.
- Do not 'dump' patients on the hospital.
- Refer patients to a specific speciality.
- Use hospital's support services (diagnostics, paramedical and so on) better than other GPs do.
- Understand how A&E works.
- Take responsibility for their own patients.

'Bad' GPs

- Are repeat 'offenders' in misusing A&E.
- Take any route to get their patient into hospital.
- Do not know how to access support services.
- Patients go to A&E when they cannot access the GP.
- Tell patients that a bed will be waiting for them.
- Often are the only GP in the practice.
- Need to re-educate their reception staff and practice nurses.
- 'Dump' patients on A&E.
- Do not use alternative PHC services.
- Habitually use deputizing services.
- Have inconvenient clinic hours.

Source: Accident and Emergency Clinical Directorates network workshop, HSMU, Manchester University (1997).

---

with long waiting times and unhelpful consultants (Glennerster *et al.* 1994; see also Dowling 2000).

NHS trusts have no standard method of segmenting GPs. Vignette 6.4 gives one segmentation of GPs referring to accident and emergency departments, transparently aimed at identifying 'problem' groups of GPs for later intervention, but also indicating recurrent problems with GPs' misuse of the referral system.

Waiting lists place NHS trusts in strong bargaining position *vis-à-vis* referrers, payers and patients – arguably, too strong a position. So although the NHS also formally respects the competent patient's right to accept or refuse an offer of secondary care, neither NHS trusts nor GPs overplay the patient's right of choice, and the shortage of beds compared with referrals puts patients in a weak position to exercise it. Although 17 per cent of patients in 1998 were given a choice of hospital by their GP, 75 per cent were not but were happy for the GP to decide. Only 7 per cent were offered no choice although they wanted one (Airey and Erens 1999); a similar pattern to earlier studies (Mahon *et al.* 1994; Anon 1995). In effect, NHS trusts offer the choice of source of secondary care to GP referrers not patients (Propper 1995a; Mulligan 1998).

The main benefits which NHS trust patients seek are: to recover; satisfactory social dealings with healthworkers; quick access to care; information about their diagnosis and prognosis; reassurance; and staff discretion and confidentiality. Most (84 per cent) are confident that the specialist they saw had the necessary information about them and their condition, although 11 per cent were not. In most trusts, four specialities (those in which private medicine is most prevalent, i.e. ophthalmology, gynaecology, general surgery, orthopaedics) are those with the longest waits. In April 2000, 1,054,000 people were on waiting lists. The average wait is a little under four months. In 1998, 36 per cent of patients referred to secondary care claimed that their condition had worsened during their wait; 35 per cent claimed that their activity had been restricted a little, and 9 per cent that it had been restricted a lot. Forty per cent waited in some, and 14 per cent in a lot of, pain. These deteriorations tended to increase as waiting times exceeded six months. Forty-five per cent of patients thought the NHS trust should have seen them sooner (Airey and Erens 1999).

Evidence conflicts as to patients' willingness to travel to hospital. A Marplan study in 1988 showed 60 per cent of patients willing to travel over 40 km, and 38 per cent willing to travel anywhere in the UK, but a study of 1992 data showed only 23 per cent willing to travel beyond 50 km.

Since 1999, NHS trusts have confronted two main purchaser 'segments': health authorities and PCG/Ts. HA purchasers appear to seek the benefits of: cheap services; a wide range of services; guarantees of technical quality and safety; monitoring information; no mid-year contract surprises; accessible services; services that are acceptable to GPs; and services that are acceptable to patients. They also require NHS trusts to help them implement the current policy guidance and priorities, especially those in the annual NHS Priorities and Planning Guidance. In descending order, HAs' past reasons for moving contracts have been: doubts about the quality of service; ease of patient travel; and the relative price of the provider's services (Mulligan 1998). PCG priorities for commissioning are: to improve waiting lists and times; to improve quality of contracted services; to implement National Service Frameworks (NSFs); and to expand services into primary care (Malbon and Smith 2000). Future contracts with both purchasers will have to conform to NICE guidance and NSFs. The first two NSFs, on coronary heart disease and mental health, were published in early 2000.

The degree of substitutability between NHS trusts varies by locality and speciality. Using the Hirschman–Herfindahl index based on market shares, Appleby *et al.* (1994) calculated for one NHS region (as then defined) that, in general surgery, 75 per cent of hospitals and 60 per cent of general surgery patients faced hospital competition in the sense of a non-monopoly by US standards. Only 8 per cent of acute service providers had a monopoly of general surgery, orthopaedics, ENT and gynaecology within a 50 km radius (Propper 1995a). Nevertheless, Hamblin (1998) found little real competition. Vignette 6.5 is an anonymized competitor analysis by an NHS trust, dating from the internal market. Shortage of capacity attenuates competition or even contestability between NHS trusts. Contestability appears to arise more from GPs' changing referral patterns than from HA or – as yet – PCT decisions.

NHS trusts have an ambivalent, problematic relationship to private healthcare. Private sector activity is concentrated in ophthalmology, gynaecology, general surgery and orthopaedics. About half of abortion is done in the private and voluntary sector. After recession in the early 1990s, private sector activity has resumed growth, more unsteadily than in the 1980s. However, NHS trusts have also been winning market share of private patients from the commercial hospitals since their nadir of 11.2 per cent in 1986–87, when pay-bed occupancy was at about one-third, to an estimated 15.1 per cent in 1994 (Laurance 1998). In descending order of importance, the loci of private competition with NHS trusts are: the opportunity to jump NHS waiting lists; treatment by a consultant; and superior 'hotel' services.

Changes in local epidemiology and demography are transmitted to NHS trusts largely from the purchasers through the medium of Health Improvement Programmes (HImPs) (see Chapter 3). Undoubtedly the most important 'soft' technology development is the spread of evidence-based medicine, in the case of NHS trusts through NICE, CHI (Commission for Health Improvement), NSFs, information sources such as the Cochrane Centre, and the increased use of protocols (or care pathway) to standardize routine treatments. Following scandals in Bristol and in Kent, NHS policy emphasizes early detection and rectification of poor clinical practice (see below).

In marketing audit terms the glaring weakness in most NHS trusts' image arises from their inability to deal with an overload of referrals. The media report stories of patients waiting in corridors and, recently, a spate of 'agism' stories about hard-pressed hospitals being willing to let elderly patients die (Tran 2000). Private healthcare promotions also depend heavily on anti-marketing the NHS by emphasizing waiting lists (Vignette 3.1). Nevertheless the adverse image has a factual basis in the under-resourcing of both A&E and inpatient services which, thanks to the 2000 review of NHS bed requirements, policy-makers are now beginning to recognize. Consultants' time for non-urgent work is another capacity constraint. Yates (1995) presents evidence of weak NHS trust management of medical staff, which at least some consultants exploit to the full in order to pursue private practice to the detriment of NHS patients.

Yet the NHS remains popular. Doctors and nurses remain highly respected occupational groups. Media coverage of major accidents rarely fails to praise the NHS staff involved.

NHS trust managers know most of this, but usually in an informal, undocumented way. NHS trusts mainly identify and prioritize service changes from central guidance and the standard data sets (see below), rather than from consumer research or market research into GPs' demands. Central guidance is of little use for marketing, nor is it intended to be. Waiting list

Vignette 6.5   An NHS trust's competitor analysis

CRITICAL SUCCESS FACTORS

Competitors / Criteria	Weighting factor	S		Y		E		C	
		Weight	Trust Total	Weight	Trust Total	Weight	Trust Total	Weight	Trust Total
CSF1 Product performance	40	9	360	9	360	9	360	9	360
CSF2 Speed of service	15	10	150	6	95	6	95	5	75
CSF3 Low costs	10	7	70	9	90	8	80	9	90
CSF4 Breadth of service	15	10	150	9	135	8	120	9	135
CSF5 Reputation/reliability	20	10	200	9	180	9	180	9	180
	100		930		860		835		840

Weighting criteria: 1 = low, 10 = high

figures have become a central managerial and political preoccupation in recent years. Analyses of what benefits patients were seeking or obtaining from NHS trust services were not common. Many trusts have completed patient surveys and taken patient opinions in other ways (focus groups and so on) but this tends to remain an exceptional, project-based activity rather than a routine input to situation analyses or equivalent activities. The first NHS National Patient Survey concentrated on primary care.

For needs assessment, HImPs should, in principle, include a population health profile, but the production of these plans started only in 1998. Previously, HAs undertook much of this work.

Marketing audit of services is equally sporadic at NHS trust level (although central government is acutely aware of it). However, the resources available to NHS trusts for identifying and using evidence-based best clinical practice (various professional and scientific journals, the Cochrane Centre, NICE, CHI) have become more visible and more influential since the late 1990s.

Marketing objectives and strategy

In so far as NHS trusts have marketing objectives and strategies at all, they have only limited grounding in the kind of situation analysis outlined in the relevant marketing model (see above). Not that NHS trusts ignore SWOT analysis and marketing grids: during the 1990s, many NHS managers took MBAs and similar qualifications, exposing them to such techniques. Inputs to these tools were partly hard data, but more often informal, even intuitive, local knowledge.

NHS trust objectives also result partly from negotiations within the dominant coalition of doctors and managers. Patient needs are often mentioned, but often as an ideological totem in negotiations.

In rural areas especially, geography often gives NHS trusts a local monopoly of hospital services. There is evidence that many GPs feel loyal to their local hospitals. Such a strong 'market' position requires little marketing to referrers and purchasers. A 'threshold' strategy (see Chapter 6) suffices. A few NHS trusts, mainly teaching hospitals and regional speciality trusts (for example Christie Hospital Manchester, Great Ormond Street, Papworth), can adopt a 'maximal' strategy of specialization and differentiation. From 1994, NHS trusts were forbidden to differentiate themselves simply by dropping services which they provided only on a minor scale or to prioritize development of private medicine. This directive limited their scope for differentiation strategies. Nevertheless, specialization (with mergers) may prove a survival strategy for community health service trusts (CHSTs) and mental health trusts which are likely to lose many of their more routine services to PCTs.

Considering the political visibility of winter overload and waiting lists, it is remarkable how few NHS trusts have adopted demarketing strategies aimed at GPs, for instance aimed at agreeing appropriateness criteria for referrals.

Marketing plan

NHS trusts rarely use the term 'marketing planning', but what matters is whether NHS trusts in fact plan their services on the basis of evidence about their users' demands and best medical practice. Hitherto, NHS trusts have planned their services by annually writing one-year operational and five-year rolling plans. Little formal research about them exists, but the author's observations are that these plans seldom use data about user preferences, GP demands on patients' behalf, or patients' experiences of the service (for example complaint patterns). NHS trust plans tend to emerge from negotiations within the dominant coalition of managers and consultants, expressing a compromise between different consultants' and managers' current expansionary ambitions no less than the data sources mentioned above. In future, patients forums will advise them.

The result is a tendency to plan service developments by adjusting the inherited pattern of existing services, with innovations focusing on the technical level in existing services. Many important innovations in models of care (i.e. those focusing on providing a new type of patient benefit rather than on implementing a new clinical technology) such as the hospice movement have originated outside the NHS. Neither have NHS trust managers often made deliberate decisions to discontinue types of treatment or service, as iatrogenic or obsolete. However, this selection is increasingly being made at national level, with NICE in particular beginning to manage more actively the range of treatments NHS trusts may provide. Increasingly, NHS trusts will choose their 'product range' from the selection predefined by NICE, NSFs, Cochrane studies and the EBM movement generally as adequately evidence-based. This trend is likely to make the use of care pathways a much more common planning method, at least for the clinical, technical aspects of care. The planning of discharge processes to prevent bed-blocking has also become widespread in response to waiting list and capacity pressures.

Some NHS trusts (Leicester General, South Tees, North Tyneside, West Middlesex University Hospital) have used care pathway methods to plan whole services at departmental level, producing some substantial improvements in speed of treatment (Dyke 1998; Department of Health 2000; see also Figure 6.4). Recent guidance specifically asks them to do this in respect of accident and emergency services (to eliminate trolley waits). Most trusts, however, can bring little consumer research data to this activity. Given the current policy focus of waiting lists and waiting times, and the above situation analysis, one would expect (from the model in Chapter 5) to see NHS trusts applying critical path analysis or process flow analysis to existing care pathways in order to identify and 'design out' the worst capacity bottlenecks. Surprisingly, it is also rare for NHS trusts to negotiate appropriateness thresholds for referrals with GPs, at least in a systematic way. *The NHS Plan* recommends that this become normal practice.

Marketing mix

Waiting times are the most palpable penalties which NHS trusts impose on their patients. NHS patients' waiting times for hospital admission are the sum of two waits. First comes the wait for a first appointment to see a hospital doctor, who decides what further treatment, if any, the patient needs and, if necessary, adds the patient to the waiting list. (Queues for first appointments are thus the waiting list for the waiting list.) To increase the penalty of inconvenience, systems by which the patient, rather than hospital staff, book the outpatient appointment time have only recently been piloted, although *The NHS Plan* intends that they should become universal. Then follows the actual waiting-list wait for admission or treatment. The recent shift towards assessing NHS trusts by their patients' waiting times instead of list size is warranted because it focuses on the most important matter for the patient. To what extent do NHS trusts use a marketing mix designed to minimize penalties to users by reducing length of stay and increasing throughput, so as to reduce waiting times?

On-site primary care provision, as an alternative to patients' using full-scale trauma services to obtain primary care, remains exceptional although a few sites (for example in the Manchester HAZ) are experimenting with different ways of providing it. No national figures appear to exist showing how far GPs' patients can use hospital-based paramedical and diagnostic services relevant to primary care without a prior specialist consultation. On purely anecdotal evidence, this arrangement seems to be more widespread although still not found in the majority of NHS hospitals. However, NHS trusts have been much more successful in substituting day-case and outpatient for inpatient care. About half NHS hospital episodes are now provided on this basis. Some NHS trusts now provide 'one-stop' outpatient diagnostic procedures – for example giving the patient same-day breast X-ray results – which minimizes inconvenience, travel and anxiety for the patient. (There appear to be no national data showing how widespread this is.) *The NHS Plan* proposes to introduce ambulatory care and diagnostic centres in which nurses and paramedical staff will play the predominant role in patient treatment and care for certain short-stay and day-case treatments. Daycare was an important means by which NHS trusts considerably reduced lengths of stay after 1990.

As noted, the systematic redesign of inpatient care pathways to reduce waiting lists does occur but appears to be exceptional. Examples of NHS hospital 'hotels' exist, but very few. (A Plymouth hospital has considered using commercial hotel accommodation for the purpose.)

There is little evidence as to how far NHS hospital patients' follow-up examinations are made by senior clinicians, although, in general, NHS hospitals still rely excessively on trainee doctors to provide routine services. In order to ensure that lengths of stay are not achieved by discharging patients prematurely, NHS trusts are monitored on unplanned readmission for the same patient for the same treatment of the same condition. Without intermediate or primary care support for discharged patients, however, there is a risk that early discharge shifts NHS trust costs to patients and their families. *The NHS Plan* announces a substantial expansion of NHS intermediate care facilities, but now this is starting from a low base: much of the 1980s and 1990s were spent closing down the community and 'cottage' hospitals which are best placed to provide such care.

NHS hospitals have generally made a slow but definite liberalization in the management of the patient's day, in terms of rules about when informal carers, friends and family can visit inpatients, choices of meals and so on. One effect of competitive tendering has been to reduce the cost, and the quality, of cleaning, laundry and catering services. NHS hospital food has been criticized not only for its quality but – astonishingly – for leaving patients malnourished. On the model of an experiment in Nottingham City Hospital, *The NHS Plan* announces that ward housekeepers will be responsible both for ordering and obtaining patients' food, and for checking its presentation and nutritive value. Commentators also ask why minor consumables such as personal stationery, mirrors and coat-hangers should be limited to the patients of private hospitals (Gilligan and Lowe 1995; Payne 1998). *The NHS Plan* says that, in future, all NHS patients will have bedside television and a telephone, being charged for telephone calls at national standard rates. There has been less success in giving patients privacy. On many NHS wards, privacy still depends on curtains and low voices because, unlike in many other countries, Nightingale wards (or in newer hospitals, multi-bed bays) rather than single rooms remain the standard design. It has been NHS policy since 1997 to end mixed-sex wards (Department of Health 1997b).

Promotional materials enabling patients to make informed choice of provider, give informed consent (or refusal) to treatment and make better use of NHS trust services appear to have gradually improved in availability since 1990, starting from a low base. Some of this material is sponsored by pharmaceutical firms and other suppliers. There have been experiments in using specially-made videos to inform patients of the outcome of surgery, for example the effects of prostatectomy and the alternative treatments. Such measures can reduce (demarket) patient uptake of referrals. Nevertheless, Williamson (1992) describes various objectionable, but not rare, communicational foibles of NHS staff. These include the use of patient forename alone or without a title ('Mrs'/'Mr' etc.), promiscuous endearments, baby talk ('pop on the bed' (Williamson 1992: 65), patronizing euphemisms ('waterworks') and dictatorial notices. The report into the Ledward affair confirmed that traces of the pre-NHS regime in which consultants provided different levels of access and even courtesy to private and public patients still exist (Anon 2000). The standard NHS consent form to surgery is worded so as to excuse the NHS trust from any obligation to ensure that the patient is operated upon by a particular (named) surgeon.

The quality of patient accommodation in NHS hospitals reflects a variegated building stock. Some of it matches hotel or normal domestic standards of decoration, furnishing, space and domestic equipment (especially in private wings), but many older buildings fall far short. NHS middle managers perennially complain of the difficulty in getting minor building maintenance works and alterations started. Arts for Health is one of the more encouraging developments of recent years and many NHS hospitals can claim credit for supporting it (Vignette 6.3). Similarly the Kings Fund and Poetry Society have launched a 'poems for waiting rooms' project. This had National Lottery funding and appears to be modelled on the 'poems on the underground' venture (replacing adverts with poetry on the London Underground).

The Labour government continues the Conservative government's policy of public–private partnerships (the Private Finance Initiative, PFI) whereby the NHS buys private sector instead of using public sector capital. A doubly short-sighted policy: not only does the NHS pay higher prices for capital and assets which it does not own than for capital and assets which it would own (implying a smaller gain of capacity for a given level of expenditure), but also it has hitherto been assumed that one way to produce commercial profits from PFI projects will be by reducing beddage and staffing – exactly opposite to the requirement to increase capacity to deal with waiting lists. In places, the policy of rebuilding NHS hospitals on greenfield, not existing town centre, sites continues. Ignoring the ecological losses, town-edge siting tends to make access for patients without cars more difficult, a retrograde step in both health and transport policy terms (Royal Commission on Environmental Pollution 1994). A few NHS trusts are so sited as to be able to install a railway, metro or tram station (for example Wythenshawe Hospital when the Manchester tramway is extended). Most NHS trusts have free telephones for patients to call taxis and 'normalized' transport such as cars, minibuses and (for example in Bristol) a courtesy bus such as hotels use. Many NHS trusts now charge for car parking, although mainly to generate income. It is rare to see parking spaces nearest the hospital or clinic allocated to patients rather than to (non-emergency) staff.

Considering waiting list pressures it is surprising how rarely NHS trusts demarket referrals. In so far as NHS trusts 'market' to GPs and PCTs, they rely heavily on relational marketing to safeguard contracts during the transition from HA to PCG/T purchasing, mainly through contact between GPs and consultants (cp. Gilligan and Lowe 1995), perpetuating in many relational links with the larger fundholding practices. More unusual past methods used by NHS trusts included: providing GP information systems that by default refer patients to the donor hospital, free pharmaceutical advice as bait to other hospital services, and 'educational' events for attracting referrals from GPs. Branding is possible only for exceptional NHS trusts such as Great Ormond Street. *Private Eye* has justly mocked other NHS trusts' attempts to follow suit. Now a national NHS 'corporate identity' service handles such matters.

Neither do NHS trusts generally do very much to counter the continual anti-marketing by private hospitals and health insurers and media

---

Vignette 6.6   Public relations in a crisis

Kent and Canterbury Hospitals received some unwelcome media coverage on learning that a story was about to appear in the *Daily Express* that some 70,000 women would have to have their cervical smear slides reviewed because quality controls indicated an unacceptably high level of false negative results. The trust had one weekend to act upon the discovery before it appeared in print on the Monday. Using a public relations consultancy, the trust senior management team meeting decided that the most important tasks were to inform the patients affected and to prevent GPs becoming swamped with enquiries. The trust therefore did the following:

- Set up a helpline for patients. Support helplines were set up over the weekend, dealing with 1300 calls on the Monday. A temporary helpline of this kind might have to deal with up to 20,000 calls during the crisis period. Counsellors were available to answer calls, and other call staff were specially trained on the Sunday evening. The lines were available 24 hours a day.
- Briefed GPs, by:
  - sending them background information immediately by fax or courier before Monday morning;
  - personal telephone calls to all GPs whose patients were affected;
  - supplying leaflets (print run of 50,000, distributed on the Tuesday) which GPs could distribute to their patients.
  The content of these messages was decided in light of advice from a GP member of the Kent cervical screening group.
- Briefed the press by holding a press conference.
- Briefed 40 trust middle managers who could then brief the staff, who are liable to be criticized and blamed in these circumstances.

The helplines had to be reopened and posters distributed to local surgeries and shops when the retest results were themselves delayed.

Source: Millar (1996).

(see Chapter 3). Instead, much promotional work in NHS trusts is the management of public relations crises. An extreme instance is Treliske Hospital which in just over one month (January–February 1995) had to respond to press coverage of how a needle left in a baby surfaced through the child's back, and how one of its surgeons had been reprimanded for letting a nurse perform an appendicectomy. Some NHS trusts are becoming more expert at dealing with press stories about trust service crises and problem-solving (Vignette 6.6).

Although it forbids loss-leading and cross-subsidies, and insists that NHS trust prices must equal their costs of provision, NHS policy is very open about costing methods. The rules in theory forbid loss-leading but do allow trusts to bundle services together. That allows tacit cross-subsidies, as does the arbitrariness of the ways of apportioning fixed costs. Consequently there are spectacular (up to six-fold) variations in unit costs (NHSE 1999c). Yet there is little evidence of price competition between NHS trusts. Trusts are free to set prices on the basis indicated for need-based incentives (separating incentives, other direct costs and capital costs – see Chapter 3), but few do. In practice, NHS trusts tend to price on an historical basis, adjusted at the margin. Nevertheless, these frequently turn out insufficient to cover their operating costs. Every year sees NHS trusts in financial difficulty. NHS trust prices are required to include capital charges, whose purpose is to enable private providers to offer comparable prices to NHS trusts. In theory (see Chapter 2), capital charging reintroduces a condition for profit maximization, but a plethora of other controls vitiate that effect.

Implementation

NHS trusts' organizational structure is typically a set of clinical director-ates, each responsible for a family of related clinical specialities or other services (Rae 1993). One consultant in the directorate becomes director, responsible to the chief executive for the directorate's budgets and various managerial tasks but remaining autonomous in clinical decision-making and influencing their peers through informal networking and persuasion. This 'product-line' structure facilitates relational marketing to GP and con-sumer marketing to patients, although it is seldom systematically used for that purpose. Control of NHS trusts thus lies in the hands of a coalition of doctors and senior managers. Although the balance of power has gradually shifted towards managers since the early 1980s, 'medical capture' persists. To challenge the consultants is fatal to a manager's career.

Consequently, medical quality has been left for doctors to manage, mainly through clinical audit (see Chapter 7). All non-clinical aspects of healthcare quality are the responsibility of the trust's general managers. This makes it difficult to coordinate the management of clinical quality with consumer research or other NHS trust marketing activities. Marketing departments, or equivalents by other names, exist in some NHS trusts but the split between medical and non-medical lines of implementation is often reflected in the coexistence of a 'quality' department (frequently nurse-managed) and a medical audit department. Following the Bristol and Kent scandals, govern-ment and NHS management have begun discussing formal annual appraisals and regular revalidation of consultants. However, these strategies still pre-sume clinical autonomy except where problems arise, when professional self-regulation is expected to supply a remedy. Usually, though, the consultant is left autonomously to achieve good quality work, service development, good relationships with patients and to balance the 'interesting' cases against more routine work which may be in greater demand (Frankel and West 1993).

When the NHS was founded, merit awards were intended to offer an incentive for innovation, replacing market rewards for consultants who devised new models of care for patients' benefit. However, control of merit awards was handed over to the medical academic establishment and, fifty years on, NHS managers are trying to reclaim the process. In all specialities, NHS trust consultants are free, and in some specialities face strong incentives, to undertake private medical practice (as opposed to writing court and insurance reports, their other main source of private income). These consultants also manage NHS trust waiting lists, creating a conflict between their own private interests and those of their NHS trust patients (Light 1998). Yates (1995) exposed some of the abuses that result as some consultants flex their rather vague conditions of NHS employment in favour of their own private practice interests. A sample of 60 consultants in ENT, ophthalmology and orthopaedics found them giving an average of two half-days a week to private work. Waiting lists are thus in part a consequence of NHS trusts' feeble management of their consultants' activity (Yates 1995). There can be little doubt what would happen to, say, a senior programmer at Microsoft who was found working for Linux even in his own time, let alone Microsoft's. However, *Supporting Doctors, Protecting Patients* mentions (just once) that private practice to the detriment of the NHS is a contractual, disciplinary matter, not within the domain of clinical judgement (Department of Health 1999).

Tracking

In one sense, NHS trusts have extensive monitoring data. Besides ad hoc data collection about specific policy initiatives such as *Patient's Charter* targets, routine monitoring is built around financial data, NHS performance tables and a common data core which track some waiting times data, but mainly activity and cost data (see Chapter 2). It is proposed to use a system awarding between one and five stars to summarize the provider's score on 20 main indicators. In contrast, NHS trusts have to track the health outcomes and user satisfaction in the face of much irrelevant data and missing seminal data, although *The NHS Plan* promises that, in future, trust incomes will partly reflect the findings of the National Patient Survey. The other routine source of user data for most NHS trusts is complaints. As noted, many ad hoc patient satisfaction and opinion surveys have occurred over the years. Beyond these, most NHS trusts collect little routine post-discharge data tracking their patients' experience, either from GPs or from patients themselves. *The NHS Plan* mentions using the bedside television system interactively to collect patients' responses about their experience of the hospital's service.

Notwithstanding the spread of EBM, few data on the health outcomes of NHS trust services are collected systematically. Patient records contain much data relevant to patients' functioning, pain, morale and satisfaction (besides a greater mass of data which is technically necessary for patient diagnosis and care but of little use for monitoring these specific outcomes). However, much of the data is held in clinical systems which, in many trusts, are still more-or-less isolated from service management systems. Routine summaries showing what change in health status was achieved for each care group of patients passing through a clinical directorate or trust are rare. Under *The NHS Plan*, CHI will externally track NHS trusts' performance against National Performance Framework criteria. There will also be independent surveys of hospital cleanliness and food quality.

NHS trusts therefore rely on 'exception management' tracking, assuming that services are generally acceptable and concentrating on finding and remedying the exceptions. Although it certainly is necessary for protecting patients, exception management does not provide a method of analysing and improving the experience of patients in services which are not egregiously bad. Recently, this weak system of tracking and redress has been strengthened by sending action teams from the NHS Modernisation Agency to 'help manage' hospitals with difficulty meeting waiting list targets. Six NHS trusts were so 'helped' during August 2000. A seventh (St James, Leeds) invited an action team in. Following an experiment in Brighton, a patient advocacy and liaison scheme (PALS) is to introduce patient advocates, charged with helping patients resolve problems and if necessary make complaints, into every NHS trust (Department of Health 2000).

However, the most important remedy is to feed tracking data back into the situation analysis, so that persistent problems in responding to users' demands or needs can be 'designed out' during the next cycle. NHS trusts have rather fragmentary elements from which to construct such a feedback loop.

In conclusion

Secondary care providers in a quasi-market require an elaborate marketing model, one that accommodates three main audiences: strategic and operational levels of marketing, specially adapted portfolio analysis, and ways of managing the inpatient day to avoid the worst effects of institutional living. The large size of most secondary providers enables them to refine the marketing uses of care pathways to include critical path analysis and tracking system design. For NHS secondary providers, the main obstacles to doing all this are the lack of consumer research information, undercapacity, limited capital investment and conflicts of consultant interest over private practice.

Questions

1 How do patients' experiences of secondary care differ from those of primary care?
2 What factors make the marketing of secondary care more complex than the marketing of primary care?
3 What physical characteristics of a hospital can be managed for marketing purposes?
4 In the short term before extra capacity can be built, what marketing activities can healthcare providers use to relieve the pressures of overdemand?

For discussion

What principles should be applied in managing the activities of publicly employed hospital doctors who also do private work?

Further reading

Frankel, S. and West, R. (eds) (1993) *Rationing and Rationality in the National Health Service: The Persistence of Waiting Lists*. Basingstoke: Macmillan.
Grönroos, C. (2000) *Service Management and Marketing*. Chichester: Wiley.
Williamson, C. (1992) *Whose Standards?* Buckingham: Open University Press.
Yates, J. (1995) *Private Eye, Heart and Hip*. Edinburgh: Churchill Livingstone.

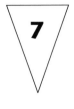

7 Quality management and clinical governance

Chapter overview

This chapter distinguishes and explains the plethora of strategies for managing the quality of services such as healthcare. It shows how the different strategies apply to different aspects of the healthcare process, how they inter-relate, and which strategies are relevant to different kinds of healthcare organization. As in previous chapters, the theory is then compared with NHS practice.

Quality management – principles and strategies

Healthcare concerns complex biological processes with ill-defined outcomes. Strong professional bodies contest outsiders' ability to measure or define healthcare quality. But the idea of needs which we have adopted makes it easy to apply one of the clearest and most influential definitions of product or service 'quality' as: 'The totality of features and characteristics of a product or service which bear on its ability to satisfy a given need' (British Standards Institute, BS4778). Here the relevant 'given need' is that of the *user*, never to be confused with the needs of governments, healthcare providers, doctors, managers or payers.

In Chapter 2 we defined users' needs as their rational demands. The healthcare which users need is the healthcare which they would demand if they were well informed about their health behaviours, health status (i.e. levels of functioning and pain), their diagnoses, what treatments are available, and the effects and drawbacks of each treatment option. We have also assumed that individuals' demands for goods and services are corrigible, either on factual grounds of incompleteness or mistake (especially in the more technical clinical matters of diagnosis, what treatments are available and what they can or cannot achieve) or on grounds of inconsistency. It follows from this and BS4778 that good quality of healthcare is the type of healthcare that the user demands, except where the user can be shown to have made one of these errors or to lack the necessary knowledge. The onus of proof is on those professionals, managers, policy-makers or carers who allege the error; but, as evidence-based medicine shows (see below), the proof can often be made. This definition of healthcare quality agrees with all those who equate healthcare quality with effectiveness in improving the patient's health status.

Unlike the need for many other consumer goods (for example, computers), important healthcare needs arise biologically, independently of the discovery of means to satisfy them. This fact cruelly exposes the technical limitations of healthcare: the inability to cure many health problems which, although often clinically unglamorous to treat, nevertheless disable millions of people (arthritis, incontinence, loss of motor function, most cancers). This is why equating needs with capacity to benefit (Stevens and Raftery 1994) is a fallacy. The only sense in which most cancer or HIV/AIDS patients are 'unable to benefit' from healthcare is that current medical technology cannot cure them. They have all too much 'capacity to benefit' in the sense of needing to recover. A fundamental dimension of healthcare quality is what disabling and prevalent conditions remain untreatable. It should not be defined out of discussions of healthcare quality and needs.

In general, quality management methods consist of setting and implementing standards for providing a product or service. Except for intersectoral activity, to which the rest of this chapter does not relate, healthcare consists of services, where production and consumption are the same process. The task of specifying the quality of a service therefore consists of specifying how it shall be produced (see Chapter 5). In healthcare, the workpiece is the patient themself, mind and body. This human raw material is highly individuated, which limits the scope for standardizing both the process of care and its outcomes. This not only affects the choice of quality indicators and quality management strategies, favouring those formulated in probabilistic, whole-population terms, but also implies that deviations from standard clinical practice can sometimes be justified by an individual patient's exceptional characteristics. This variation is a strong argument for giving health-workers discretion (with due safeguards) in making and implementing clinical decisions, i.e. clinical autonomy (Jamous and Pellouille 1970; Jackson 1999). On this basis, quality management in healthcare will prove more successful in changing clinical behaviour and services to the extent that it admits quality management methods which accommodate such indeterminacies (i.e. peer review, quality circles, continuous quality improvement, and so on).

Nevertheless, the implications of variations between patients can be overstated. Differences of individuals' shapes and sizes do not stymie 'Fordist' or 'McDonaldized' quality management techniques (a standard range of products; codified, routinized and partly automated production methods;

1 **Planning stage**

Consumerist methods
Evidence-based medicine
Standard-setting
Risk management
Total quality management

2 **Implementation stage**

(A) *Inputs*:
Quality assurance
Accreditation

(B) *During service delivery*:
Inspection
Quality circles

3 **Tracking stage**

Quality control
Statistical process control
Audit
Benchmarking
Complaints management

Figure 7.1 Main strategies for quality management and their place in the marketing cycle.

guaranteed minimum standards of product or service) in the production of, say, clothes. Healthcare professionals claim, rightly, that healthcare practice is the application of scientific knowledge. If so, Fordist methods have at least some application to the management of healthcare quality.

Quality management literature generally, and in healthcare especially, has a rather variegated character because different writers make divergent assumptions on these points. Debates occur between advocates of routinized, 'scientific', Fordist approaches and those who prefer semi-formal ways (for example using quality circles) of devising quality standards and managing their implementation. Views also differ as to whether managers, users or professionals have the greater knowledge or legitimacy and should therefore dominate the process.

Juran's (1993) 'quality trilogy' in effect orders the different strategies around stages in the product life cycle. Figure 7.1 adapts this idea to health-care by grouping the main quality management strategies according to where in the marketing cycle they occur.

Many of these methods are complementary. Those which focus on pro-vider or professional interests can be seen (in one sense) as complementary to those focusing on patient interests. Those focusing on, say, the planning or inputs of service production complement those with a tracking focus. Many hybrids have also emerged. For instance, accreditation can take service outcomes as well as processes into account; consumer preferences can be used as a source for standard-setting and benchmarking; total quality management (TQM) methods can be used to generate standards, and so on. All the strategies noted in Figure 7.1 can be evidence-based. Where they differ is in what evidence they apply. Many (especially standard-setting, consumerist strategies, TQM, statistical process control, benchmarking) require formal quality indicators. Present-day evidence-based medicine (EBM) draws heavily on elements of the quality assurance, statistical process control, quality control, benchmarking and expert review strategies. But to keep the presentation clearer, the next step is to outline briefly the principles so as to establish (see Chapter 2) how far each is relevant to healthcare and what adaptations are necessary for use in a quasi-market whose purpose is to meet healthcare needs.

Planning stage

Consumerist methods generate feedback and service quality standards from the public or users (through market research, consultation processes, patient panels and so on) then either implement these (with corresponding promotion campaigns) or 're-educate' consumers to expect different quality standards. Managers sometimes worry that patient groups who are consulted may not be representative. But not representative of whom? To consult users who are not representative of managerial or professional interests but of their own, is the whole point of consumerism. Some patient groups have expert knowledge of good practice and can be consulted to gain this knowledge although (indeed, because) it makes them unrepresentative of other patients. Lastly, it depends on the managers themselves whether a representative range of patients' views is taken (for example, by using the relevant consumer research methods).

Evidence-based medicine in essence consists of reviewing scientific and clinical evidence, where available, to discover whether a given clinical procedure does patients more good than harm. If so, reviews of clinical evidence can then be used to determine which of the clinical procedures that survive this test produces the largest outcome, where there are alternative ways of treating (or diagnosing or preventing) the same condition. To decide, one must know how strong the evidence for or against a particular clinical procedure is. Organizations such as the Cochrane Centre have published the following:

- 'hierarchies' of evidence;
- methods for finding published evidence relevant to a specific care group or procedure;
- methods for systematically reviewing published evidence;
- ready-made reviews of the evidence relating to common procedures and care groups (for example, for coronary heart disease);
- databases of health status and outcome indicators;
- guidelines for the design, ethics and conduct of clinical trials and managerial advice on how to put EBM findings into practice.

Clinicians, epidemiologists and (other) natural scientists are bound to be the predominant agents of this work. Whilst 'craft' forms of EBM relying on clinicians to be self-critical of their practice exist, the predominant forms of EBM are bureaucratic and implemented through formal channels – line management and prescriptive guidelines.

A great strength of EBM is that it focuses on the benefit which is central to patients' needs for healthcare: the clinical impact of treatment. It exempts no aspect of clinical practice from scrutiny. It insists on scientific evidence as the sole warrant for clinical interventions. Healthcare is a distress good which exacts penalties from its users (sometimes very large penalties, sometimes a very large probability of more modest penalties), placing the onus of proof on those who propose treatment. EBM offers scientific ways of accepting or rejecting claims that treatment is warranted.

Given the account of needs used here, any criticism of EBM is not at the level of principle but of practice. One such question is what evidence is considered. We have assumed that, for patients, the prime benefit of healthcare is restoration of function, removal of pain, and providing the mental equivalents of these benefits. At this level of outcome measurement, indicators developed for social and long-term care indicators are often relevant, for instance showing the number of activities of daily living (bathing, dressing, bed-to-chair transfer and so on) and instrumental activities (heavy housework, shopping) the patient can undertake, besides measures of the 'plagues' of institutional care – loneliness, helplessness, boredom (De Friese and Hogue 1999). Assuming that patients have privileged knowledge not only of non-clinical but also of many of the most fundamental clinical outcomes of care, EBM reviews should include evidence of consumers' own experience, and evaluation, of the clinical procedures reviewed. Secondly, EBM reviewers should concentrate on the most disabling, chronic and prevalent conditions (Muir Gray 1997). Many of these (arthritis, incontinence, chronic disease, degenerative disease, physical and mental disability) are not necessarily those where expertise attracts the highest prestige amongst clinicians or academics. Thirdly, by its nature, EBM reviews existing clinical procedures showing, in many cases, how small or uncertain a health outcome they produce. EBM methods can be used to indicate care groups for whose needs it is necessary to develop new, more effective clinical procedures and therefore the concomitant basic and applied research. Critical conclusions of this kind, however, require extending the purview of EBM reviews beyond evidence on existing clinical procedures. EBM principles can also be applied to health promotion and intersectoral planning, including anti-marketing methods (see Chapter 3), although most EBM activity concentrates on acute, indeed secondary, care.

Standard-setting means writing and implementing a minimal specification of what quality of health service to provide, although the term is often extended to cover protocols, pathways of care and the documentation of nursing procedures (Zander 1988). Promulgation and implementation has to be done at ward, clinic or department level. In other sectors, bodies such as the International Organization for Standardization (ISO) and the European Commission set substantive minimum quality standards for such goods as, say, electrical equipment. With the exception noted below, no such standards yet exist for healthcare, where quality standards can instead be set by any combination of:

- managerial or political decision;
- EBM review of the relevant clinical procedures;
- consumer or market research, or through public consultation, patient panels etc. (Hallas 1976; Williamson 1992);
- staff at ward, clinic or department level;
- benchmarking (see below);
- recommendation of professional bodies;
- recommendation of consumers' organizations, patient or carer groups and accreditors (see below);
- law or regulation (for example on informed consent to treatment);
- documenting current practice.

Even if 'craft' methods such as local consultation and debates are used to derive the standards, implementing them is nearly always a Fordist activity of training, standardization of workplace procedures and monitoring, typically accomplished through line-management hierarchies. If they are at all specific, standards are a ready-made tracking system: one simply compares the actual service with what the standard stipulates.

Here the critical question is, who sets the standards and how (Williamson 1992). The great risk is that standard-setters fail to adapt the standards quickly, or at all, as patients' needs and demands change. In practice, standard-setters often seem tempted to write pointlessly overdetailed standards. The 1986 *Sbornik* (compilation) of Soviet healthcare norms, still used in the 1990s, has 675 pages, most of them containing between five and fifteen norms each (Burenkova 1986). Standard-setting can also offer professional bodies a means of controlling day-to-day healthcare provision. Whether the resulting standards correspond to users' preferences is then mere chance. The most active and influential standard-setters tend to be governments, healthcare purchasers (for example, national associations of sick-funds in the Netherlands), and professional bodies. It is less common for users or informal carers, or their organizations, to have the decisive voice.

By the law of large numbers, any healthcare provider's patients will sooner or later suffer catastrophic medical negligence, serious hospital-acquired illness or injury, or some other serious mishap. *Risk management* consists in trying to predict the most likely and the most serious disasters that can arise whilst providing a service (here, healthcare) and in making contingency plans to deal with such an event. In each main area of work, the healthcare manager enumerates the most serious risks faced, considering both the probability of each kind of disaster and the scale of its consequences. Preventive measures can then be taken (for example, routinely checking the calibration and reliability of anaesthetic machines), and contingency plans made. The resulting precautions and contingency plan are typically implemented through Fordist line-management methods. The purposes of risk management are to:

- minimize the effects of such a calamity should it occur;
- enable healthcare managers to document that they took all reasonable steps to anticipate and prevent the calamity and mitigate its effects;
- prevent any recurrence.

In countries whose law of negligence follows English models, risk management also minimizes the provider's liability for compensation, punitive damages and adverse publicity.

Risk management, like standard-setting, offers consumers an explicitly guaranteed minimum service quality. It is applicable to all aspects of healthcare provision (i.e. to both clinical and 'hotel' aspects), but because managers decide which calamities it is worth trying to avoid, there is no guarantee that they will focus on the risks and consequences that matter most to patients, or the most clinically serious. American risk management seems intended as much (if not more) to protect providers from litigious patients as to protect patients from unlucky or inept providers. The greatest limitation of risk management, though, is that it defines quality primarily in terms of risk avoidance, not positive health outcomes or the other user needs, i.e. too narrowly to constitute a comprehensive quality strategy in healthcare.

Quality assurance means assuring the quality of services by using inputs only of a predetermined quality. It assumes that high-quality inputs will produce correspondingly high-quality outputs. It includes:

- Ensuring healthworkers are properly trained, qualified, registered and their skills are periodically updated, and that they comply with ethical and professional disciplinary codes.
- Physically testing equipment and consumables. Many consumables (for example, sterile packaging) can only be tested on a sample basis. Here, statistical process control methods can be applied (see below).
- Testing the completeness, reliability and accuracy of data collection, records and the management systems which use them.
- More sophisticated approaches also assure the design of the process of giving healthcare (the 'care pathway', 'quality chain', 'protocol'; in short, technical knowledge) in advance by using EBM methods (see above).

Because quality assurance assumes a causal relation between service inputs and outputs, it tends to be carried out predominantly by technical experts and managers, with a consequent focus on technical suitability of the inputs, their reliability and costs. Again there is no guarantee that their conceptions of what dimensions of quality are important will match the consumers'. The emphasis on formal testing tends to make the implementation of quality a comparatively Fordist activity. In large enterprises, quality assurance is often implemented through a specialized, separate department.

To suppose that good quality inputs produce good quality outputs assumes that the actual process of production will occur as planned – a doubtful assumption in a sector whose main technology is still handicraft treatment of a highly individuated, human workpiece, especially in health systems where, after initial professional qualification and registration, clinicians have a high degree of autonomy. The risk is not so much that the professional loses practical skills (which tend to improve with use) but that their knowledge and practice gradually become outdated or drift away from current standards. Continuing education methods, however, vary in their value as a remedy. Academic detailing seems the most effective (Davis *et al.* 1995). Consumerists and feminists have (again) criticized the tendency of professional quality control criteria to become divorced from users' main interests and needs (see, for example, Faulder 1985; Foster 1995).

Accreditation is a strategy for managing quality of inputs at whole-provider level. Healthcare providers seek accreditation, either voluntarily so as to gain a competitive advantage (as in Australia some years ago), or as a legal requirement for operation, or because it is practically impossible to attract patients or payments without it (as in the USA). An independent accrediting body determines which providers meet its standards of service quality. The accrediting organization may be a public body (as is the French Agence Nationale d'Accréditation et d'Évaluation en Santé), or an independent organization financed by charging providers for its accreditation inspection (for example, JHACC in the USA). Typically the accreditor obtains background and documentary information about the provider, followed by site visits to observe services, interview staff (and, possibly, patients) and to obtain other information. Afterwards the accreditor issues a report either refusing accreditation, granting it, or (frequently) granting accreditation subject to the provider's making specified changes in working procedures or services. Accreditation is usually for a fixed period, during which the accreditation standards themselves are likely to be revised to accommodate clinical and organizational innovations.

Various non-health bodies also accredit whether a healthcare provider meets formal standards such as ISO9000 or BS5750. Accreditation under these standards confirms not that services reach a certain level of effectiveness or safety, but that the provider's management systems enable it to set, monitor and document whatever substantive quality standards it decides to set for itself.

By itself, a polar yes–no indicator of quality is too simple a basis on which technically well-informed purchasers or referrers would choose providers. Rather, accreditation is best adapted as a mechanism for regulating new providers' entry to the health system. How relevant that function is to a quasi-market therefore depends upon how open the quasi-market is to new providers. However, in nearly all health systems the state also regulates provider entry. Further accreditation therefore seems redundant, unless to advertise service quality as being above the legal minimum. A worldly consumer might also ask what safeguards ensure that the accreditor's decision

Each gap indicates a point in the management cycle where a firm's product specification can diverge ever further from the customers' quality requirements.

Gap 1: Managers misunderstand what quality specification the customer expects.

Gap 2: Product or service specifications then fail to articulate accurately the managers' (mis)perception of what quality specification the customer expects.

Gap 3: The service actually provided does not match the (erroneous) service specification.

Gap 4: External communications (promotions and so on) to the customer do not resemble the service actually provided.

Gap 5: Service which the customer receives differs from what they wanted and what the promotions promised.

Figure 7.2 Gap analysis.
Source: Zeithaml *et al.* (1990).

is not unduly influenced by the fact that the provider itself pays for the accreditation review.

Total quality management (TQM) was a great managerial fashion of the 1990s, becoming rather ill-defined as many variants appeared, with their own brand names (for example, 'continuous quality improvement' (CQI)) and unique selling points. The core idea is that product quality is managed systematically throughout the management cycle, from the specification of product design to operation of the production process, monitoring the resulting goods and rewarding successful realization of the desired quality standards (Crosby 1979; Berwick 1989; Wilson 1992). Implementation is through firms' formal line-management system, optionally supplemented with quality circles (see below). TQM texts tend to emphasize the importance of briefing, training and persuading staff to implement the firm's quality policy, advocating strong internal communications about it, mission statements and the like. Albrecht and Zemke (1986) say the essential ingredients of TQM are a well-conceived service strategy, 'customer-friendly systems' and suitably trained frontline staff. They commend SAS (Swedish Airlines) for ensuring that all 20,000 frontline staff received two weeks' training (during the 1980s) on how to implement the airline's quality strategy. (BA and other airlines have done likewise.)

Additionally, TQM writers have invented more specific algorithms and techniques. Gap analysis (Figure 7.2) shows how the managerial cycle of deciding and implementing the quality specification for a product or service can break down.

The 'total' in total quality management signifies that the firm simultaneously manages the quality of its products at three levels:

• Preventing or remedying accidental deviations from normal working practices. Thus quality assurance, standard-setting and quality control (see below) are sometimes subsumed within TQM.

- Reviewing existing production methods to identify and remove short-comings in the ways in which normal (as opposed to deviant) working processes fail to realize the firm's current quality specifications, for example by reviewing protocols and nursing 'procedures'.
- Reviewing the quality specifications themselves. TQM writers frequently state that quality specifications should reflect consumers' demands and needs.

Slogans advanced to promote TQM often reveal whose standpoint is central to it. Crosby's (1979) slogan 'Quality is free' means that the cost of quality management measures are less than the costs of reworking, complaints and lost customers which the firm's management would incur in their absence. A minor irritant to many healthworkers, who tend to be well-educated, is the patronizing, inflated style of much TQM material (Chambers 1991).

During service delivery, two more strategies become applicable: inspection and quality circles. *Inspection* by external experts varies according to the inspectors':

- rights of access to workplaces, records, samples and individuals and whether they can access them without prior notice;
- remit, hence what is inspected (or not). For instance it may cover the safety of buildings and equipment but not that of clinical practices;
- powers of redress – whether they have legal powers to order the cessation of unsafe practices, to close the workplace, prosecute managers or secure redress in other ways, or whether redress depends on the inspectee's voluntary cooperation.

Like risk management, inspection aims to guarantee for workers and consumers a minimum standard of service quality, typically focused on safety (hygiene, temperature, noise, pollution). Inspectors are independent of the provider, hence able to be incisive and critical. Inspection is an important means of ensuring transparency in verifying the realization of quality standards and as a means of redress. However, the inspection guarantees only a minimum level of quality. It involves testing providers against fixed standards which may or not reflect the user's own needs and demands, or change as they do. Inspection allows only an episodic control of quality standards, unlike the more continuous methods such as quality assurance. Its effectiveness also depends, in a more subtle way, on the relationships between inspectors and inspectees. The method is weakest where this relationship becomes too close, comfortable and uncritical. Again, the crucial questions are, to whom is the inspectee accountable – government, managers, profession or users – and who defines the inspector's remit?

Quality circles derive from the action research methods pioneered by Revons and colleagues in the 1960s. The method is to create and train ad hoc groups (circles) of workers to identify and remodel defective working practices (Collard 1988; Ishikawa 1991; Juran 1993). Each quality 'circle' consists of workers who directly operate a particular process of production (in healthcare, a care pathway), or part thereof. Depending on the technology involved, the circle may include various occupational groups and various strata of the organization (for example, middle managers alongside casual workers). After training, the circle pursues the marketing cycle in miniature, starting with a critical analysis of what they are producing and how; an informal marketing audit and SWOT analysis. In service industries, frontline production workers directly witness consumers' experiences of the services. On this basis, the group then invents an improvement (perhaps a different booking system, new staff rota system) and tries to implement it. Then the circle monitors implementation and – the distinctive feature – attempts to learn from practical experience which factors have aided or impeded implementation in particular and their operation of the cycle in general. The circle is informally managed, with a coordinator or facilitator rather than a manager. It attempts to harness the participants' uncodified, practical 'craft' knowledge of how to raise quality standards and to solve particular problems in maintaining or raising service quality.

Quality circles thus provide a way for sensitizing service workers to users' experiences of the service. They can review and revise all aspects of service quality. They provide a way to integrate the review of service production methods in organizations – often found in healthcare – whose hierarchies are structured by profession not product-line. Indeed, the very necessity for quality circles points to inadequacies (for these purposes) of the formal organizational hierarchy. Quality circles are also a way of involving professional bodies, trade unions and other 'informal organizations' in the management of quality. By the same token, it is harder to involve consumers in quality circles and a matter of chance whether the quality circle's solutions reflect consumers' demands or needs.

At the tracking stage, four more quality management strategies become available.

Quality control consists of checking goods and services after they have been produced, to identify and rectify any which fail to meet predetermined quality standards: an 'exception management' approach. In healthcare it includes untoward incident analysis, complaints systems, informal peer pressure (the 'quiet word'; Rosenthal 1995), disciplinary procedures of licensing or registration bodies ('striking off') and juridical or quasi-juridical processes (for example judicial reviews, civil prosecution). For healthcare applications, the US Agency for Healthcare Policy and Research recommends combining:

- medical review criteria of the form 'for all patients in a given care group, clinical procedure X should be carried out';
- performance measures, i.e. investigating what percentage of eligible patients actually received X;
- quality standards, i.e. the performance levels of X-giving that trigger investigation or reward.

Quality control tends to be a highly Fordist activity of checking services and products against pre-existing standards. Typically it is performed by line managers or, in large organizations, by a specialized managerial department. Given suitably specific quality standards, product or service compliance can (depending on the case) be checked by observation, measurement, physical testing, from documentation (such as medical notes) or by asking the consumer (for example, 'Did the doctor ask whether you have any allergies?'). By creating systems which enable the firm to trace either who was responsible for each piece of work, or who verified that its quality was satisfactory, it is possible to link quality controls with personal incentives – or, more often, penalties – for individual workers.

Assuming there is a practically irreducible minimum of clinical mishap and mistake, users need health systems to have quality control systems for rectifying them. But in healthcare the great limitation of quality control is that the harm done by badly performed or unnecessary clinical procedures is often irreversible and serious, at worst death by clinical mishap or negligence. This makes quality control a second-best strategy compared with the 'right first time' approaches of the EBM, TQM and standard-setting approaches. Quality control also reveals what problems arise with existing quality standards rather than how to implement the standards more successfully or raise them.

Statistical process control (SPC) is the most sophisticated and Fordist variant of quality control. It is a set of interpretive and statistical techniques for analysing data showing how far a firm realizes predetermined quality standards. The analyses show, firstly, whether any patterns at all emerge in the data comparing the actual service with its predefined quality standards. If not, service production is 'out of control', i.e. allows too much individual variation and discretion to enable any single predetermined quality standard to be implemented. Where a pattern does emerge, the commonest form is a normal distribution. Thus clinic waiting times, for instance, will have a normal distribution around a central tendency, which can then be compared with the quality standard. In healthcare, SPC is most readily applied to frequently performed, rather standardized clinical activities such as cataract removal (Vignette 6.2). But it also has numerous non-clinical uses, such as waiting time management. Various texts explain the techniques more fully (see Deming 1986).

SPC thus focuses on the quality of populations of goods and services. Unlike quality control, its remedial emphasis is on redesigning the systems of producing goods and services rather than on rewarding, retraining or punishing individual workers. These uses of statistical analyses are readily compatible with those of EBM and epidemiology. The main difference is that EBM and epidemiological approaches focus (at best) on the health outcomes and benefits of care, whereas SPC is a way to manage the quality of goods or services during and at the end of the process of producing them. By its nature, the standards and remedies used in SPC are controlled by the firm's managers, reflecting the incentives they face. They may or may not respond to users' demands or needs.

Audit is the expert review of the work of a healthcare provider, a group of professionals or a single professional within it, by fellow professionals. Various approaches are used, but typically audit follows a cycle similar to the one used by quality circles albeit with a narrower focus and more formal structures and documentation. In clinical contexts, a typical process would be as follows:

1 Decide which care group or clinical procedure(s) to audit.
2 Select the cases to analyse.
3 For each, evaluate the quality of treatment, looking for causal relationships and patterns.
4 Devise proposals to improve any quality shortcomings revealed (for example education, changes in clinical practice such as revised criteria for when a given clinical procedure is appropriate or wider changes in service design such as new admissions policies).
5 Implement the proposed solutions.
6 Monitor the results by repeating the audit.

Audits vary according to whether a single profession is involved or several, and whether the audit is purely internal to the provider or whether fellow professionals from outside undertake the review. Audits have the option to analyse only cases which exhibit a particular problem (for example, reviews of unexpected readmissions), or a sample of normal cases, or a mixture. The audit results may be restricted to the group involved. If they are reported externally, the auditors may opt to do so in summary and anonymized form. Above all, audits vary according to the criteria by which quality is evaluated. These may be EBM-based, formal consensus criteria, predetermined standards of care or the intuitive, uncodified 'craft' criteria which working clinicians acquire through practice. Audit strategy lends itself more readily to a 'craft' than a Fordist approach, especially when implemented by professionals rather than managers or patients.

Much depends on which experts undertake the review, to whom they are accountable, and therefore what review criteria they employ. Common criticisms of intra-professional audit are that professionals are reviewed by colleagues who share their interests and empathize with the pressures they face – factors likely to make a review more cosy than incisive. A professional audit may or may not focus on outcomes, but it inevitably scrutinizes the inputs and process of healthcare. But in doing so, audit often focuses on one profession's inputs rather than the service as a whole. Evidence as to how far audits actually change clinical practice is equivocal (Davis *et al.* 1995).

Benchmarking is a surrogate for competition as a strategy for raising quality standards, provided quality standards, the corresponding indicators and quality control data are publicly available (Pantall 2001). In benchmarking, these data are compared not only with a given provider's performance but also with what other providers are achieving. Like statistical process control, benchmarking focuses on populations (in the statistical sense), not individual providers or healthworkers. But benchmarking analyses the distribution of achieved quality performance standards across whole populations of providers rather than within a single provider. From the range of providers' results, a benchmark is then chosen as a normative quality standard. The important point is that the benchmark quality standard is defined not in absolute terms (as with standard-setting) but in terms of its place within the distribution of providers. The reason for defining the benchmark as (say) the lower quartile is that, as the providers who currently fail to meet that benchmark either lose patients to providers above the benchmark or improve their performance, the absolute quality standard which the benchmark represents is automatically forced upwards.

To illustrate; a group of GPs might observe from performance data that the lowest quartile of hospitals have an average length of stay of more than three days for an uncomplicated cataract extraction. Using this benchmark, they could then decide not to refer any more patients to hospitals in that lowest quartile. The effect would be that the lowest quartile hospitals lost patients to those in the upper three quartiles who treat uncomplicated cataracts in less than three days. But this change would itself reduce the average length of stay. In doing so, it would also change the absolute level of the lowest-quartile benchmark, reducing it to, say, two-and-a-half days, so that next year the process can be repeated.

The impact of benchmarking depends upon what incentive the providers face to set and reach a benchmark which raises their current quality standards. Such incentives are at their most powerful when purchasers or referrers do actually use benchmarks as a criterion for shifting work from the lower- to the higher-quality providers, rather than as a merely informational stimulus.

That many of the above strategies are complementary, and some presuppose others, argues for a judicious mixture of them rather than reliance on a single strategy. In a quasi-market, some of these strategies are more relevant to some organizations than others. Healthcare purchasers have only limited access to the detailed operations of healthcare providers, and the rationale for a purchaser–provider split anyway is that detailed operational matters are, on the whole, best left to the providers, not decided higher up the health system. The purchasers' role is to focus on the general level and direction of development of quality standards, ensure that minimum quality standards are met, and to redress shortcomings. Quality strategies most relevant to them therefore are:

- Consumerism
- Evidence-based medicine
- Standard-setting
- Benchmarking
- Inspection
- Quality control
- Quality assurance.

In combination these strategies are the kernel of a TQM package relevant to purchasers. Hardly surprisingly, a wider range of strategies applies to healthcare providers in a quasi-market. They are:

- Consumerism
- Evidence-based medicine
- Standard-setting
- Quality assurance
- Quality circles
- Audit
- Statistical process control
- Benchmarking
- Quality control.

Together these strategies constitute a TQM package relevant to service providers. All these strategies, however, are ill-adapted for managing inter-sectoral demarketing, anti-marketing and social marketing. What most of these quality strategies lack is any guaranteed, decisive representation of consumers' own quality interests and standards.

One would therefore evaluate whether each organization uses the mix of quality strategies relevant to it against four main criteria:

- How widely evidence-based medicine is used.
- How far the evidence used includes both healthcare experts' standards for the technical effectiveness of clinical procedures *and* users' rational demands about what standards of quality they desire from health services in the round.
- Taken together, whether the quality strategies include strategies for ensuring existing quality standards are implemented as well as strategies for raising the quality of services for care groups whose clinical care is least effective.
- How far quality management is integrated with other aspects of healthcare marketing.

How does NHS practice compare?

Quality management in the NHS

Part of the settlement by which the NHS was established was an understanding between government and the medical profession to the effect that, provided they accepted that government would set the overall financial constraints within which the NHS operated, doctors would be free to practise as they pleased at the clinical level (Klein 1983). Doctors also were given privileged representation on management boards, executives, committees and authorities throughout the NHS. With the core of medical activity outside managerial control, NHS managers had only a 'diplomatic' relationship with doctors (Harrison and Pollitt 1994). Exceptional negligence or accidents apart, clinical practice and its quality were beyond NHS managerial scrutiny or knowledge.

Between 1976 and 2000, British governments tried hard to curtail NHS spending; and attempts to curtail NHS spending were bound, sooner or later, to involve attempts to manage doctors' clinical activity. The strengthening of NHS management since the early 1980s caused increasing interest in, and attempts to import, quality management methods used in other sectors of the economy, including sporadic efforts to involve patients in NHS management. Senior doctors were also gradually incorporated into NHS management by giving them control of some budgets; clinical directorates (see Chapter 6); through introducing 'clinically pertinent' information systems; and, of course, through systems for managing the quality of clinical work. NHS management is highly centralized. Many of the processes it uses to manage healthcare quality are concentrated at national level, but despite these trends the medical profession is still largely 'semi-detached' from NHS management. Patients remain rather marginal figures in managing the quality of NHS services. The result has been a separation of the management of clinical quality from responses to patients' demands and from other aspects of quality management.

Variations in clinical practice were first investigated in depth by Wennberg (1986) and others in the USA, and in Britain during the 1990s (Evans 1990). Instances where medical incompetence caused large numbers of serious injuries and deaths surfaced in several NHS hospitals (Bristol, Kent), whilst the case of a doctor who was convicted of murdering 15 patients and is accused of murdering many more, suggested weak quality control – or almost none – in general practice. Not only did these events occur at a moment when the UK government was, for electoral reasons, reviewing methods of managing clinical quality in NHS services, but there was a rare coincidence of scandals, with the consequent pressure and opportunity for reform, in both general practice and hospital medicine.

NHS bodies now have a statutory duty to ensure the quality of their services. For the first time this duty falls to the organizations, personified by their chief executives, besides individual doctors who have a long-standing personal legal duty to treat their patients competently. The means by which NHS organizations discharge this duty have been collectively labelled:

> Clinical Governance: A new initiative . . . to assure and improve clinical standards at local level throughout the NHS. This includes action to ensure that risks are avoided, adverse events are rapidly detected, openly investigated and lessons learned, good practice is rapidly disseminated and systems are in place to ensure continuous improvements in clinical care.
>
> (Department of Health 1997: glossary)

So broadly defined, 'clinical governance' covers all the quality management strategies outlined earlier in the chapter.

Professional registration has been the mainstay of *quality assurance* in British medicine since 1858, spreading to nursing and many of the paramedical occupations. British medical registration is peculiar in that the

General Medical Council (GMC) which registers, disciplines and strikes off doctors is not part of the Department of Health (health ministry) but a semi-autonomous statutory body dominated by the profession itself. In the scandals mentioned above, GMC intervention has occurred after other bodies (in the NHS or a public inquiry) have already investigated. This tardiness has enabled doctors already suspended from NHS work to continue private practice. It places the GMC very much in the second line when it comes to protecting patients from legitimately registered doctors who have 'gone wrong'.

Reform, indeed the very future, of the GMC has therefore come into question. Two revisions of the medical registration system are under discussion. One is a common registration system for all healthcare professions. This would give an opportunity to modernize medical registration and that of other clinical professions (much as the registration system and ethical code for British nursing were simplified in the 1990s), placing them all on a common and more transparent footing. It would also ease the transition for those who wish to acquire the qualifications of another professional group (for example nurses wishing to retrain as doctors). (In addition, it would be an opportunity to harmonize with systems elsewhere in the EU.)

Revalidation of doctors is the latest refinement to this strategy. It is proposed that every consultant and GP will have to have their clinical skills revalidated every five years if they are to continue practising in the NHS. Revalidation will be on the basis of a portfolio showing what the doctor has done to maintain their clinical knowledge and skills, regular appraisals of their work and the results of clinical audit. This approach relies on each doctor implementing their own professional and personal development plan for keeping their clinical competence up to date. In general practice, the current problem is to try to produce a convergence between the NHS revalidation schemes and a parallel revalidation scheme proposed by professional bodies.

For non-clinical consumables, quality assurance hardly exists in the NHS in any systematic form, except that all new pharmaceuticals have to undergo testing for safety before they can be marketed, under arrangements dating from the thalidomide tragedy in the 1960s. The National Institute for Clinical Excellence (NICE) evaluates new healthcare technologies, including drugs, for safety, effectiveness and cost-effectiveness, using both original research and a rapid appraisal method relying heavily on past research and other evidence in the public domain. In practice, NICE approval has become necessary before the NHS will take up a new product. One of NICE's first rapid appraisals was of an anti-influenza drug, Relenza. NICE initially advised:

> health professionals should not prescribe zanamivir (Relenza) during the 1999/2000 influenza season. The NHS should encourage, and where possible, support the manufacturer in the conduct of the four additional clinical trials which are currently underway.
>
> (www.nice.nhs.uk/nice-web/Article-asp?a=427&c=12476
> accessed 2000)

Glaxo (the manufacturer) responded by threatening to withdraw investment from the UK. The following year, NICE moderated this advice, citing 'new evidence' and allowing NHS prescribing of Relenza to adults 'at risk' (www.nice.nhs.uk/nice-web/pdf/NiceZANAMIVAR15guidance.pdf, accessed 2000).

NICE inherited work in progress on clinical guidelines about psychological therapies in primary mental healthcare, pressure sores (bedsores), primary care management of completed myocardial infarction (heart attack), early management of schizophrenia, non-insulin-dependent diabetes, management of speech and language impairment, foetal monitoring and induction of labour. NICE is also instigating production of guidelines for hypertension (raised blood pressure), multiple sclerosis, peptic ulcer and dyspepsia, referral cues, routine preoperative investigations, and urological, haematological and colorectal cancers. These guidelines are produced in collaboration with the NHS Health Technology Assessment (HTA) programme. National Service Frameworks (see below) are becoming their standard form of dissemination into NHS management practice. NICE also promulgates suitable ready-made guidelines.

The scientific quality of these projects is beyond serious question. The next question is therefore how far they evaluate treatments on the basis of patient-led outcomes as well as expert-defined (technical, intermediate, instrumental) outcomes. Systematic reviews of existing research contain patient evaluations only to the same extent as the original research. Few, if any, studies exist showing how far published clinical research uses patients' own evaluations to define the outcome of treatment in clinical trials, or about the extent to which clinical trial focus on the kinds of outcome that would be perceptible and valuable to patients – pain, function, prognosis, longevity. It appears that these aspects of outcome are often evaluated, but still only in a minority of cases, and patients' own evaluations of outcome less often again. But this is speculation; the question remains an important gap in knowledge about health technology development.

A connected question is how far these activities focus on treatments for the most disabling and prevalent forms of illness, with a view to forcing the pace of development of these technologies. In the short term this is a harsh criterion to judge NICE or the HTA programme by. Both have had little time yet to set their own stamp on the range of treatments they research. They also have to evaluate new technologies (drugs, treatments, equipment) promoted by firms outside the NHS and clinical enthusiasts within it, in essence a reactive agenda. Since June 2000, NICE has concentrated on evaluating cancer treatments, an issue of great current interest to politicians.

Since these bodies are separate from the healthcare providers, one must also ask how far their recommendations are implemented. There can be little doubt that their guidance reaches NHS trusts and PCG/Ts. Indeed, the greatest danger is that clinical guidelines lose visibility amongst masses of other guidance. Next the guidance has to reach the clinicians and be put into practice. Experience of the TQM Initiative and NHS clinical audit suggests this is more problematic. How – or whether – GPs put NICE and similar guidance into practice is the subject of an NPCRDC (National Primary Care Research and Development Centre) research project which is only just beginning.

Turning to *quality control* in the NHS, patients can complain informally to a manager or other member of staff before launching the formal complaints system (usually started by sending a letter to the chief executive or other senior manager or clinician). NHS rules stipulate that the patient receives an acknowledgement within 2 days and a full response within 20 (10 for general practices).

Whilst the standard NHS system is spreading from hospital and community health services into general practice (see Chapter 4), two big cleavages remain. One is the separation of clinical from non-clinical complaints. Non-clinical complaints are investigated by the chief executive (or one of their managerial staff). How effective this system is depends on how vigorously the individual manager investigates and arranges a resolution. Nevertheless, it provides a relatively swift and flexible mechanism for most purposes, including making, where necessary, an apology to the patient (which is often all the redress they want).

NHS hospital consultants are personally legally accountable for their treatment decisions. But those complaints against them which never go to law are handled separately from non-clinical complaints and can be decided at NHSE regional rather than provider level. In law, NHS hospitals or community health services are vicariously liable for other clinicians' decisions. Complaints about them are usually investigated by a similar system to that used for non-clinical complaints unless the healthworker's professional competence and registration are called into question, in which case the relevant professional body becomes involved. A few GPs are employed (through PMS contracts) under similar terms to NHS hospital consultants. Most, however, still work under an older contract whose fundamentals have changed little since 1947. It accommodates only three rather limited complaints procedures. As for any UK doctor, a complainant can try to initiate a GMC disciplinary enquiry (see above) or take the matter to court – extreme and exceptional measures. Otherwise, the doctor is liable only for failure to comply with the terms of their NHS contract, which is vague about clinical quality and offers the complainant little hope of redress.

There has been an upward trend in the number of court cases brought by patients, and a sharper upward trend in the sizes of damages awarded, principally for the increased cost of caring for damaged patients. The total cost to the NHS exceeds £200 million annually (Perry 2000). Otherwise, patients can complain to the health ombudsman, whose remit was extended in 1996 to clinical matters. The ombudsman has considerable powers of investigation and reports directly to Parliament. Unlike ombudsman systems in other countries, though, British citizens cannot make their appeal directly; their MP must do so for them, so this mechanism too is rather exceptional.

The number of complaints the ombudsman handles is rising slowly, but is only some 2000 annually. Without giving much detail, *The NHS Plan* says that NHS complaints procedures will be reviewed, and it announces the introduction in each hospital of patient advocates, whose duties will include complaints-handling (see Chapter 6).

Clinical audit is the other established method of quality control, dating from the 1950s when an annual Confidential Enquiry on Maternal Deaths was launched, based on the (initially voluntary) reporting and confidential medical review of maternal deaths in NHS hospitals. This system was later extended to peri-operative deaths (CEPOD), stillbirths and deaths in infancy. By the 1980s, individual experts and enthusiasts were also making local clinical audits. Mrs Thatcher's government achieved 'voluntary' NHS-wide use of clinical audit partly by veiled threats of legislation and partly by making clinical audit non-threatening to doctors. Policy documents introducing medical audit to NHS presented it as a medically private domain and initially 'soft-sold' it as a self-managed educative activity (Department of Health 1990).

In theory, NHS managers can initiate clinical audits, but in practice the participating doctors generally control the clinical audit agenda, usually in a rather ad hoc way (Kerrison *et al.* 1994). Clinical audit still depends heavily on individual medical enthusiasts to promote and manage it, despite the hospital's providing (typically) a manager and a small support staff. Multi-disciplinary audits do occur, but uni-disciplinary audit is more common. Medical Audit Advisory Groups in general practice normally consist of 12 GPs although NHS guidance says they may co-opt other members (NHSME 1991). Because NHS clinical audit often relies on specially collected data, and it is often laborious to extract data for clinical audit purposes from NHS hospital information systems, audits tend to rely on small, one-off surveys or case reports. They are most often criterion based, but if EBM guidelines are either unavailable or not used, the audit tends to reflect consensus medical opinion. Junior doctors, consultants in other specialities and non-doctors (when present) are unlikely to criticize much. Eyewitness accounts are rare, but one reports: 'The doctors attending played the role of audience to a performance rather than participants in a decision making process' (Kerrison *et al.* 1994: 162). This observation is consistent with Bosk's (1979) suggestion that, whatever its practical use, clinical audit in the USA at least has the important symbolic use of showing doctors to be concerned with patient care.

Neither is it often clear what the follow-up action is or who is to take it. For these purposes, indeed, hospital clinical audit is of limited use because the audit cycle is often longer than British junior doctors' normal six-month training placement in a given speciality. NHS trusts' annual reports on clinical audit to their local health authority usually anonymize doctor and patient identifiers. Neither is it clear how far lessons drawn from clinical audit are applied in general practice. These modest results should, however, be seen in perspective. In America meanwhile:

the QA activity of the majority of HMOs is fairly modest. Typically, in a medium-sized plan caring for 50,000 persons, several doctors meet every other month and a staff person performs one or two medical audits on about 30 patients each. The focus of the audits is usually a very specific clinical issue (e.g. appropriate use of antibiotics for patients under treatment for urinary tract infection).

(Weiner and Ferris 1990: 22)

Paradoxically, NHS clinical audit may have been too non-threatening for the medical profession's own good. The Bristol, Shipman, Kent, Exeter and other misfortunes exposed its weakness as a means of quality control and fuelled demands for more incisive ways of managing clinical quality.

After these events, risk management was bound to appeal to NHS managers and clinicians. Proposals for an NHS-wide risk management system have appeared under the name 'controls assurance', consisting of 17 sets of standards covering activities ranging from estates management to catering, infection control and 'professional and product liability', although the emphasis is non-clinical. For each area, the main risks are identified (for example, 'Patient falling out of the back of an ambulance'), the likelihood of the event's occurring and the seriousness of its consequences are evaluated and a 'risk rating' calculated. The NHS provider then invents systems to minimize the likelihood of the event's occurring and the adverse consequences if it does. It remains to be seen how controls assurance will fare as a means of preventing harm to patients.

The proposals in *Supporting Doctors, Protecting Patients* focus on identifying exceptionally poor medical performance and rectifying it early. They are intended to forestall such events as this:

Dr. I was a senior consultant radiologist who was known to be moody and unpredictable. He was regarded as difficult to get on with, so had few friends within the hospital. When he was reading X-rays he never allowed anyone into the room with him. Radiographers in the department tolerated his moods and his eccentricities. One day a new radiographer heard a commotion coming from Dr. I's office and went in. She described Dr. I as laughing like a hyena, skimming through X-rays at breathtaking speed shouting 'normal!', 'normal!' into the dictaphone. Dr. I was suspended and was persuaded by his wife to seek medical care. He was diagnosed as suffering from severe manic depression. An external review of his X-ray reports in the previous five years found a huge error rate and patients had to be recalled for reassessment.

(Department of Health 1999: 35)

A doctor whose performance 'appears to give cause for concern' can be referred by colleagues or managers, or self-refer, to an assessment centre outside the doctor's usual workplace. The centre will investigate and remedy whatever aspect of the doctor's practice has given cause for concern, a quicker and simpler response to borderline medical work than the present formal investigations.

Standard-setting has likewise had several avatars. Parts of the NHS, for instance ambulance services, have long-established national operating standards (for example the ORCON activation and response times standards). In the 1990s, many organizations, especially professional bodies, created extensive, indeed voluminous, systems for checking nursing standards at ward or clinic level (*Monitor*, the *Phaneuf* system and others). Some purchasers have produced standards schemes of their own. The Barking and Havering example contains a hierarchy of:

1 core standards applied to all providers (including statutory requirements, *Patient's Charter* standards and other national requirements (Department of Health 1992));
2 care group standards representing best practice for the care group in question and applying to all providers for this particular purchaser;
3 service-specific standards, which are particular to individual providers and local stakeholders (Squires 1999).

Some patient and voluntary bodies, such as the National Association for the Welfare of Children in Hospital (NAWCH), also promulgate care standards.

As NHS management gained electoral salience, governments joined in. *Patient's Charter* standards are publicized nationally to patients, not just internally to NHS staff. Besides reiterating seven existing patient rights, it added three new rights, nine national charter standards, and five prescribed 'local standards' which NHS organizations could supplement with further local standards. Most concern speed of access to NHS services. Those most relevant to other aspects of service quality include rights to an explanation of a treatment's nature and risks, and the alternatives; information on local health services, their quality standards and waiting times; full, prompt written replies to complaints; 'respect for privacy, dignity and religious and cultural beliefs'; adequate hospital directions; NHS staff in patient contact to wear name badges and the right to receive one's general practice's leaflet. With modifications (such as shorter maximum waiting times), these rights remain, but work proceeds on an *NHS Charter* to replace it (Dyke 1998).

Until recently, NHS policy said little about how NHS contracts should specify service quality. National Service Frameworks (NSFs) are standard frameworks around which NHS purchasers and providers are to formulate their Service Agreement and Financing Frameworks (sc: service contracts). The first two frameworks were formulated quite differently. The one for coronary heart diseases stipulates specific clinical interventions in detail, covering the whole episode from risk to rehabilitation, with a list of guidelines and 'service models' (in fact, recommendations about service settings and managerial tasks). The one for mental health describes examples of good practice, specifies access to services, activities and inputs, but also gives a set of outcome indicators stating how to use them for tracking purposes (NHSE 1999b, 2000). The forthcoming framework for diabetes will reportedly be considered the prototype for subsequent NSFs.

Further quality standards are publicly compared in the *National Framework for Assessing Performance* and the corresponding league tables (see Chapter 3). Despite some odd inclusions (for example mortality rates, which are mostly rather unresponsive to health service activity), the emphasis on health outcomes has increased compared with earlier performance indicators as has emphasis on delays to access. *The NHS Plan* mentions creating a national care standards commission to set and monitor standard for domiciliary and nursing home care.

Inspection has tended to be a marginal instrument of NHS quality management. Health authorities inspect nursing homes as a preliminary to licensing them and the Health Advisory Service (HAS) inspects NHS providers of long-term care for people with learning difficulty. Their power to expose any shortcomings in service quality is limited to the practice of giving prior notice of visits. HAs can withhold the registration necessary for a nursing home to operate legally, but the HAS is purely advisory. Inspection as a quality strategy has been much strengthened by creating the Commission for Health Improvement (CHI), with statutory rights of access to premises, persons and documents. Indeed, the Health Act 1999 makes it a criminal offence to baffle CHI's investigations. CHI also has statutory powers to require an NHS body responsible for inadequate services to make remedies, report back to CHI and undergo further inspection. If necessary, the Secretary of State can remove services from its control or disband it. It remains to be seen how CHI will use its (on paper, formidable) powers and to what effect. *The NHS Plan* implies that inspections of NHS hospitals by NHS bodies such as CHI, and by patients' forums, may be unannounced and have full access to services.

Evidence-based medicine has increasingly become available to support NHS quality management strategies generally. Indeed, the NHS can claim to have helped invent it. Cochrane's founding work (Cochrane 1972) helped stimulate such enterprises as the UK Clearing House on Health Outcomes. The Cochrane Centre has become an international centre for both substantive reviews and methodological advice on evidence-basing. More specialized centres for EBM also exist for child health (London), dentistry (Oxford), mental health (Oxford) and nursing (York). One of the first attempts to apply EBM to healthcare purchasing was the work of the Welsh Health Forum, whose pioneering work in the early 1990s was justly recognized in Europe more widely (see Chapter 3). NICE, the National Service Frameworks and, in another way, CHI have also helped promote EBM. As yet, this infrastructure has concentrated on reviewing existing research, in which an inverse relationship tends to hold between the incidence and prevalence of a disease or condition and the amount of evidence about it (Inglis 1983; Frankel and West 1993). Consequently, EBM is most developed in acute secondary care, much less so in primary and long-term care.

Other NHS quality management strategies have so far made uneven use of EBM. NSFs use it, as do the more modern, but certainly not all, forms of

NHS quality assurance and standard-setting. Its use in NHS medical audit appears to be limited (see above); its use in quality control and inspection still more so. Yet EBM is likely to continue to spread through the NHS for the same reasons as it has in other health systems. It opens up the quality clinical practice to public, governmental and managerial scrutiny, besides being a demonstrably effective way of improving the outcomes which clinical practice achieves.

Such are the mainstream NHS quality management strategies. There have also been more fitful attempts to use the others.

An NHS-wide policy initiative promoted *total quality management* in the early 1990s. It instigated diverse experiments including quality circles, some forms of accreditation and consumerism (see below), standard-setting and quality assurance (see above). A favourite approach was to emphasize the internal communications aspect of TQM, especially staff training programmes. This is understandable considering that clinical practice was a nearly-closed world to NHS management and EBM much less developed than now. Neither were the mechanisms for responding to consumer demands very strong. In most cases, therefore, the term 'total' was a misnomer. Activities tended to focus on the implementation and adjustment of existing working practices. Nevertheless, 're-engineering' projects aimed at reconstructing care pathways also began to appear during the late 1990s.

Of *consumerist* strategies, current NHS policy states: 'the NHS Executive will involve users and carers in its own work programme' (Department of Health 1997). Generally, the NHS has tended to prefer including lay members on boards and authorities to consumer choice of services or doing routine consumer research. In the past these were mostly either local worthies (representatives of local government, leaders of voluntary organizations, individual healthcare experts) or, increasingly during the 1990s, political appointees (Hallas 1976; Widgery 1979; Sheaff and West 1997; Wilkin *et al.* 2000). NICE has 4 out of 7 lay board members and a partners panel of 45 members, of whom 11 are patients or carers (the rest being representatives of professional bodies and such like). *The NHS Plan* says that NICE will acquire an advisory 'citizens council'. Up till now, however, there is little sign that lay representation on NHS bodies countervails the voices of government, managers and doctors. There are scraps of evidence that patients who become 'involved' also become domesticated, in the sense of coming to 'understand' and accept the managerial and medical 'problems' in changing services. Lay membership of authorities and board is only a weak and circuitous channel for consumer influence on NHS services. *The NHS Plan* proposes to appoint patient advocates to assist hospital patients to solve problems and pursue complaints.

Consumer research became much more prominent in the NHS during the 1980s. This established a pattern, which continues, of numerous fragmented, local surveys of patient and public views of NHS services. At local level, a minority of general practices and some HAs and hospitals have run patient consultation groups. As noted in Chapter 5, the National Patient Survey of

1998 substantially extended the data available to NHS organizations. What is less clear is how much use NHS organizations make of the resulting data for quality management purposes. The plethora of local surveys still tend to be one-off events, somewhat marginal to the main planning and management cycles. However, Kerrison *et al.* (1994) reported that 37 per cent of audits included patient views.

Benchmarking is from time to time mooted in NHS management circles. Until recently it has been hampered by the paucity of relevant nationally collected data, and publication of what data are available has been in forms and through channels intended for managers rather than the general public. However, the performance ('league') tables mark a shift towards making the tables' content and presentation more relevant to users' interests. In future, NHS managers will be expected to focus on 20 main performance standards, selected for their public (indeed electoral) salience and published in the national press. However, there is still heavy emphasis on using benchmarking to control costs:

> The requirement for benchmarking will encourage rigorous scrutiny of NHS Trusts' costs and performance. All NHS Trusts will in future publish the costs of the treatments they offer, so that inefficient performance can be identified and tackled.
>
> (Department of Health 1997a)

In practical terms, mechanisms for making the weakest performers either improve or leave the system are weak, partly because of the undercapacity in NHS hospitals and, in some places, in primary care. Whether this component of benchmarking will also be strengthened remains to be seen.

Accreditation has had a patchy history in the UK. Scrivens (1995) did much to develop the idea, and two NHS regions embarked on experiments. A number of NHS organizations (ambulance services, hospital ancillary services, a few general practices) obtained BS5750 accreditation. Private nursing homes have also to be licensed by the HA for their territory, an arrangement which extends to private hospitals. Before hiving them off into a separate organization (Hospital Quality Services), the Kings Fund marketed its services for reviewing hospital, and later general practice, management and organization as 'organizational audit', in essence accreditation by another name. To side-step controversy, it concentrated on organization not clinical standards, and accredited whole hospitals. By contrast, the then South East Thames Regional Health Authority accredited particular services within hospitals on the basis of clinical standards and practice. However, accreditation has had limited influence in England although a proposal to apply organizational audit throughout Wales is under discussion.

Statistical process control is rare in the NHS outside specialized areas such as the production of intravenous fluids and sterile packs – surprisingly, given the spread of EBM. So far as the author knows, there are no NHS applications (even experimentally) to the process of patient care itself. One aspect of statistical process control which is quite widely used, though, is the managerial tactic of concentrating on improving the lowest tail of the normal distribution of performance. Applied to clinical practice (for example, lengths of stay for particular illnesses or referral rates), this incremental approach enables doctors and managers to recruit the support of the majority of doctors to bring the practice of the less able 'minority' of doctors into the line with the rest.

Quality circles also appeared in the NHS as a result of the 1990 TQM Initiative. NHS clinical audit is carried out very much on quality-circle lines (see above). Evaluations of the TQM Initiative suggested that such activities achieved some modest local successes, removing minor workplace irritants and time-wasting caused by poor working technologies or systems and staff overload. Although much was made of quality circles at the time, it is unknown how many have survived the TQM Initiative itself.

Taken together, how does this collection of activities compare with the criteria outlined at the start of the chapter?

Hospital doctors have had clinical autonomy to decide, on an individual basis, what type and quality of care the patient should receive. Consequently the quality and safety of NHS clinical care has largely been managed by exception, tacitly assuming that standards of clinical quality are usually satisfactory. Detection and correction of substandard practice has been left to the medical professional organizations with, in extreme cases, the remedy of striking off incompetent or criminal doctors. Recent events have discredited reliance on clinical audit and exception management alone. Inquiries (in Bristol and Kent) revealed instances where, for years, individual consultants had autonomously continued practising dangerous surgery with high rates of death and iatrogenesis. Other doctors and managers who knew about it were unable to expose the problem except at risk to their own careers. The dangers were exposed by staff whistleblowers and patients' complaints; despite NHS management systems and professional self-regulation, not by them. Although it concerns an extreme dereliction of duty, the report into the Ledward case exposed not only the personal failings of one doctor but also – more seriously – system failures in identifying, facing and resolving the problem. The system failures were:

- Weak systems for collating complaints and detecting patterns.
- Unwillingness of staff, including medical staff, to report and pursue their knowledge of clear derelictions.
- Managers' unwillingness to confront the problem. This reflects managers' precarious tenure compared to consultants'.
- Absence of systems for promptly stopping an apparently dangerous clinician.
- Underlying cultural problems. One was the doctor's attitude to patients, his NHS post and his private practice (an extreme but not isolated case). Another was an interpretation of clinical autonomy which extended it from discretion to make the best treatment decisions for the patients into freedom from scrutiny, criticism or accountability either to patients or the NHS.

Two NHS responses have been rather traditional: stronger quality assurance (revalidation) and a stronger, more supple version of exception management (Department of Health 1999). These measures circumscribe the external limits of clinical autonomy more firmly. Within those limits, EBM is becoming more widely used, indeed a mainstay of NHS quality management. However, the use of EBM for quality management in the NHS still focuses on secondary acute care.

Inclusion of consumer demands in NHS quality management remains the exception rather than the rule. Consumer research remains a patchy, rather marginal activity for most NHS organizations. The committee-based 'user involvement' approach appears inadequate to the task of managing the user-led quality aspects of NHS services. Neither is it clear that consumers' evaluations of health outcomes (function, pain, prognosis, impacts on daily life, quality of patient experience of healthcare) have much impact on the development of EBM in the NHS.

However, the most important policy conclusion in this domain is that it was a legislative and structural strategy, not a management strategy which breached English doctors' resistance to medical audit (Dent 1995).

In conclusion

Many of the different strategies for managing service quality are complementary. A healthcare organization in a quasi-market requires a combination of strategies relevant to its role in the health system. The main difficulties with quality management in the NHS are the semi-detached nature of medical management (clinical governance), its separation from other aspects of quality management, and the underdevelopment of EBM. Nevertheless, quality control and quality assurance systems are being strengthened, especially the applications of EBM. Hitherto these developments have occurred more in secondary than primary care.

Questions

1 Which quality management strategies are most suited to long-term care for people with mental health problems?
2 Are Fordist or 'craft' strategies of quality management better suited to healthcare? Why?
3 What marketing approaches might reduce the division of quality management between clinical and non-clinical domains?
4 Why is clinical quality so difficult to manage in the NHS?

For discussion

Should patients, government or doctors have the last word in setting healthcare quality standards?

Further reading

Davis, D.A., Thomson, M.A., Oxman, A.D. and Haynes, R.B. (1995) 'Changing physician performance. A systematic review of the effect of continuing medical education strategies', *Journal of the American Medical Association*, cclxxiv(9), 700–5.

Donabedian, A. (1980) *The Definition of Quality and Approaches to its Assessment.* Ann Arbor: Health Administration Press.

Muir Gray, J.A. (1997) *Evidence-based Healthcare.* Edinburgh: Churchill Livingstone.

Rosenthal, M.M. (1995) *The Incompetent Doctor.* Buckingham: Open University Press.

Wilson, C.R.M. (1992) *Strategies in Health Care Quality.* Ontario: Saunders.

8 Consumer research in healthcare

Chapter overview

All the marketing methods discussed in previous chapters require evidence about what healthcare users want from health services, their health beliefs and behaviours. This chapter outlines the main methods of consumer research necessary to obtain that evidence, showing how the use of research to inform decisions influences the choice of consumer research methods.

Types of consumer research in healthcare quasi-markets

Health professionals are becoming increasingly research-literate. This makes it necessary to highlight three differences between consumer research for practical, managerial purposes and scientific research. Consumer research is often largely secondary. Its aim is to answer specific questions about consumer behaviour (see the situation analyses outlined in earlier chapters). If answers can be found in published sources or existing administrative data rather than new primary research, so much the easier, quicker and cheaper. Consumer research is often descriptive. The simplest data are often the most practically useful: who is using which services and who is not; what reasons they give; which alternatives they considered, and so on. Crude results are often sufficient for managerial purposes. If one is trying to estimate mean waiting times, a margin of error of 5 minutes for waits which average 30 minutes (i.e. plus or minus 16 per cent) is likely to be of little practical consequence.

The separation of users and purchasers in healthcare quasi-markets makes market research there in one way wider, and in another way narrower, than in commercial settings. Health organizations need to know the demands and experience of people who actually use health services, why people who do not take up healthcare do so (why there are 'icebergs' of need which do not translate into demand), and proxy consumers' demands. This requires fairly conventional consumer research, making a wide literature readily applicable to the healthcare quasi-market setting (see, for example, Prince 1982; Crimp 1985; Luck *et al.* 1988). Additionally, though, health services need to know how to demarket demands for needless healthcare, and why consumers consume 'bads' produced by firms outside the health sector. In a quasi-market, healthcare organizations have much use for consumer research, but little for *market* research. They tend to confront relatively small numbers of purchasers who, at least in theory, are pursuing objectives congruent with their own and with whom there are often both formal and 'relational' channels through which information about purchasers' and government's demands can flow.

The consumer research process

Consumer research follows the sequence outlined below.

Consumer research brief

Whether the research be done internally or externally, a consumer research brief can be used to define the task. It specifies the following:

- What decisions the consumer research is to inform, for example, from how far away it was worth a particular hospital's trying to attract referrals.
- What research questions are to be answered, i.e. what information the decision turns on. In the present example, the decisions turned upon two questions: how far were the potential patients willing and able to travel to hospital; and were GPs just beyond the hospital's existing catchment area willing to refer patients to it? The research question in turn indicates what target populations to research, and which aspects of their beliefs, behaviours, and so on. Figure 8.1 shows what information the Consumers' Association require from product tests.
- Who the results go back to, and by what deadline.
- Who sponsors the research and thus has authority to vary the research brief.
- What specific, concrete information is required and, if statistical results are required, their permissible confidence intervals and significance levels (see below).
- Ethical constraints, for example requirements for data confidentiality, anonymity, permission for access to patients.
- Who owns the resulting data and report, any budgetary or payment details, confidentiality and rights of copyright and resale of the results.

The brief for external consumer research must also stipulate the price for the work, who meets incidental expenses and on what scale, and which

- Safety
- Ease of use
- Comfort
- Performance, efficiency
- Adjustability
- Reliability
- Servicing
- Other factors:
  – Possible misuses of product
  – Day-to-day use and treatment of product

Figure 8.1 Product testing – Consumers' Association.

aspects of the work are the responsibility of the contractor and which of the healthcare organization sponsoring the work. As a clear and agreed starting-point for the next stages, and for managing the project, it is a false economy of time and trouble to skip or underprepare the consumer research brief.

Consumer research generally has to be done periodically if much is to be gained from it by way of detecting trends or the impacts of service changes. How periodically depends upon the types of decision being supported. Thus, tracking data to check whether services are being delivered to standard have to be collected at short intervals, say weekly or monthly. For analyses of health behaviours to decide anti-marketing strategy, annually or perhaps once every two or three years suffices. Exceptionally, consumer research will be once-off, usually for such purposes as evaluating experimental or pilot services or promotions. Often the frequency has to match that of the meetings to whom the results are reported, or other managerial purposes such as contracting, planning, reporting or financial cycles.

Research design

Where possible, secondary research is preferable, i.e. reusing data which have already been published or collected for other administrative reasons. Nowadays the standard method of secondary research is a systematic review. Because EBM also uses this research design, texts on it (for example, Muir Gray 1997) outline the method more fully than is possible here. It consists of the following steps.

1 Define the subject matter using keywords used in the main databases that will be searched (see below). For the previous example, obvious choices are such phrases as 'patient mobility', 'patient travel', 'travel times to hospital', 'referral patterns', 'hospital access'.

2 Select the period and places about which one wants data. The obvious choice is to focus on the particular locality one is interested in, or, if data are likely to be scarce, about similar localities. Thus if one was interested in, say, north-east Cornwall one would select the relevant place-names as

keywords, but then consider places whose geographical characteristics were sufficiently similar to make their patients' travel patterns relevant (for example north Devon, mid Wales). In defining a period, it is necessary to make assumptions about how stable the relevant consumer behaviours and preferences are. For travel patterns, data 15 years old might still be informative because car ownership and public transport patterns have not changed much, nor the dispersal of health service facilities. But for a subject such as young persons' alcohol consumption, only the more recent past might be relevant.

3 Identify suitable databases and libraries to search, both electronic and paper. The databases most familiar to health professionals (Medline, for example) tend to concentrate on clinical effectiveness, so with a librarian's advice one might for consumer research purposes widen the search to include such sources as the NHS National Patient Survey, the census or general household survey, *British Social Attitudes* and the commercial opinion survey firms. Commercial databases record mainly companies' financial activities but some relevant to the health sector exist, mainly covering such areas as pharmaceuticals, equipment and private hospitals. They mainly collect and sell raw data, but some will also sell data analysis and interpretation services.

4 Sort the material found according to its relevance (see above) and the strength of the evidence. All else being equal, surveys with more responses and higher response rates are more valid descriptive evidence than those with the opposite, as (for analysing trends) are longitudinal surveys over a longer period and repeated at closer intervals. The sampling methods that yield stronger evidence are outlined below. Although the following hierarchy of evidence (shown in descending order) was devised for mental health settings (*Bandolier*, www.jr2.ox.ac.uk/Bandolier), a similar ranking, but reflecting the larger amount of evidence available, would apply in other domains:

- Type I evidence – at least one good systematic review, including at least one randomized controlled trial (RCT);
- Type II evidence – at least one good randomized controlled trial;
- Type III evidence – at least one well designed intervention study without randomization;
- Type IV evidence – at least one well designed observational study;
- Type V evidence – expert opinion.

In practice there is only limited scope for using RCTs in consumer research, so much of the published evidence is likely to be at the weaker end of the range.

Secondary research rarely yields all the information required, especially about very narrowly defined care groups (for example, deaf and blind people), localities (north-east Cornwall), or periods (for example, likely effects of the 2002 Commonwealth Games on demand for health services for tourists). Then the consumer researcher themself has to select a research method for producing the desired information from primary data.

The type of research question determines what research design is required. Table 8.1 indicates the main possibilities for each of the research topics indicated in earlier chapters.

'Qualitative methods' means the use of methods such as focus groups and interviews to elicit users' own accounts of their reasons for their health behaviours, patterns of service use, ideas and attitudes about health and healthcare. 'Technical evaluations' means research designed to compare the effectiveness of services with their main competitor or substitute. They investigate, and where possible quantify, the causes of the effectiveness (or ineffectiveness) in healthcare. Various research designs are suitable for this purpose, and the EBM literature explains and ranks these in order of their validity.

Recurrent entries in Table 8.1 are descriptive surveys and qualitative methods. It is standard practice to use qualitative methods to identify initially what issues and problems are important to respondents, and their reasons, knowledge, attitudes and preferences. Pursuing the example above, a consumer researcher might use patient focus groups or interviews to answer such questions as:

1 For what reasons do patients decide they will go, or not go, to a particular hospital?
2 What influence does the GP's recommendation have on the patient compared with other factors?
3 How important are transport, distance and accessibility amongst the factors which influence patients' preferences amongst hospitals?
4 How far are patients willing to travel to hospital? What factors influence their willingness or the distance they are willing to travel?

A second round of qualitative research would be required for local GPs, reformulating questions to numbers 1, 3 and 4 to focus on the reasons why GPs refer to particular hospitals and how footloose these referrals are. By identifying the main issues which concern GPs and patients, the qualitative research can be used to produce a more structured, focused survey questionnaire which, typically, would be used to check how far the population at large, or the other local GPs, shared the views which emerged at the qualitative stage.

This instance shows the advantages of combining two or more research designs. One can obtain both interpretive depth in the results by qualitative methods, to discover why users think and behave as they do, and breadth using a survey to give a population-wide overview. It is also possible to cross-check results derived from different data sources ('triangulation'). This is often a wise precaution: comparing questionnaire figures on newspaper purchasing with sales figures indicates that many consumers claim to read the more respectable and cerebral broadsheets (*The Times*, *Guardian* and so on) but actually buy middle-range papers and tabloids (*Daily Mail*, *Sun*

Table 8.1 Quasi-market consumer research designs

Topic	Possible designs
Consumption of bads: pseudo-benefits, counter-benefits	Descriptive survey Qualitative methods
Antagonists' marketing methods	Content analyses of trade press, managerial documents
Service (and proxy) users: benefits sought, segments	Descriptive survey Qualitative methods
Media representation of health and healthcare	Content analysis of media, discourse analyses, user surveys and qualitative methods
Media channels: patients' use, credibility to patients	Surveys of media sales Descriptive survey Qualitative methods
Users' demands for 'how-to-use' information on services, self-care instructions	Descriptive survey Qualitative methods
'Icebergs' of care: user disincentives to access PHC	Descriptive survey Qualitative methods
Referring doctors: benefits sought, appropriateness thresholds	Descriptive survey Qualitative methods
Purchasers: benefits sought, income	Qualitative methods Content analyses of policy documents
Competitor analysis: entrants, loci of competition, substitutes	Content analyses of trade press and competitors' publications User surveys Analysis of utilization data
Technology scanning	Content analyses of technical press, EBM sources
Business grid	Utilization data EBM sources Technical press Qualitative methods
Mapping care pathways	Observational study
Product and promotion testing, acceptability testing	Comparative technical evaluation Descriptive survey
Tracking: gap between marketing objectives and actual services	Descriptive survey Analyse utilization data Technical evaluations
Benchmarking providers	Descriptive survey Analyse utilization data Technical evaluations

Qualitative methods

Critical incident analysis
Psychometry (e.g. repertory grid, semantic differentiation)
Interviews
Focus groups
Consumer panels
'Ghost shopping'
Study visits
Content analysis of media (e.g. press cuttings and other media watch)
Inspections
Image profiling
Blind testing of products/services
Consultation with user, interest groups and pressure groups
Staff consultation
Public meetings
Industrial espionage

Quantitative methods

Direct observation and measurement
Questionnaire surveys (e.g. opinion polling, telephone surveys)
Technical evaluations (clinical trials etc.)
Routine managerial data (activity, case mix etc.)

Figure 8.2 Consumer research data collection methods in healthcare – an incomplete list.

and so on). The best research design, or combination of designs, depends on the specific research question and has to be decided case by case. It is the hardest part of any research.

Data collection

Data collection methods have now to be chosen, and the data collected. What method of data collection is required depends on the research question and research design. An important first check is whether the research design requires one also to collect data on comparator services or user groups (for benchmarking, competition analysis, technical evaluations), control data (for technical evaluations) or baseline data (for technical evaluations, tracking, analysing trends).

Consumer research tends to rely heavily on focus groups, questionnaires and routine administrative information (such as data from cash registers, in the case of shops). For many purposes these are the relevant methods, but many public managers tend to have a rather narrow view of the possibilities, especially for qualitative research. Figure 8.2 gives an incomplete list of options.

Critical incident analysis consists in asking very open questions (such as 'What happened when you went to outpatients?') to elicit what patients spontaneously recall as the most memorable events, the best and the worst, presumed to be the events most important to them (Caple and Deighan 1986). It is useful for discovering the 'critical points' in care pathways. Psychometric techniques such as repertory grid are used to profile users' attitudes and motivation of service users with a view to finding any psychological segmentation, and for assessing users' reaction to promotional materials. Semantic differentiation shows how respondents regard a service in terms of verbal contrasts (friendly versus impersonal; organized versus chaotic). Focus groups are group discussions which a single researcher 'focuses' (steers) towards the main research questions (Henderson 1995). Patient panels can have either a permanent membership or one replaced by rota. 'Ghost shopping' consists in getting a researcher, volunteer or actual user to become a patient and report what happens to them, having been briefed about what to observe and how. Obviously, this is not practicable for all services (for example, mortuaries). A substitute is to follow a selected patient or client through the system. These methods are useful for mapping care pathways and for monitoring. Vignette 8.1 is an old example, but ghost shopping is still a rare event in English long-term care settings.

Vignette 8.1 What it's really like

To assess the quality of care in its residential homes for elderly people, Norfolk Social Services arranged for 37 elderly volunteers to be admitted as residents for a week in 37 of the Council's 46 homes. The volunteers were recruited by a newspaper advertisement and paid expenses and a small fee. As far as possible, their admission arrangements imitated those of any other resident, except that staff in the homes were told in advance of the experiment. The 'ghost shoppers' experiences were recorded in diaries and in debriefing interviews after the week's residence.

Their findings give a rich, qualitative picture of life in the homes. New residents' welcome to the home was usually warm although some of the admission procedures showed scope for improvement. The daily routine, especially meals, was found to run earlier than the new residents were used to at home. The importance of food and mealtimes became very evident. For instance, cups of tea are valued as a symbol of care and (if the residents were able to make their own tea) of independence. The importance of the building layout also became evident. The residents valued a layout which allowed them to form small social groups – suggesting that domestic-scale modern buildings and converted older houses are the optimal type of home building, provided the rooms are not too small. Data on privacy, security, choice and relations with staff emerged, as did the comparators against which residents compare elderly persons' homes: hospitals, hotels, prison or workhouse or schools. Enabling staff and residents to work towards extending residents' choices and influence over the services required further, more subtle methods than user participation in a standing consultative committee.

Source: Casey (1989).

Public meetings allow detailed discussions with the most interested members of the public. These are often unrepresentatively well informed and critical; at best, therefore, a worthwhile source of ideas for service development. Similarly, pressure group and interest group (for example NAWCH, Age Concern, Mind) opinion is often valuable precisely because it is not representative of most users' views but better informed, expressing well-researched views on good practice, the acceptability of new services and the most glaring failures in existing service provision.

For quantitative data, direct observation (including the use of security video tapes) and measurement give objective data on such matters as waiting times, food or room temperatures, patterns of telephone use, and when patients are woken (from power surges as lights and other equipment are switched on). They are most obviously useful as tracking data but can also be used to compare users' perceptions or complaints with the reality. For tracking purposes, Gilligan and Lowe (1995) recommend 'evaluation cards', i.e. short questionnaires periodically collected in small numbers over a long time.

If a survey is to be made, the consumer researcher has to choose a sampling strategy and design the questionnaire.

A sampling strategy is the choice of a sampling frame and sampling method. The ideal sampling frame is one which covers all and only the user group one wishes to sample, such as a census, a population register (including those for sub-populations, such as all cancer patients or a list of employees or prisoners) or a patient or subscriber database. Specialist firms sell mailing lists, others will mail questionnaires to respondents selected randomly or by specific criteria. These lists will have been prepared for commercial purposes and, depending on the sources, may under-record low-income groups, people who do not use credit, and similar.

The sampling frame is the pool of potential respondents to which a sampling method is applied to draw a sample. There is a clear hierarchy of sampling methods, here listed in descending order of the strength of evidence they provide about the population being studied. (Here 'population' is used to denote the whole user group being studied, which may or not be a population in the everyday sense of all the inhabitants of a region.)

1 *Census*, i.e. selecting the whole population for study. Technically a census is not a sample but is included here as the obviously preferable way (if feasible) to collect data about a population because it pre-empts any sampling error (i.e. the risk that the sample might not represent the population in some important characteristic). Population size is an obvious practical limitation on making a census, but consumer researchers are often interested in populations which are small enough to make a census of (for example, everyone who has used a particular service during the last month, all GPs in a locality).

2 *Probability sampling*, in which every member of the target population has an equal chance of being selected as a source of data, and the total

population size is known. Probability sampling can therefore be applied to exhaustive sampling frames such as admissions lists, subscribers, employees. It is preferable if statistical processing of results beyond simple descriptions is intended.

3 *Random sampling* differs from probability sampling in that the total population size is unknown, narrowing the scope for statistical analysis. The simplest way is to use random numbers to select respondents from a list, but other ways include:

(a) *systematic sampling* ('file sampling'), which consists in selecting a first respondent randomly from a list (sampling frame) and then every *n*th name thereafter. What fraction of names one selects (i.e. the size of *n*) is obtained by dividing the population size by the desired sample size (see below);

(b) *cluster sampling*, which divides the target population into clusters which are as similar as possible then samples clusters at random. For instance, one might take a non-bank holiday weeks' throughput of patients as the clusters;

(c) *stratified random sampling*, which divides the target population into strata and then samples randomly within each stratum. The resulting data then have to be weighted by the size of each stratum to produce statistics about the whole population.

4 *Quota sampling* also divides the population according to the differences within the target population which are assumed to differentiate their attitudes, behaviour, or whatever else the research is studying. Thus accident and emergency patients might be stratified by age, sex, GP and occupation. A quota of each sub-population are then sampled, the size of each quota reflecting how large a proportion of the whole population each sub-population is.

5 *Convenience (or 'accidental') sampling* is simply completing the required number of observations or questionnaires in the most accessible or convenient way.

Various statistical texts expound these more fully. The choice of sampling method also depends on the size and character of the user group one wants to research. Neither probability nor random sampling of a large target population is an easy (or cheap) way to collect data about small minorities of users such as sufferers from rare conditions or diseases. Stratified random sampling enables the researcher to make such groups one of the strata, so that a large number of them can be questioned or observed without distorting the results for the wider population as a whole. Quota sampling presupposes that the researcher already has evidence about which differences (age, sex, illness) within the target population are likely to differentiate their attitudes, behaviour, or whatever else the researcher is researching. In practice, the data collector has to judge which quota a respondent belongs to, so if data are being collected on, say, the street or at the hospital entrance, there is a danger that data collection will collapse into a form of convenience sampling because it relies heavily on the data collectors' powers of stereo-typing. 'Convenience sampling' usually offers more of convenience than of sampling, because a sample which is unrepresentatively convenient to collect may also be unrepresentative in more important ways (for example, orthopaedics patients may be heavily over-represented in a Tuesday clinic).

When a sample is randomly chosen from a population, there are trade-offs between the margin of accuracy (confidence interval) of the conclusions drawn about the population from the sample; the risk (probability) that the true figure for the whole population lies outside that margin (the signifi-cance level of the results); and the sample size (and thus the time, difficulty and cost of the research). A standard formula connects sample size, margin of error and risk of error:

$$n = \frac{s^2 \cdot Z^2}{E^2}$$

where: n = sample size
s = standard deviation in the sample
E = margin of error
Z = the number of standard deviations corresponding to a given probability that the statistic calculated for the sample lies within E of the true figure for the population.

Z thus quantifies the risk that the sample's characteristics are more than plus or minus E away from the true figure for the whole population that the sample was taken from. Using statistical tables, a calculator or computer software, Z can be translated into p (the significance level) which states the probability that the result from the sample lies *outside* the true figure for the whole population. Thus the smaller p is, the smaller that risk of error and the stronger the evidence which the sample gives. Standard deviation is a measure of the dispersal of the individual sample answers (or measures, observations).

This formula has some intuitively obvious implications. The more dis-persed (less consistent) the sample results are, the more of them one needs in order to estimate a figure for the whole population to within a given accuracy. A bigger sample will produce a narrower margin of error and a smaller likelihood that the true figure for the population falls outside that margin. If one specifies a smaller margin of error, one makes it less probable that the true figure for the whole population really lies inside that margin, and so on.

What are not so intuitively obvious are the rates of trade-off that the formula implies. All the figures on the right-hand side are squared. So, to halve the margin of error one must not double, but quadruple, the sample size. To reduce the probability of error by nine-tenths, say from 10 per cent (i.e. $p = 0.1$) to 1 per cent (i.e. $p = 0.01$) requires a sample 100 times larger. Furthermore, a larger sample size in one study is not automatically more representative than a smaller sample size in another. A small (say 10 per cent) sample may be more representative and thus stronger evidence if it comes from a more homogeneous population (lower standard deviation) than, say, a 20 per cent sample. A 10 per cent probabilistic sample is also likely to yield more trustworthy results than a 20 per cent convenience sample.

The choice of sample size thus depends on what degree of accuracy and certainty the researcher wants in the results, but these rates of trade-off imply that the small increases in accuracy and certainty can demand much larger increases in data collection. Consumer researchers tend to apply conventional rules of thumb about what sample sizes (and therefore significance levels and confidence intervals) are good enough for most practical purposes.

- For significance level, a round figure is usually chosen, most often $p = 0.05$ (5 per cent risk of larger error) or $p = 0.01$.
- Alternatively, one can choose a margin of error and accept whatever significance level follows. Gallup accept a margin of error up to ±3 per cent on a 1000-person sample (Heald and Wybrow 1985).
- Sample sizes of greater than 200 will rarely be necessary for exploratory, first-time consumer research because the probability that a sample result lies outside a given margin of error (E in the above equation) declines very slowly once sample size grows above 200.
- In many statistical calculations the risk of error grows rapidly once sample size falls below 30, so the smallest segment of the sample which it is intended to analyse independently should not be smaller than this.
- To the sample number calculations (above) one must add a compensation for respondents who drop out or fail to respond. Piloting and past experience indicate what response rates are likely.

Here, too, numerous texts are available to explain the reasoning and mathematics underlying this formula (see, for example, Crimp 1985), and what statistical analyses one can perform of different types of sample. The above formula assumes a normal distribution of the data and that the data come from a randomly selected sample. Different formulae are required for qualitative data and for non-normal distributions.

A survey also requires a questionnaire or other data collection instrument (observation checklist, diary and so on). An increasing range of such instruments are now available in the health research literature and, in some cases, commercially (for example, the Nottingham Health Profile is marketed through Galen Plc).

Adopting a ready-made instrument is worthwhile if, but only if, the data it records are relevant to the research question, the instrument has been validated, and one knows how to use it. Many instruments require special training to ensure that different data collectors record reliably (i.e. consistently). Using a ready-made instrument may also enable one to compare one's own data with findings from other services and groups. Modifying someone else's instrument can, however, give the worst of all worlds. One

- Aim not to exceed 30 questions for a member of the public; fewer if possible.
- Check each question is unambiguous, i.e. elicits only one piece of information. 'Were the doctors polite?' is preferable to 'Were the doctors and nurses polite and helpful?' (The user may want to reply that the doctors were helpful but not polite, and the nurses the reverse.)
- Move from more general to more specific questions ('funnelling').
- Leave personal questions (about age, occupation etc.) until last.
- Sequence questions so that replies to earlier questions do not bias replies to later questions.
- Minimize 'filtering', i.e. routing respondents or data collectors to the next question according to earlier answers ('If "yes" go to question 8').
- Avoid questions requiring embarrassing, self-incriminatory or socially expected answers.
- Avoid leading questions such as 'When did the nurses wake you up?'
- Avoid very difficult or demanding questions, for example, about trivial events which happened long ago.
- Include explanatory definitions or instructions ('Take "doctor" to mean "family doctor", "school doctor" or "hospital doctor"').
- Draft questions to match the general public's reading age of around nine. Drafts can be checked for this by an educationalist or psychologist.
- Always pilot test the questionnaire.

Figure 8.3 Rules of thumb for questionnaire design.

not only loses a validated instrument and has to repeat the process of testing and validating the adapted model, but also risks ending up still using an instrument that was not originally designed for the present purpose.

Questionnaires, in particular, seem easier to design than they really are. Since they are so useful and ubiquitous in consumer research, however, Figure 8.3 gives some rules of thumb for designing them. These rules are particularly important for questionnaires which the user will have to fill in without help from the researcher (for example postal questionnaires, evaluation cards).

Piloting should include data coding, computer entry and a data analysis, to check whether the data collected are usable and whether the questionnaire spreads the users' responses. (If all patients score the mid-point of, say, a satisfaction scale then these data are unlikely to be very informative.) Piloting a questionnaire can indicate the likely response rate in practice, the time required to select the sample, collect, enter and analyse the data. Data entry is also becoming more automated, using machine-readable questionnaire or other consumer research data collection documents (for example, the Patsat system developed by CASPE in Bloomsbury in the 1990s) and, more recently, automated interview transcription using voice-recognition software.

In non-anonymous surveys one can use reminders and replace non-responders in order to raise the response rate to the level required for any sampling. As rules of thumb, in a field such as healthcare, which in Britain has a quite high public interest and sympathy, response rates of 50 per cent should be possible (compared with about 10 per cent for most consumer surveys outside healthcare). To compare with the USA, Berkowitz (1996) cites examples of response rates of 13 per cent for postal surveys but 85 per cent for telephone surveys.

Analysis and report

Without interpretation, consumer research results are almost uninformative and may mislead. 'Eighty per cent of patients found the doctors' explanations helpful' may induce complacency until it is compared with a figure of 85 per cent for three months ago and 95 per cent for the neighbouring practice. Table 8.2 shows the main analyses of consumer research data relevant to a healthcare quasi-market. Earlier accounts (Chapters 2–6) of what situation analyses healthcare marketers require elaborate more fully.

Image profiling consists in reconstructing the 'image' (i.e. the totality of beliefs and impressions) users have of a given product or service from questionnaires, interviews and so on. 'Strategic gap' simply means the gap between marketing objectives and actuality, i.e. comparing the actual data with a normative standard. The main techniques to inform environmental analysis are trend extrapolation and correlation, dynamic modelling, cross-impact analysis, scenario analysis, demand forecasting, hazard forecasting and Delphi studies (in essence, syntheses of the opinions of panels of experts). 'Technical evaluation' means analyses intended to show which services produce which benefits (effectiveness, user satisfaction) and to what extent. This is the hardest analysis. In general it is easier to show that service standards or user behaviour or attitudes exist than to demonstrate that their existence is due to the marketing activities which were intended to produce these (or possibly different) changes. 'Benefit analysis' is a comparison of the range of benefits which a given provider offers its users, user segment by user segment.

'Benefit segmentation' means describing the benefits which each user (or proxy user or purchaser) segment is seeking, and in the case of care icebergs, the disbenefits they are avoiding by not taking up healthcare that they need. User segmentations can be revealed by combining associations amongst data sets with the results of qualitative research. The former suggest correlations between sets of user characteristics (age, sex, educational level, what types of healthcare users seek) and the latter help explain their motives and attitudes (for example, using hospitals because it is hard to get a familiar GP out of hours). Alternatively, one of the established consumer segmentation methods can be used. Two useful ones for healthcare purposes are:

- ACORN (A Classification of Residential Neighbourhoods), a multivariate correlation of demographic characteristics taken from Office for National Statistics census data. Each of 36 neighbourhood types has a characteristic profile in age, sex, household composition, employment, income, housing, family structure, cars and hence consumption patterns. ACORN then classifies each neighbourhood (enumeration district) according to which of these profile most closely approximates.

Table 8.2 Analyses of healthcare consumer research data

Topic	*Analyses*
Consumption of bads: pseudo-benefits, counter-benefits	Market share of bads and goods: segmentation by pseudo-benefit
Antagonists' marketing methods	Analyses of antagonists' marketing activity; anticipate antagonists' SWOT analyses
Service (and proxy) users: benefits sought, segments	Benefit segmentation of users, utilization trends
Media representation of health and healthcare	Image profiling
Media channels: users' use, credibility to users	Readership analyses
Users' demands for 'how-to-use' information on services, self-care instructions	Benefit segmentation of users, compared with content analyses of existing materials
'Icebergs' of care: user disincentives to access PHC	Benefit segmentation of users
Referring doctors: benefits sought, appropriateness thresholds	Benefit segmentation of GPs (or equivalents)
Purchasers: benefits sought, income	Benefit segmentation of purchasers
Competitor analysis: entrants, loci of competition, substitutes	Environmental analysis, 'market' shares and trends, anticipate competitors' SWOT analyses
Mapping care pathways	Critical incident analysis; observational description
Technology scanning	Environmental analysis, comparative technical evaluation
Deciding marketing strategy	Business grid
Product and promotion testing, acceptability testing	Comparative technical evaluation
Tracking; gap between marketing objectives and actual services	'Strategic gap' analysis
Benchmarking providers	Comparative technical evaluations, benefit analysis

- JICNARS (Joint Industry Committee for National Readership Surveys) analyses periodicals' readerships by class (using the registrar general's classification of television company region, demography and special interests).

During the 1990s many new lifestyle-based segmentations appeared, often with colourful acronyms for particular consumer segments ('Yuppies', 'Dinky', even 'wrinkly').

Consumer research findings are typically presented in dual form. An 'executive summary' presents the practical implications of the findings to managers or other decision-makers who want to know the practical implications and how strong the evidence is, on which they are based, without needing to know more about how they were reached. It is presented as briefly and clearly as possible, often using graphs and graphics rather than text, but appending references and data in greater depth to substantiate any surprising conclusions or controversial recommendations. It draws upon the full report. This latter typically states:

- The remit of the research, what decisions it supports and the consequent research questions it answer.
- An account of the research design and method, noting any ways in which these limit the strength of the evidence and conclusions.
- The population studied, its size and any sampling methods, stating when and where the samples were taken.
- What data were collected.
- Assumptions made and any statistical methods used in analysing the data.
- Results of the analyses.
- How much reliance can be placed upon these results, noting any possible causes of bias such as groups omitted from data collection (for example, patients too ill to answer), any ambiguous results and what further research would be required to resolve the ambiguities.
- Practical implications and managerial options, with the advantages and disadvantages of each, any recommendations and the reasons for them.

Recommendations, and the reasons for them, should be separated from statements of facts, as should any matters of conjecture or opinion. Report readers who are as research-literate as many health professionals are will usually be able to find some methodological objection, not only to truly methodologically weak research but also to methodologically sound research whose results they dislike. So far as possible, it is prudent for the report-writer to anticipate the most obvious objections when drafting and preparing a report whose findings are likely to be unwelcome. One way to soften the blow (and abreaction) is to give positive and negative feedback about services as nearly equal weighting as the facts will allow.

Consumer research in the NHS

Earlier chapters will have prepared the reader for the revelation that an account of consumer research in the NHS today is likely to be brief. Not much consumer research occurs, not much is known about the consumer research which does occur, and some of what is known has already been stated in earlier chapters. Only a few overviews of consumer research have been made, mostly in the mid 1990s or earlier.

Except for the NHS National Patient Survey and some other national opinion surveys cited earlier, most NHS consumer research takes place at a local level, on a small scale and on a once-off special project basis whose occurrence depends on the initiative and drive of individual enthusiasts. One of the main sources of such research, the Community Health Councils, are, however, being abolished under the 2000 *NHS Plan*. When pursuing their consumer research projects, these researchers have tended to encounter the following problems.

One has been the absence or weakness of a research brief, reflecting unformed or ill-formed expectations because managers have no coherent view of what they want to use the consumer research results for or of how to apply them in healthcare planning and management, or because consumer research is being used tokenistically, as a sign of concern for users' demands. In that case, what matters is that some research occurs, not what it covers or whether it is subsequently used. Another common practice is that of starting from a consumer research technique, frequently a data collection technique such as a favourite questionnaire or an interest in focus groups, and then seeking ways to use it: the reverse of the approach recommended above. Enterprising managers also often undertake consumer research not so much for the sake of the information it yields as in hope of inventing resaleable questionnaires, data collection instruments or software. (This hope is either naïve or requires a powerful and expert partner; if the plan is to produce resaleable software, the researcher should remember that they will be competing with Microsoft.) In all these cases it proves hard to formulate the research questions because answering them was not really the purpose of the research.

Other problems concern the management of consumer research projects in the absence, in most NHS organizations, of a managerial infrastructure intended for that purpose or even very familiar with it. Consequently, control over consumer research projects tends to be divided amongst several members of a project team, leading to uncoordinated control and overconsultation, itself a recipe for delay and compromise. Because they are liable to raise interesting, controversial issues, NHS consumer research projects are also prone to interference from uninformed third parties. For instance, one Welsh researcher was advised by her hospital manager to combine random and non-random data sets so as to get a larger sample. Not least amongst the interferers are sluggish, even obstructive ethics committees. Ethics committees exist, and necessarily, to protect patients from the dangers of needless, ill-conceived and poorly conducted clinical trials and experiments. But consumer research seldom, if ever, exposes patients to physical danger. (It is a challenge to imagine how it could.) The greatest risk is of breaching the confidentiality of some types of patient information, nearly all administrative (for example, that a person was admitted for treatment of a mental disorder or sexually transmitted disease) or, conceivably, diminish patients' privacy. It hardly requires a committee of senior clinicians to detect and thwart these dangers.

The other problems tend to be more technical, often reflecting inexperience. They have included unrealistic timescales and costings such as forgetting to include the cost of data entry; not allowing for non-responses; neglecting to collect baseline, comparator or control data; poor instrument or questionnaire design; and misinterpreting data (for example, interview data about waiting times tell you how long patients *think* they waited; observational data are necessary to tell you how long they *did* wait). Many healthcare outcome indicators are available (at least 400 quality of life indicators, for instance (Miles and Lugon 1996)), and many variants of consumer questionnaire, but few are standardly used, making it difficult to track data over time or compare providers. Among the exceptions are Thompson's questionnaire on inpatient experiences and the Patsat system (both popular in the 1990s but now fallen out of use) and, being developed, the GPAS (General Practice Assessment Survey) questionnaire for use in general practices. However, few manual, let alone automated, systems for routine consumer data collection exist. Until recently there has been no British equivalent to the USA National Research Council's *Healthcare Market Guide*, a routine periodic 100,000-respondent survey.

Nevertheless, there are some more positive trends. Thanks to EBM, more secondary research on the effectiveness and some other aspects of patient experience of healthcare is readily available and usable. If the National Patient Survey is repeated regularly, and in ways that enable its analyses to be taken down to PCG/T and larger NHS trust level, the biggest gap in NHS consumer information will have been filled. The EBM movement also has the potential to place future consumer research in the NHS on an altogether more systematic and scientific footing.

The overall picture is thus of NHS consumer research as a somewhat marginal, minority interest amongst managers, quite widespread but also quite fragmentary and idiosyncratic. Considering the lack of incentives for consumer research in the NHS, and the medical, financial and managerial slant of its planning and control systems, a cause for guarded optimism is not how little consumer research has taken place but, in the circumstances, how much.

In conclusion

Consumer research is required for a gamut of purposes in the various marketing models outlined in earlier chapters, especially for situation analyses, testing new services and promotions, and tracking. It differs in several ways from clinical research, relying more heavily on a range of qualitative methods, survey methods and, where possible, secondary data. NHS consumer research has had a very fragmentary, sparse and occasional character but the National Patient Survey represents a potentially significant improvement.

Further reading

Health Education Authority (1992) *Marketing Research for Local Health Promotion.* London: HEA.

Henderson, N.R. (1995) A practical approach to analyzing and reporting focus group studies: lessons from qualitative market research, *Qualitative Health Rsearch*, v(4), 463–77.

Luck, M., Lawrence, B., Pocock, B. and Reilly, K. (1988) *Consumer and Market Research in Health Care.* London: Chapman and Hall.

Worcester, R. and Downham, J. (eds) (1986) *Consumer Market Research Handbook.* London: McGraw-Hill.

9 Marketing in a post-market system

Chapter overview

This postscript gathers the conclusions of earlier chapters, using them to draw wider conclusions about how to make publicly funded health services, and public services generally, more responsive to users' needs.

Theory and practice

For use in the public sector, conventional commercial marketing models have to be modified much more radically than most writers suppose because the purposes and organizational structures of public services are quite different from commercial purposes and contexts. The resulting modified models are implicitly a theory of how to make publicly funded services more responsive to their users' rational demands, i.e. to users' needs (see Chapter 2). As such, they make testable, empirical claims. To test these claims it is necessary firstly to develop the theory to the point where it can be applied in practice. The first sections of Chapters 3–7 attempt that. Next one must stipulate what would count as evidence that applying the resulting theory does indeed produce the intended effects on user-responsiveness. Then it becomes possible to try to apply the revised marketing model in practice and compare the actual effects with those predicted, enabling one to modify the model as necessary.

The simpler way to apply and test a (revised) marketing model is through conventional research and development activity. One attempts to create artificially the conditions which the marketing model predicts will improve user-responsiveness, in a pilot or experimental scheme. This method pre-supposes, though, that it is possible to start implementing the model; for instance that current regulations do not prevent it, sufficient budget is available, there will be no political interference or obstruction by professional bodies. Because these conditions cannot always be met, it is sometimes necessary to fall back to relying on natural experiments. One scrutinizes (in this case) health services' own activities to find any which by chance approximate to an implementation of the relevant marketing model, and note the effects of doing so, making allowance for the effects of any obstructing (or potentiating) confounding factors. In particular, the model may only have been implemented in part, for instance when organizations collect data about users' demands but cannot change payment systems in response. What natural experiments are available to study is limited by the historical accidents of what policies, organizational structures and managerial arrangements have existed. However, one compensating benefit is that health services innovate ideas which theorists did not think of. The natural experiments which actually occur test a wider range of models than marketing theorists devise. Similarly, natural experiments include negative lessons, those of measures which produced the opposite effects to those the revised marketing models are trying to produce (for example the creation of perverse incentives for surgeons).

Earlier chapters indicated what sorts of management activity would be evidence of attempts to implement the quasi-marketing models outlined. Evidence of attempts to collect users' views of health and health services routinely and systematically, to incorporate that evidence into service specifications, to invent new models of care, and to implement the corresponding service changes would be evidence that using the model had produced more user-sensitive planning and management processes. (The second parts of Chapters 3–7 summarized evidence of that kind from the NHS.)

Evidence that the resulting services conform more closely to users' reasonable demands is what would confirm the relevant marketing model(s). Improved satisfaction ratings would tend to confirm the models, as would smaller numbers of complaints and a shift in their distribution towards more trivial matters (for example about ward decor rather than about long waits on a trolley for a bed). Where objective indicators of user-led standards are available (waiting time, length of stay, unfilled GP vacancies), improvements in these indicators would be confirmatory evidence, as would evidence of greater levels of self-care and declining use of private health care. Shifts of referrals and self-referrals towards providers that had more fully implemented the marketing models outlined above would be confirmatory behavioural evidence. Evidence of promotional activities aimed at strengthening users' self-care and their ability to get full benefit from public health services would also tend to confirm the models. So would evidence of greater user involvement, particularly of patient groups, in the management of public services, and greater transparency of public services' management at all levels to public scrutiny.

Now we can return to a question left in abeyance (see Chapter 2). The second part of Chapters 3–7 outlined how far the English NHS has implemented, and to that extent tested, the marketing models outlined above. From the historical, natural experiments occurring in the NHS, we can draw some conclusions about methods which do not work as means of making publicly managed health services responsive to users' needs, and a smaller number of positive lessons.

Lessons of NHS experience

Analysts often remark that the NHS has attempted two broad strategies for making its services user-responsive: strategies based on the notion of citizenship and so-called consumerist strategies (Lupton *et al.* 1998; Pickard 1998). Citizenship strategies are so called because they rely on the claims which patients and members of the public putatively have as citizens and taxpayers to monitor and influence what public services do. In fact, the NHS has used two variants of citizenship strategy. One relies on account-ability to Parliament, the other on lay participation in decision-making bodies.

The 'bedpan doctrine' is that NHS services – or, more exactly, the health-workers providing them – are managed by managers accountable to the Department of Health, the Department of Health is responsible to minis-ters, ministers to Parliament, and Parliament to users in their capacity as electors. The experience of the 1990s suggests that applying the bedpan doctrine does, in certain political climates, put ministers under pressure to resolve the main problems of public health service access and quality. It produces strong responses to users in regard to the most electorally contro-versial issues, although they are political marketing responses as much as service development. However, there are many links in this accountability chain between NHS providers and users, and every link in it has to work. A single loose link vitiates the whole process. To be sure, the 1990s saw a considerable tightening of managers' accountability to the Department of Health, and sustained but incremental attempts at making doctors more accountable to managers. But several other links are loose. Notwithstand-ing the changes of the 1990s, doctors remain largely outside this system of accountability, having privileged legal status and powerful but auto-nomous occupational organizations. The relationship between senior civil servants and minister has long been recognized as ambivalent. Whatever the formal position may be, in reality it is not always clear who manages whom. Ministerial accountability to Parliament is still weaker; for Parliament to overturn a ministerial, civil service or managerial decision is the excep-tion not the rule, and for it to dismiss a minister for the poor quality of public services is rare indeed. MPs usually become electorally accountable to voters only at long intervals (in Britain, at a time the government chooses, within five years of the previous election). The quality of a given public service becomes one of many election issues, rarely the decisive one. The act of choosing someone to be an MP is anyway far too crude a process to enable voters to select specifically how a particular public service will be provided at operational level. Lastly, not all public service users are voters and not all voters are service users. NHS accountability chains are constructed to give strong managerial accountability to government, not users (Allsop 1984; Mulligan 1998). They also inhibit NHS managers from making even constructively critical comments about NHS services, which is hardly conducive of transparency of decision-making and information for public and users. Applying the bedpan doctrine is too clumsy, slow, erratic and circuitous a system for getting NHS services to make continual day-to-day adjustments and sustained improvements and innovations in service design.

Lay participation in managerial boards and committees is the other main citizenship strategy. NHS authorities, boards, executives and similar committees have included lay membership since 1974, and in many cases since 1947. Usually, most members are lay, in the sense of being neither clinicians nor career managers. Mostly, however, they are local dignitaries and party nominees. A paradoxical effect of the Nolan Report (Committee on Standards in Public Life 1995) and subsequent efforts to improve the transparency and fairness of English public administration is that NHS managers and civil servants, and not politicians, now control the initial stages of selecting these lay members. It is express policy that lay members are not selected to represent any particular interest, let alone particular patient groups. But even where lay representatives originate from such groups, a dilemma arises. Compared with clinicians and managers, incoming lay members are usually at an initial disadvantage in terms of knowledge, experience and self-confidence, not to mention the time and access to management information. Even when lay members are the majority they are in a weak position to challenge managers', and especially doctors', judgements about how to develop services. In acquiring these skills, there is always the risk that lay representatives become domesticated, in the sense of adopting managers' and clinicians' views about how services should be provided. Lay involvement in healthcare planning is necessary to give artificial voice to the demands and needs of patients and others who are unable to use mechanisms for choosing providers, participating in consumer research and taking part in the political process (see Chapter 3). It is also another way of increasing the transparency of management in public services. As a way of making services responsive to users' reasonable demands, however, it seems, on the basis of NHS experience, too weak a voice to countervail the interests of doctors, managers and government and therefore of limited value as a mechanism for making services user-responsive.

Having a statutory and regulatory basis, both forms of citizenship-based strategy have been applied across the NHS as a whole. Except for the patient's right to refuse treatment, the same cannot be said of the consumerist strategy. It relies on using consumer information, consumer choice and routine use of consumer research and other suitably adapted marketing methods to make services more responsive to users' needs. The quasi-marketing models outlined previously are consumerist methods.

Earlier chapters indicated how far the NHS has implemented the relevant marketing models. So far as the commissioning model is concerned, NHS purchasers (HAs, and PCG/Ts in their commissioning capacity) undertake parts of the situation analysis shown in the model (mainly those dealing with population needs) and critically review existing services' effectiveness. The National Patient Survey substantially strengthens their data about users' demands and experiences. A few purchasers make SWOT analyses for deriving their objectives for local services. NHS purchasers plan quite systematically the range and volume of services to be made available, by whom, and, in broad terms, plan ways of checking that the services follow acceptable clinical practice. Tracking mechanisms for the purpose of ensuring accountability to government are strong and they are beginning to focus more on the clinical effectiveness of NHS providers and, on some specific matters (above all waiting lists), service qualities which users demand. These developments have been instigated above all by central government pressure, reflecting the government's electoral and political marketing interests. Beyond this, few NHS bodies collect data about users' demands and experiences and the data which are collected are not necessarily used for planning services and selecting providers. In general, the whole area of consumer research and the concomitant aspects of service design and planning are under-resourced and undermanaged. In PCG/Ts especially, this situation reflects a lack of management resources. More widely, it also reflects NHS managers' training, payment and promotion systems. Ways of measuring health outcomes, especially those which matter to users, and health services' impact upon health remain technically underdeveloped (although developing). It remains to be seen how far PCG/Ts will be able to replicate the effect of fundholding in making NHS hospitals more responsive to GPs.

British health promoters have developed and used a wide, sophisticated range of marketing and anti-marketing activities. Not only have they applied the relevant adaptation of marketing models comprehensively but their activities have made it possible to extend and develop the models themselves.

The range of primary care providers has widened considerably since 1997, partly in response to central government initiatives but also through initiatives within primary care itself, instigated by GPs, nurse practitioners and voluntary organizations. Many general practices make considerable efforts to implement a balanced marketing mix, complementing their clinical services, promotional (informational) material, attention to the staff mix, location of services and quality of premises. National-level bodies have focused objectives and tracking on some variables (waiting times, out-of-hours access) which matter to consumers. Users can choose their healthcare provider and most general practices are paid accordingly (by capitation). New pricing and contracting systems are being introduced with potential to accelerate these developments. Complaints systems have improved. On the other hand, there is a little user participation in management and the mechanisms for enabling patients to choose their primary care provider operate only weakly. Partly this is because patients value continuity of care and do not change GP lightly, and changing a person's nursing home is upsetting enough to reduce the scope for using contestability as a tool of control in long-term care (De Friese and Hogue 1999). Partly it reflects barely sufficient primary healthcare capacity, in the cities especially. Similarly the mechanisms which enable GPs to choose secondary service on their patients' behalf are attenuated by the shortage of secondary care capacity. GPs, like patients, are also fairly set in their referral habits. Furthermore, it is often the GP rather than the patient who chooses the hospital, partly because many patients abdicate the decision.

In NHS secondary care, situation analysis techniques are getting stronger in respect of the effectiveness of services and there are occasional user surveys. Some providers use forms of SWOT analysis and business grid to derive their objectives. There is greater medical involvement in the formation of objectives and in service planning, and a gradually sharpening focus on the effectiveness of services. Care pathways are spreading as a means of service planning. The range of services is wide, their psychological impact and physical setting at their best appear to satisfy patients, and at its best, their public relations activity is competent. Tracking arrangements reflect purchasers' concerns. On the negative side, NHS trusts' incomes depend hardly at all on how many referrals they attract. For hospital consultants, obviously perverse incentives operate, giving them an interest in promoting private practice. Yet consultants are still permitted to control their own NHS waiting lists. 'Concordat' proposals to use private hospitals for NHS patients are liable to make matters worse. NHS trusts' management of how consultants reconcile their private with their NHS work is weak and lax. There is a palpable shortage of capacity and of investment from public sources in NHS secondary care.

In both primary and secondary care providers, methods for managing service quality are gradually becoming more incisive, and shifting from a focus on exception management towards designing and specifying clinical quality in an evidence-based way. NHS organizations themselves are dominated by a coalition of managers and doctors, who have a privileged role in NHS management. In HAs, managers dominate the coalition, in PCGs doctors do, and in trusts the position is more balanced. This arrangement opens up clinical effectiveness of services to critical scrutiny and active management, provided it does not simply cause medical 'capture' of NHS management, with the opposite effect on critical scrutiny of medical effectiveness. The dominant coalition also dominates the EBM movement. It rightly emphasizes clinical effectiveness, but effectiveness is seldom taken to mean 'effectiveness in satisfying users' reasonable demands in general'. The incentives which NHS organizations and staff face are oriented towards producing responsiveness to government. Unless government itself is so minded, they are only weak incentives to make services either more clinically effective or more user-responsive.

In results as in implementation, health promotion is the exception. For smoking control, quasi-marketing methods have been put to a sustained practical test and shown remarkable success in influencing consumption patterns. UK cigarette sales peaked (at 137 billion) in 1973. UK prevalences of smoking fell from 53 per cent for females and 80 per cent for males in 1948–52 to 39 per cent for males and 33 per cent for females in 1998. Tobacco-related deaths among middle-aged people (ages 35–69) fell from 80,000 in 1965 to 43,000 in 1995 (Peto *et al.* 2000). On a more modest scale, because of the later start, a similar pattern emerges with certain other health behaviours, most notably diet and exercise. The anti-marketing model at least can claim substantial empirical validation.

GP fundholding (GPFH) was the main natural experiment in linking hospital incomes to the referrals they attracted. Leaving aside the ambivalent evidence as to whether fundholders' patients received preferentially short waiting times, the most obvious lesson of GPFH is how dramatically changes in governance structures can change providers' behaviour and services. A behavioural mechanism operated by proxies for the patient, outside the hospitals' or managers' control, produced (in London and other large cities) service reprofiling and behavioural changes in providers of a scale and pace that decades of political and line-managerial effort failed to achieve.

Outside these spheres, however, the marketing models have not been implemented in anything like a total, systematic form. In NHS healthcare purchasing, NHS primary care and NHS trusts, many elements have been applied fragmentarily, usually as special projects initiated by enthusiasts or opportunistically in response to national 'initiatives' and the money that goes with them. As earlier chapters indicate, they have been numerous and the range is wide, from national level (for example the National Patient Survey) to one-principal general practices, covering activities from consumer research to service redesign, communications and staff training programmes, and many kinds of quality management activity, both clinical and non-clinical. Rarely has this been done with any perspective of developing and testing generalizable models of how to do healthcare marketing in a quasi-market. Scientific evaluations of the projects are very much scarcer than the projects themselves. For such results we have to look largely to parallel enterprises in other countries such as the USA, with only limited relevance to the British health system and consumer culture. In Britain, such evidence as exists consists largely of small case studies – a few used in the vignettes above – and 'grey' material (unpublished managerial reports and similar documents). Nevertheless, the NHS projects that have occurred suggest at least the practicality of implementing many of the ideas mooted in the theoretical parts of earlier chapters. In certain cases it is possible to show tangible improvements in services as a result, with evidence of user satisfaction and changed behaviour.

The only way to remedy this dearth of evidence about the validity of the quasi-marketing models outlined above is to implement them experimentally, research the results and refine the models accordingly.

How can publicly managed services be made more responsive to users?

Meantime we must be duly cautious in suggesting how to make publicly managed services more responsive to users. With that proviso, the historical and theoretical materials outlined above suggest at least the framework of an answer.

NHS attempts to make services user-responsive have for the most part been an exceptional, marginal activity. This marginalization seems to reflect a lack of knowledge about the subjects treated above: lack of regular systematic consumer research, lack of knowledge of how and why to apply it in service design, management and monitoring. But this pattern in turn reflects the incentives and constraints which NHS staff and managers face, and therefore the governance structures which create these incentives and constraints. The problem is fundamentally a structural one of how to design public service governance structures; of what arrangements of property-relations, incentives, resources and knowledge flows make public services respond to users' needs and changes therein.

A prerequisite governance structure is one that gives users access to services freely and as needed. The next requirement is a governance structure that routinely and automatically feeds users' demands back to the service providers and motivates providers to respond promptly and fully to users' reasonable demands. The internal regimes of the providers from whom it is necessary to produce this response are, perforce, dominated by non-user interests: of government, managers, professions and other occupational groups. We cannot naïvely assume that their interests will spontaneously coincide with users' needs. Consequently the main feedback and reward structure has to lie under users', rather than providers', control. Assuming that it should make providers respond to the reasonable demands of all service users, it must also be a structure that operates whenever a person obtains services. Ideally, the use of this structure would also impose the minimum practicable penalty upon users. These requirements strongly favour users' choice ('lateral re-entry' – Saltman and von Otter 1992), or a close proxy for it, as the structure for feeding knowledge of users' demands back to service providers. Users make their feedback at least in the practical, behavioural way of selecting which available provider to use. As an incentive to respond, a large part of providers' income has to reflect this feedback. This does not require that any cash or vouchers should pass through users' hands; only that incentives to providers strongly reflect how many users (or proxy users such as relatives, friends or referrers) demand their services. This argument for using user choice as the structure for making public service providers responsive to users' demands applies whenever users' demands are well-informed and consistent; that is, when users' demands reflect users' needs.

Yet there are also domains in which user choice is likely to be under-informed at best, and irrational at worst (for example the choice of treatment plan and of health behaviours, respectively). In those mainly technical domains beyond their capacity for informed demand, users themselves need some other, expert body to select which services, and by implication which providers, may enter the health (or education, transport, housing) system. This further governance structure selects what service designs are made available to users, excluding designs (and by implication their providers) which are ineffective by current technical standards or dangerous. More positively, users also need this governance structure routinely and automatically to feed back data on providers' standards of technical competence and safety, and to motivate providers to raise current standards.

Together these two governance structures would effect a dual process of selection amongst service designs and therefore providers. In effect, users would select services and providers by the criterion of conformity to users' reasonable demands. An expert body would select providers by the criterion of technical effectiveness, and pay them by both selection criteria. Conversely, the providers least responsive to users' reasonable demands or least technically effective, or both, would be deselected, leading to a reduction of their activity, even their eventual exclusion. Both selection processes rely upon the contestability of providers. Making service provision contestable in this double way has, however, some radical implications.

To begin with, the volume of provision must be sufficient to ensure real contestability of providers. Otherwise, neither users nor the public body admitting new providers has much practical scope for shifting work (and therefore income) from the less responsive and effective to the more responsive and effective providers. Neither hopes of gaining nor fears of losing incentive payments are credible to providers then. There must be not only sufficient volume but also a sufficient variety of providers if the dual selection is to occur. If we assume that users' reasonable demands – their needs – differ from segment to segment, a variety of service designs (and thus providers) offers users the means to select which one best meets their own demands (in those matters where users' demands are well informed). Similarly, a variety of providers is also necessary for enabling new technical designs for public services to emerge and be tested against each other and existing services. Provided current safety and effectiveness minima are satisfied, this implies a presumption in favour of encouraging new, non-commercial providers to enter public services, in particular cooperative, charitable, public and voluntary providers, including provision of services by users themselves.

What is critical, therefore, is not to restrict provider entry more tightly than by imposing minimum standards of safety and technical effectiveness. This is a *prima facie* objection to any one occupation or provider's having, in principle, a monopoly of service provision. Who can provide services safely and effectively is an evidential question. The admission of new providers should, on preceding arguments, be decided on that criterion alone.

It follows from the dual process of provider selection that the other governance structure required for making public services user-responsive is an incentive structure that rewards providers equally powerfully for user-responsiveness and for technically effective services. The former implies that providers be paid partly according to the number of users they attract. The latter implies they be paid partly according to the health (or education, or transport etc.) outcomes that they produce, remembering the technical complexities of disentangling what the provider has achieved from the effects of confounding factors. Concomitantly, it is necessary for these incentive structures to focus on rewarding only these two achievements and not others. Investigating what combination of financial and non-financial incentives is most effective is a substantial future research programme in its own right, as is the question of how much excess capacity amongst service providers is just enough to make them aware of the contestability of their position.

All these conditions have further implications for the internal organization and managment of providers of healthcare and other public services. They imply, for example, internal managerial regimes which are flexible enough to allow new service designs to be invented, tested and adopted. Besides the more obvious implications for minimizing regulations, occupational demarcations and budget virement rules, they also imply the removal of professional vetoes on service redesign. The measures outlined above also imply strengthening the capacity of patients (and their counterparts in other public services: students, tenants, passengers) to obtain information about services, select providers and articulate their own demands in respect of service design. In short, they imply promoting users' self-help, as co-producers of healthcare and other services and helping users become discerning, well-informed consumers. That requires making the management of public services transparent to users and the public, with the onus of proof on those who advocate secrecy beyond the confidentiality of personal records.

In summary, making public services user-responsive is above all a matter of constructing the right governance structures. These include making services free at the point of use, a system open to all safe and competent providers, and incentives that reward effectiveness and user responsiveness (and only these outcomes) with equal force. Sufficient volume of provision to make provision contestable is also necessary, and transparency of management information. Lastly, it is also necessary for healthworkers and policy-makers to know how and why to combine consumer research with technical evidence-basing in service design, and what the purposes and methods of making public services more user-responsive are: a task which this book offers a contribution to.

There is much scope for improving the user-responsiveness of publicly funded services such as the NHS. For most users, privatizing public services such as the NHS would be a self-defeating, retrograde step. The only solution is to learn how to make publicly funded services more adaptive, innovative and user-responsive. To mark this point of no return to the market it would incidentally be desirable (and in itself a minor task) to invent a new terminology speaking not of 'marketing' or even 'quasi-marketing' but of, say, 'consumption management' or 'public service' since the purpose of the new corpus of theory and evidence is to improve the user-responsiveness of public services, not increase the sales of firms in markets. Healthcare has many specific characteristics, but none of them is unique to healthcare (Sheaff 1999). Developing marketing – or rather, consumption management – for post-market economic systems is a task of wider importance still.

References

Abbott, S. and Gillam, S. (2000) 'Health improvement', in D. Wilkin, B. Leese and K. Smith, *The National Tracker Survey of Primary Care Groups and Trusts. Progress and Challenges 1999/2000*. Manchester: NPCRDC, pp.47–50.

Airey, C. and Erens, B. (eds) (1999) *The National Health Service (NHS) Patients Survey*. London: National Centre for Social Research.

Aitken, P.P. and Eadie, D.R. (1990) Effectiveness of Advertisements on Children, *British Journal of Addiction*, lxxxv, 399–412.

Albert, T. and Chadwick, S. (1992) 'How readable are practice leaflets?' *British Medical Journal*, 21 November 1992.

Albrecht, K. and Zemke, R. (1986) *Service America*. New York: Dow Jones Irvine.

Allsop, J. (1984) *Health Policy and the National Health Service*. London: Longman.

Anderson, D.C. and Near, R. (1983) 'Something may not be working in the hospital – but is it marketing?', *Journal of Health Care Marketing*, iii(1), 49–55.

Anon (1989) Good Stuff, Nicotine, *Economist*, 26 August.

Anon (1992) A Breathtaking Affair, *The Health Summary*, ix(7–8), 1–2.

Anon (1995) 'What makes a good GP?', *Which*, June, 18–19.

Anon (1999a) 'Find the right GP', *Which*, April, 21.

Anon (1999b) 'In an emergency', *Health Which*, February, 8–11.

Anon (2000) *An Enquiry into Quality and Practice Within the National Health Service Arising from the Actions of Rodney Ledward*. London: Department of Health.

Ansoff, H.I. (1957) 'Strategies for diversification', *Harvard Business Review*, xxv, September, 113–24.

Antonanzas, F., Rovira, J. and Correia, A. (eds) (1992) *Intersectoral Action for Health*. Navarra: Spanish Health Economics Association.

Appleby, J., Smith, P., Ranade, W., Little, V. and Robinson, R. (1994) 'Monitoring managed competition', in R. Robinson and J. Le Grand (eds) *Evaluating the NHS Reforms*. Newbury: Policy Journals, pp.24–53.

Arts for Health (n.d.) *Arts and Health*. Manchester: North Western RHA.

ASH (Action for Smoking and Health) (1991) *Briefing: Children and Young Persons (Protection from Tobacco) Bill. Clause 5: Prohibition of Tobacco Advertising on Shop Fronts.* London: ASH.

Ashton, J. and Seymour, H. (1988) *The New Public Health.* Milton Keynes: Open University Press.

Audit Commission (1994) Trusting to the Future. Towards an Audit Agenda for NHS Providers. London: HMSO.

Bailey, J., Black, M. and Wilkin, D. (1994) 'Specialist outreach clinics in general practice', *British Medical Journal*, 308, 1083–6.

Bailey, J., Glendinning, C. and Gould, H. (1997) *Better Buildings for Better Services: Innovative Developments in Primary Care.* Manchester: NPCRDC.

Baker, M.J. (1988) 'The Chief Scientist reports . . . Marketing Health'. Edinburgh: SHHD.

Bartlett, W. and Le Grand, J. (1994) The performance of trusts, in R. Robinson and J. Le Grand (eds) *Evaluating the NHS Reforms.* Newbury: Policy Journals, pp. 54–73.

Bassett, M. (1993) *A Health Cheque For All.* Manchester: European Policy Forum.

Baum, N. and Henkel, G. (1992) *Marketing your Clinical Practice.* Gaithersburg: Aspen.

Benato, R., Clarke, A., Holt, V. and Lack, V. (1998) 'Women and collective general practice. The Hoxton experience', in L. Doyal (ed.) *Women and Health Services.* Buckingham: Open University Press, chapter 14.

Berkowitz, E.N. (1996) *Essentials of Health Care Marketing.* Gaithersburg: Aspen.

Berwick, D. (1989) Continuous improvement as an ideal in health care, *New England Journal of Medicine*, cccxx, 53–6.

Biswas, B. and Sands, C. (1987) Reasons for attendance at child health clinics. Leicester (unpublished).

Black, M., Gosden, T., Leese, B. and Mead, N. (1996) *The Costs and Benefits of Specialist Outreach Clinics in General Practice in Two Specialties.* Manchester: NPCRDC.

Bitner, M. (1989) *Designing a Winning Service Strategy.* Chicago: American Marketing Association.

Boersmd, G. (1996) 'Ours to reason why', *Health Service Journal*, 10 October.

Bosk, C.L. (1979) *Managing Medical Failure.* Chicago: Chicago University Press.

Boston Consulting Group (1968) *Perspectives on Experience.* Boston: BCG.

Boustani, P. and Mitchell, V.W. (1990) 'Cereal bar: A perceptual, chemical and sensory analysis', *British Food Journal*, lxxxxii(5), 17–22.

Bowling, A. (1991) *Measuring Health.* Buckingham: Open University Press.

Bowling, A. (1993) *What People Say about Prioritising Health Services.* London: Kings Fund.

Boydell, L., Scally, G. and Scott, M. (1991) 'Advertising for health?' *Health Education Journal*, l(1), 31–3.

Bradshaw, J.S. (1972) 'Taxonomy of social need', in G. McLachlan (ed.) *Problems and Progress in Medical Care: Essays on Current Research.* Oxford: Oxford University Press.

Broadbent, S. and Jacobs, B. (1984) *Spending Advertising Money.* London: Business Books.

Brooks, R.M. (1998) 'Top of the charts', *Health Management*, August, 20–1.

Burenkova, S.P. (ed.) (1986) *Сборник штатных нормативов и типовых штатов учреждении здравоохранение* [Sbornik shtatnykh normativov i tipovikh shtatov uchrezhdenii zdravookhraneniye]. Moscow: Meditsina.

Calnan, M. (1983) 'Social networks and patterns of help-seeking', *Social Science and Medicine*, xvii(2), 25–8.

Calvert, J. and Johnston, L. (1999) 'The tales of cruelty that defy belief', *The Express*, 6 September, p.5.

Cantrill, J.A., Jaohannesson, B., Nicolson, M. and Noyce, P.R. (1996) 'Management of minor ailments in primary school children in rural and urban areas', *Child Care, Health and Development*, xxii(3), 167–74.

Caple, T. and Deighan, Y. (1986) *Managing Customer Relations. Taking a Snapshot.* London: North West Thames Regional Health Authority.

Cartwright, A. (1979) 'Minor illness in the surgery: a response to trivial, ill-defined or inappropriate service?', in *Management of Minor Illness*. London, Kings Fund.

Casey, B. (1989) *Tell Us What It's Really Like to be a Resident in Local Authority Care in Norfolk in 1988*. Norwich: Norfolk County Council.

Chambers, N. (1991) Report on the Total Quality Management Initiative at Derbyshire Family Health Services Authority. Derby.

Chambers, N. (1998) *Nurse Practitioners in Primary Care*. Oxford: Radcliffe Medical.

Charatan, F. (2000) 'New York votes to post doctors' details on net', *British Medical Journal*, 321 (8 July), 69.

Chisnall, P. (1975) *Marketing: A Behavioural Analysis*. London: McGraw-Hill.

Christopher, M., Payne, A. and Ballantyne, D. (1993) *Relationship Marketing*. Oxford: Butterworth Heinemann.

Cochrane, A. (1972) *Effectiveness and Efficiency*. London: Nuffield Provincial Hospitals Trust.

Collard, R. (1988) *Total Quality*. London: IPM.

Committee on Standards in Public Life (1995) *First Report of the Committee on Standards in Public Life* [Nolan Report]. London: HMSO.

Consumers Association (1998) *Health Which*, October.

Contreras, R., Greenspan, B. and Levanthal, R.C. (1994) Medical care in the discount aisle, in P.D. Cooper (ed.) *Health Care Marketing*. Gaithersberg: Aspen, chapter 32.

Cooper, P.D. (ed.) (1994) *Health Care Marketing*. Gaithersburg: Aspen.

Cooper, P.D. and Miaoulis, G. (1994) Altering corporate strategic criteria to reflect the changing environment: the role of life satisfaction and the growing senior market, in P.D. Cooper (ed.) *Health Care Marketing*. Gaithersberg: Aspen, chapter 22.

Corney, R. (1999) 'Changes in patient satisfaction and experience in primary and secondary care: the effect of general practice fundholding', *British Journal of General Practice*, xxxxix, 27–30.

Crimp, M. (1985) *The Marketing Research Process*. Englewood Cliffs, NJ: Prentice Hall.

Crofton, J. and Wood, M. (eds) (1985) *Smoking Control: Strategies and Evaluation in Community and Mass Media Programmes*. London: Health Education Council.

Crosby, P.B. (1979) *Quality is Free*. New York: McGraw-Hill.

David, F.R. (1989) 'How companies define their mission', *Long Range Planning*, xxii(1), 90–7.

Davidson, H. (1987) *Offensive Marketing*. Harmondsworth: Penguin.

Davies, J. (1998) 'Centre stage', *Health Services Journal*, 5 November (supplement), 1–5.

Davis, A. (2000) Making choices in emergency settings – does HTA promote action or social justice? Paper presented to the International Society for Technology Assessment in Health Care Conference, The Hague, 21 June.

Davis, D.A., Thomson, M.A., Oxman, A.D. and Haynes, R.B. (1995) 'Changing physician performance. A systematic review of the effect of continuing medical education strategies', *Journal of the America Medical Association*, cclxxiv(9), 700–5.

De Bruxelles, S. (2000) 'Private heart surgery for NHS patients', *The Times*, 8 June, p.8.

De Freise, G. and Hogue, C. (1999) An orientation to long-term care policy in the USA. Seminar, NPSRDC.

Deming, W.E. (1986) *Out of the Crisis*. Cambridge, MA: MIT Press.

Dent, M. (1995) 'Doctors, peer review and quality assurance', in T. Johnson, G. Larkin and M. Saks (eds) *Health Professions and the State in Europe*. London: Routledge.

Department of Health (1990) Working paper 10: [Clinical Audit]. London: DoH.

Department of Health (1992) *The Patient's Charter – a summary* (leaflet HPC2). London: HMSO.

Department of Health (1993) *Executive Letter*, (93)10 (12 February).

Department of Health (1997a) *The New NHS. Modern Dependable*. London: HMSO.

Department of Health (1997b) *New Drive to Rid NHS of Mixed Sex Hospital Accommodation*. London: DoH.

Department of Health (1999) *Supporting Doctors, Protecting Patients*. London: DoH.

Department of Health (2000) *The NHS Plan*. London: HMSO.

Dixon, P. and Carr-Hill, R. (1989) *The NHS and its Customers. Customer Feedback Surveys*. York: CHE.

Doll, R. and Hill, A.B. (1950) 'Smoking and carcinoma of the lung', *British Medical Journal*, 30 September, 739–48.

Doll, R. and Hill, A.B. (1954) 'The mortality of doctors in relation to their smoking habits', *British Medical Journal*, 26 June, 1451–5.

Donabedian, A. (1980) *The Definition of Quality and Approaches to its Assessment*, Vol. 1. Ann Arbor: Health Administration Press.

Douglas, J. (1998) 'Meeting the needs of black and minority ethnic communities', in L. Doyal (ed.) *Women and Health Services*. Buckingham: Open University Press, chapter 4.

Douglas, M. and Isherwood, B. (1996) *The World of Goods*. London: Routledge.

Dowling, B. (2000) *GPs and Purchasing in the NHS: The Internal Market and Beyond*. Aldershot: Ashgate.

Dubois, B. (1981) *Le Marketing-management Hospitalier*. Paris: Berger–Levrault.

Dyke, G. (1998) *The New NHS Charter. A Different Approach*. Leeds: Department of Health.

Enthoven, A. (1999) *In Pursuit of an Improving National Health Service*. London: Nuffield Trust.

Evans, R.G. (1990) 'The doc in the night-time'; medical practice variations and health policy, in T.F. Andersen and G. Mooney (eds) *The Challenge of Medical Practice Variations*. Basingstoke: Macmillan.

Faulder, C. (1985) *Whose Body Is It?* London, Virago.

Ferlie, E. (1994) The creation and evolution of quasi markets in the public sector: early evidence from the National Health Service, *Policy and Politics*, xxii, 105–12.

Fisher, A. (1991) Why Marlboro has warmed to the colour red, *Financial Times*, 15 August.

Foster, P. (1995) *Women and the Healthcare Industry*. Buckingham: Open University Press.

Fox, N.J. (1992) *The Social Meaning of Surgery*. Buckingham: Open University Press.

Frankel, S. and West, R. (eds) (1993) *Rationing and Rationality in the National Health Service. The Persistence of Waiting Lists.* Basingstoke: Macmillan.

Freake, D., Crowley, P., Steiner, M. and Drinkwater, C. (1997) Local heroes, *Health Services Journal*, 107(5661), 28–9.

Genillard, A. (1992) Czech Tobacco Group Draws Bids, *Financial Times*, 9 April.

Gilligan, C. and Lowe, R. (1995) *Marketing and Health Care Organizations.* Oxford: Radcliffe Medical.

Glendinning, C. (1999) GPs and contracts: bringing general practice into primary care, *Social Policy and Administration*, xxxiii(2).

Glendinning, C., Bailey, J., Burkey, Y., Gosden, T. and Kirk, S. (1996) *An evaluation of primary care resource centres in the north west of England.* Manchester: NPCRDC.

Glennester, H., Matsanganis, P., Owens, P. and Hancock, S. (1994) 'GP fundholding: wild card or winning hand?', in R. Robinson and J. Le Grand (eds) *Evaluating the NHS Reforms.* Newbury Policy Journals.

Goodwin, N. (1998) Fundholding, in J. Le Grand, N. Mays and J. Mulligan (eds) *Learning from the NHS Internal Market. A Review of the Evidence.* London, Kings Fund.

Gravelle, H., Dusheiko, M. and Sutton, M. (2000) *Rationing by Time and Money in the NHS: Variations in Admission Rates.* York: Centre for Health Economics.

Green, J. and Dale, J. (1992) 'Primary care in accident and emergency and general practice: a comparison', *Social Science and Medicine*, xxxv(8), 987–1005.

Griffin, J. (1994) *Health Information and the Consumer.* London: OHE.

Griffiths, S. and Bradlow, J. (1998) Involving women as consumers: the Oxfordshire health strategy, in L. Doyal (ed.) *Women and Health Services.* Buckingham, Open University Press, chapter 15.

Grönroos, C. (2000) *Service Management and Marketing – A Customer Relationship Management Approach.* Chichester: Wiley.

Gulland, A. (1997) 'Behind the smokescreen', *Nursing Times*, 18 June.

Hallam, L. (1994) Primary care outside normal working hours: review of published work, *British Medical Journal*, 302(6969), 1621–3.

Hallam, H., Wilkin, D. and Roland, M. (eds) (1996) *24 Hour Responsive Health Care.* Manchester: NPCRDC.

Hallas, J. (1976) *Community Health Councils in Action.* London: NPHT.

Ham, C. (1998) Financing the NHS, *British Medical Journal*, 316, 212–13.

Ham, C. and Pickard, S. (1998) *Tragic Choices in Health Care.* London: Kings Fund.

Hamblin, R. (1998) Trusts, in J. Le Grand, N. Mays and J. Mulligan (eds) *Learning from the NHS Internal Market. A Review of the Evidence.* London, Kings Fund.

Hammond, E.C. and Horn, D. (1954) Relationship between human smoking habits and death rates, *Journal of the American Medical Association*, 7 August, 1316–28.

Hammond, E.C. and Horn, D. (1958) Smoking and death rates, *Journal of the American Medical Association*, 8 March, 1159–72, and 15 March, 1294–308.

Harris, A. (ed.) (1997) *Needs to Know: A Guide to Needs Assessment for Primary Care.* Edinburgh: Churchill Livingstone.

Harrison, S. (1997) NHS management, in *NHS Handbook 1996–7.* Birmingham: NAHAT.

Harrison, S. and Pollitt, C. (1994) *Controlling Health Professionals.* Buckingham: Open University Press.

Hart, J.T. (1971) The inverse care law, *The Lancet*, 405–503.

Hassell, K., Harris, J., Rogers, A., Noyce, P. and Wilkinson, J. (1996) *The Role and Contribution of Pharmacy in Primary Care*. Manchester: NPCRDC.

Heald, G. and Wybrow, R.J. (eds) (1985) *The Gallup Survey of Britain*. London: Croom Helm.

Health Care Advisory Board (1992) *Physician Bonding*. Washington, DC: The Advisory Board Company.

Helms, D., Lindsay, W.N., Gauthier, A.K. and Campion, D.M. (1992) *Marketing Strategies and Methods to Influence the Sale of Group Health Insurance Products to Uninsured Small Businesses*. Washington, DC: Robert Wood Johnson Foundation.

Henderson, N.R. (1995) A practical approach to analyzing and reporting focus group studies: lessons from qualitative market research, *Qualitative Health Research*, v(4), 463–77.

Hinde, S. (1998) New supermarket GPs threaten NHS surgeries, *Daily Express*, 29 March.

Hudson, B. (1999) Decentralisation and primary care groups: a paradigm shift for the National Health Service in England?, *Policy and Politics*, xxvii(2), 159–72.

Hunter, D.J. (1995) Rationing: the case for muddling through elegantly, *British Medical Journal*, 311, 811.

Hutton, W. (1996) *The State We're In*. London: Vintage.

Inglis, B. (1983) *The Diseases of Civilization*. St Albans: Granada.

Ishikawa, K. (1991) *Introduction to Quality Control*. London: Chapman and Hall.

Jackson, P. (1999) *The Language of Quality: Developments in the Perception of Heath Care*. PhD thesis, University of Teesside.

Jamous, H. and Pelouille, B. (1970) Professions of self-perpetuating systems? Changes in the French hospital system, in J.A. Jackson (ed.) *Professions and Professionalism*. London: Cambridge University Press.

Jarman, B. (1983) Identification of underprivileged areas, *British Medical Journal*, 284, 1705–9.

Jewett, J.J. and Hibbard, J.H. (1996) Comprehension of quality of care indicators: differences among privately insured, public insured and uninsured, *Health Care Financing Review*, xviii(1), 75–94.

Jones, K. (1995) *Accountability Not Ownership – Labour and the NHS*. London: Fabian Society.

Juran, J. (1993) *Quality Planning and Analysis*. London: McGraw Hill.

Karpf, A. (1988) *Doctoring the Media*. London: RKP.

Katz, B. (1988) *How to Market Professional Services*. Aldershot: Gower.

Kennedy, A. and Robinson, A. (1999) *A Handy Guide to Managing Ulcerative Colitis*. Manchester: NPCRDC.

Kerrison, S. and Corney, R. (1998) Private provision of 'outreach' clinics to fundholding general practices in England, *Journal of Health Services Research and Policy*, iii, 20–2.

Kerrison, S., Packwood, T. and Buxton, M. (1994) Monitoring medical audit, in R. Robinson and J. Le Grand (eds) *Evaluating the NHS Reforms*. Newbury: Policy Journals.

Khayat, K. and Salter, B. (1994) Patient satisfaction surveys: a market research tool for general practice, *British Journal of General Practice*, xxxxiv, 215–19.

Kickert, W.J.M., Klign, E-H. and Koppenjan, J.F.M. (eds) (1997) *Managing Complex Networks*. London: Sage.

Klein, N. (2000) *No Logo*. London: Flamingo.

Klein, R. (1983) *The Politics of the NHS*. Harlow: Longman.

Klein, R., Day, P. and Redmayne, S. (1996) *Managing Scarcity: Priority Setting and Rationing in the National Health Service*. Buckingham: Open University Press.

Kotler, P. (1991) *Marketing Management*. Englewood Cliffs, NJ: Prentice Hall.

Kotler, P. and Clarke, R. (1987) *Marketing for Health Care Organizations*. Englewood Cliffs, NJ: Prentice Hall.

Kotler, P. and Levy, S.J. (1969) Broadening the concept of marketing, *Journal of Marketing*, xxxiii, 10–15.

Kreitz, H.J. (n.d.) *Social-Marketing. Marketing für gesundheitspolitische Ziele*. Bonn: BDW.

Laber, E. (2000) Designer drugs, *The Sciences*, July/August, 8–9.

Laughlin, S. (1998) From theory to practice: the Glasgow experience, in L. Doyal (ed.) *Women and Health Services*. Buckingham: Open University Press, chapter 16.

Laurance, B. (1991) Filtering out the Propaganda, *Guardian*, 2 March.

Laurance, J. (1998) Hospitals lose £100m a year in pay bed income, *Sunday Times*, 18 December, p.A7.

Laurance, J. (1999) NHS is ageist, say patients, *The Independent*, 19 April.

Lee, J., Gask, L., Roland, M. and Donnan, S. (1998) Total purchasing and extended fundholding of mental health services. Manchester: NPCRDC (unpublished).

Lee, T.J. (2000) *Incentive Payments and the Quality of Services Provided by Primary Care Physicians*. PhD thesis, University of Manchester.

Leese, B. and Gillam, S. (2000) in D. Wilkin, B. Leese and K. Smith, *The National Tracker Survey of Primary Care Groups and Trusts. Progress and Challenges 1999/2000*. Manchester: NPCRDC, pp.27–30.

Leiss, W., Kline, S. and Jhally, S. (1986) *Social Communication in Advertising*. London: Methuen.

Levine, S. and Lilienfeld, A. (eds) (1987) *Epidemiology and Health Policy*. London: Tavistock.

Levitt, T. (1976) The industrialization of service, *Harvard Business Review*, September/October, 67–74.

Lewton, K.R. (1995) *Public Relations in Health Care*. Chicago: AHA.

Light, D. (1998) *Effective Commissioning: Lessons from Purchasing in American Managed Care*. London: OHE.

Locock, C. (2000) The changing nature of rationing in the UK National Health Service, *Public Administration*, lxxviii(1), 91–109.

Luck, M., Lawrence, B., Pocock, B. and Reilly, K. (1988) *Consumer and Market Research in Health Care*. London: Chapman and Hall.

Lumsden, Q. (1992) Shares. Tobacco fills the coffers, *The Independent on Sunday*, 1 November.

Lupton, C., Barnes, R. and Peckham, S. (1998) *Managing Public Involvement in Healthcare Purchasing*. Buckingham: Open University Press.

McCarthy, E.J. (1978) *Basic Marketing: A Managerial Approach*. Homewood: Irwin.

McDonald, M. and Miles, C. (1995) The potential for marketing planning in an NHS trust, *British Medical Journal*, 18 March, 719–24.

McKeown, T. (1979) *The Role of Medicine*. Oxford: Blackwell.

MacStravic, R.S. (1989) Market and market segment portfolio analysis for hospitals, *Healthcare Management Review*, xiv(3), 25–32.

Madeley, R.J., Gillies, P.A., Power, F.L. and Symonds, E.M. (1989) Nottingham Mothers Stop Smoking Project – baseline survey of smoking in pregnancy, *Community Medicine*, xi(2), 124–30.

Maguire, K. (2000) Tobacco company faces inquiry into smuggling, *The Guardian*, 7 March, p.2.

Mahon, A., Wilkin, D. and Whitehouse, C. (1994) Choice of hospital for elective surgery referral, in R. Robinson and J. Le Grand (eds) *Evaluating the NHS Reforms*. Newbury: Policy Journals.

Majaro, S. (1982) *Marketing in Perspective*. London: Allen & Unwin.

Malbon, G. and Smith, J. (2000) Commissioning, in D. Wilkin, B. Leese and K. Smith, *The National Tracker Survey of Primary Care Groups and Trusts. Progress and Challenges 1999/2000*. Manchester: NPCRDC, pp.39–42.

Marshall, M.N., Shekelle, P.G., Leatherman, S. and Brook, R.H. (2000) Public release of performance data. What do we expect to gain? A review of the evidence, *Journal of the American Medical Association*, cclxxxiii(14), 1865–74.

Maturen, V.L. and Zander, K. (1993) Outcomes management in a prospective pay system, *Caring*, June, 46–54.

Maxwell, R. (1984) Quality assessment in health, *British Medical Journal*, cclxxxviii, 12 May.

Miaoulis, G. and Corson, R. (1994) Benefit segmentation: a marketing tool to enhance the physician process for hospitals, in P. Cooper (ed.) *Health Care Marketing*. Gaithersburg: Aspen.

Miles, A. and Lugon, M. (eds) (1996) *Effective Clinical Practice*. Oxford: Blackwell Science.

Millar, B. (1996) False positive, *Health Services Journal*, 8 August, 13.

Miller, P. (1997) Are GP fundholders wasting money?, *Health Service Journal*, 6 March, 28–9.

Mitchell, K. and Tayler, W. (1988) *You May Quote Me*. London: IHSM.

Moore, W. (1992) Smoking them out, *Guardian*, 17 July.

Moreira, J. (1998) *Applied Social Marketing and Health Promotion: A Theory of Discourse Management*. PhD thesis, University of Manchester.

Muir Gray, J.A. (1997) *Evidence-based Healthcare*. Edinburgh: Churchill Livingstone.

Mulligan, J. (1998) Locality and GP commissioning in J. Le Grand, N. Mays and J. Mulligan (eds) *Learning from the NHS Internal Market. A Review of the Evidence*. London, Kings Fund, chapter 5.

Nader, R. (1965) *Unsafe at Any Speed: The Designed-in Dangers of the American Automobile*. New York: Grossman.

Nelson, E. and While, D. (1992) Children's awareness of cigarette advertisements on television, *Health Education Journal*, li(1), 34–7.

Nettleton, S. (ed.) (1995) *The Sociology of Health and Illness*. Cambridge: Polity.

Nettleton, S. and Bunton, R. (1995) Sociological critiques, in R. Bunton, S. Nettleton and R. Burrows (eds) *The Sociology of Health Promotion*. London: Routledge, chapter 4.

New, B. and Le Grand, J. (1996) *Rationing in the NHS. Principles and Pragmatism*. London: Kings Fund.

NHSE (1999a) *NHS Primary Care Walk-in Centres*, HSC 1999/116. Leeds: NHSE.

NHSE (1999b) *Mental Health. National Service Framework*. Leeds: NHSE.

NHSE (1999c) *The New NHS – 1998 Reference Costs*. London: NHSE.

NHSE (2000) *Coronary Heart Disease. National Service Framework*. Leeds: NHSE.

NHSME (1991) HC(91)2, January.

NHSME (1992) *Executive Letter*, (92)21, 2 April.

NICE (2000) *Referral Practice*. London: NICE (pilot version).

Nicolaas, G., Rogers, A., Elliott, H. *et al.* (1997) *Population Health, Pathways into Primary Care and the Use of Health Care: Phase 1 – A Report of Reviews.* Manchester: NPCRDC.

Normann, R. (1984) *Service Management*. Chichester: Wiley.

O'Dowd, A. (1998) GP lost as BUPA scheme fails, *Pulse*, 25 April.

Office of Health Economics (1998) *Compendium of Health Statistics*. London: OHE.

Osborne, D. and Gaebler, T. (1992) *Reinventing Government*. Reading, MA: Addison-Wesley.

Packard, V. (1960) *The Waste Makers*. London: Longman.

Pantall, J. (2001) Benchmarking in healthcare, *Nursing Research*, vi(2), 568–80.

Payne, A. (1993) *The Essence of Services Marketing*. Hemel Hempstead: Prentice Hall.

Payne, S. (1998) 'Hit and miss': the success and failure of psychiatric services for women, in L. Doyal (ed.) *Women and Health Services*. Buckingham: Open University Press, chapter 5.

Perry, K. (2000) Doctors warn after record £77m paid out to patients, *The Guardian*, 7 August.

Peto, R., Darby, S., Deo, H. *et al.* (2000) Smoking, smoking cessation, and lung cancer in the UK since 1950: combination of national statistics with two case-control studies, *British Medical Journal*, 321(5 August), 323–9.

Pickard, S. (1998) Citizenship and consumerism in health care: a critique of citizens juries, *Social Policy and Administration*, xxxii(3), 226–44.

Pickard, S. and Sheaff, R. (1999) Primary care groups and NHS rationing: implications of the Child B case, *Health Care Analysis*, viii, 37–56.

Pickard, S., Williams, G. and Flynn, R. (1995) Local voices in an internal market: the case of community health services, *Social Policy and Administration*, 29, 135–49.

Picken, C. and St Leger, S. (1993) *Assessing Health Need using the Life Cycle Framework*. Buckingham: Open University Press.

Porter, M.E. (1981) *Competitive Strategy: Techniques for Analysing Industries and Competition*. New York: Free Press.

Prince, M. (1982) *Consumer Research for Management Decisions*. Chichester: Wiley.

Propper, C. (1995a) Agency and incentives in the NHS internal market, *Social Science and Medicine*, 40, 1683–90.

Propper, C. (1995b) Regulatory reform of the NHS internal market, *Health Economics*, iv, 71–83.

Rae, C. (ed.) (1993) *Managing Clinical Directorates*. Harlow: Longman.

Raw, M., White, P. and McNeill, A. (1990) *Clearing the Air: A Guide for Action on Tobacco*. London: BMA.

Rawstorne, A. and Hill, A. (1991) Tobacco ad ban faces a bumpy ride, *Financial Times*, 20 May.

Redmayne, S., Klein, R. and Day, P. (1995) *Priorities in Hard Times*. Bath: Centre for the Analysis of Social Policy.

Rhein, R. (1993) Environmental smoke causes cancers, says US agency, *British Medical Journal*, xxxvi(16 January), 163.

Ritzer, G. (1996) *The McDonaldization of Society*. Thousand Oaks, CA: Pine Forge Press.

Roberts, H. (1992) Professionals' and parents' perceptions of A-and-E use in a children's hospital, *Sociological Review*, xxxx(1), 109–31.

Robertson-Steel, I.R.S. (1998) Providing primary care in the accident and emergency department, *British Medical Journal*, 316, 409–10.

Robinson, R. and Steiner, A. (1997) *Managed Health Care: US Evidence and Lessons for the NHS*. Southampton: Institute of Health Policy Studies.

Rogers, A. and Nicholaas, G. (1998) Understanding the patterns and processes of primary care use: a combined quantitative and qualitative approach, *Sociological Research Online*, iii(4).

Rogers, A., Hassell, K. and Nicolaas, G. (1999) *Demanding Patients? Analysing the Use of Primary Care*. Buckingham: Open University Press.

Roland, M. (1999) Primary Care Groups and Primary Care Trusts, *Journal of the Royal College of Physicians*, xxxiii, 337.

Rosenthal, M.M. (1995) *The Incompetent Doctor*. Buckingham: Open University Press.

Royal Commission on Environmental Pollution (1994) *Transport and the Environment*. London: HMSO.

Royal Commission on the NHS (1979) *Access to Primary Health Care*. London: HMSO.

Salisbury, C. (1989) How do people choose their doctors?, *British Medical Journal*, cclxxxxix, 1 September, 608–10.

Saltman, R. and von Otter, C. (1992) *Planned Markets and Public Competition*. Buckingham: Open University Press.

Sarafino, E.P. (1999) *Health Pyschology*. Chichester: Wiley.

Sasser, E.W., Olsen, P.R. and Wycoff, D.D. (1978) *Management of Service Operations*. Boston: Allyn and Bacon.

Scrivens, E. (1995) *Accreditation. Protecting the Professional or the Consumer?* Buckingham: Open University Press.

Sheaff, R. (1991) *Marketing for Health Services*. Buckingham: Open University Press.

Sheaff, R. (1996) *The Need for Healthcare*. London: Routledge.

Sheaff, R. (1998) What is 'primary' about primary healthcare?, *Health Care Analysis*, vi, 330–40.

Sheaff, R. (1999) 'Last time buyers': markets and marketing in services for the elderly, in A.H. Lesser (ed.) *Aging, Autonomy and Resources*. Aldershot: Ashgate.

Sheaff, R. and Lloyd-Kendall, A. (2000) Principal–agent relationships in general practice: the first wave of English PMS contracts, *Journal of Health Services Research and Policy*, v(3), 156–63.

Sheaff, R. and Peel, V. (eds) (1995) *Managing Health Services Information Systems*. Buckingham: Open University Press.

Sheaff, R. and West, M. (1997) Marketisation, managers and moral strain, *Public Administration*, lxxv(2), 193–210.

Silver, R. (ed.) (1985) *Health Service Public Relations*. London: Kings Fund.

Simon, B. (1991) Smokers Fight to the Very Last Gasp, *Financial Times*, 11 July.

Smee, C. (1992) *Effect of Tobacco Advertising on Tobacco Consumption: A Discussion Document Reviewing the Evidence*. London: Department of Health Economics and Operational Research Division.

Smith, K., Dickson, M. and Sheaff, R. (1999) Second among equals, *Nursing Times*, 95(13), 54–5.

Squires, A. (1999) *Stakeholder quality and health care*, City University, London (PhD thesis).

Starkey, F. (1998) Maternity and health links: an advocacy service for Asian women and their families, in L. Doyal (ed.) *Women and Health Services*. Buckingham: Open University Press, chapter 8.

Stern, A. (1992) Tobacco Industry Tries to Smoke out the Eurocrats, *The Guardian*, 7 March.

Stevens, A. and Raftery, J. (eds) (1994) *Health Care Needs Assessment*. Oxford: Radcliffe Medical.

Stirling, A. (2000) Paid role for GPs in NHS-led private health services, *Pulse*, 18 March, 4.

Summers, D. (1992) Ashes to ashes as smoking bites dust, *Financial Times*, 17 January.

Syme, S.L. and Guralnik, J.M. (1987) Epidemiology and health policy: coronary heart disease, in S. Levine and A. Lilienfeld (eds) *Epidemiology and Health Policy*. London: Tavistock, chapter 3.

Taylor, P. (1984) *The Smoke Ring*. London: Sphere.

Tobacco Advisory Council (n.d. (a)) *Sports Sponsorship by Tobacco Companies. A Working Partnership*. London: TAC.

Tobacco Advisory Council (n.d. (b)) *Hear the Other Side*. London: TAC.

Tobacco Institute of Australia (n.d.) *Workplace Smoking Policy Guidelines: New South Wales*. TIA.

Tran, M. (2000) NHS under fire for 'allowing older patients to die', *The Guardian*, 13 April.

Tye, J.B., Warner, K.E. and Glantz, S.T. (1988) Tobacco advertising and consumption: evidence of a causal relationship, *World Smoking and Health*, (Winter), 6–16.

Ungoed-Thomas, J. and Dignan, C. (1999) The NHS dials 999, *Sunday Times*, 9 January, p.10.

Venning, P., Durie, A., Roland, M., Roberts, C. and Leese, B. (2000) Randomised controlled trial comparing cost effectiveness of general practitioners and nurse practitioner in primary care, *British Medical Journal*, 320 (15 April), 1048–53.

Vidal, J. (1992) The true price of development, *Education Guardian*, 26 May.

Weiner, J.P. and Ferris, D.M. (1990) *GP Budget Holding: Lessons from America*. London: Kings Fund.

Welsh Office NHS Executive (1989) *Strategic Intent and Direction of the NHS in Wales*. Cardiff: Welsh Office.

Wennberg, J. (1986) Which rate is right?, *New England Journal of Medicine*, cccxiv(5), 310–11.

WHO (World Health Organisation) (1990) *It Can Be Done*. Copenhagen: WHO Europe.

Widgery, D. (1979) *Health in Danger*. London: Macmillan.

Wiggins, D. (1985) Claims of need, in T. Honderich (ed.) *Morality and Objectivity*. London: Routledge.

Wigzell, H. (2000) Biotechnology – a threat or a promise for managing healthcare? Paper presented to the European Healthcare Management Association Conference, Örebro, 28 June.

Wilkin, D., Leese, B. and Smith, K. (2000) *The National Tracker Survey of Primary Care Groups and Trusts. Progress and Challenges 1999/2000*. Manchester: NPCRDC.

Williams, S.J. and Calnan, M. (1991) Key determinants of consumer satisfaction with general practice, *Family Practice*, viii, 237–42.

Williamson, C. (1992) *Whose Standards?*, Buckingham: Open University Press.

Wilson, C.R.M. (1992) *Strategies in Health Care Quality*. Ontario: Saunders.

Wohl, S. (1984) *The Medical–Industrial Complex*. New York: Harmony.

Wolf, C. (1979) A theory of nonmarket failure: framework for implementation analysis, *Journal of Law and Economics*, xxii(2), 107–39.

Wolfe, C. (1994) A new model for marketing health care and senior housing services, in P.D. Cooper (ed.) *Health Care Marketing*. Gaithersburg: Apen.

Wollnitz, G. (1983) *Marketing in der Gesundheitsvorsorge*. Baden-Baden: Nomos.

Wood, B. (1999) The politics of disease-related patients' association: an Anglo-American comparison. Paper to annual meeting of the American Political Science Association.

Yankelovich, D. (1964) New criteria for market segmentation, *Harvard Business Review*, xxxxii, 83–90.

Yates, J. (1995) *Private Eye, Heart and Hip*. Edinburgh: Churchill Livingstone.

Zander, K. (1988) Nursing case management: strategic management of cost and quality outcomes, *Journal of Nursing Administration*, xviii(5), 23–30.

Zeithaml, V.A., Parasuraman, A. and Berry, L.B. (1990) *Delivering Quality Service*. New York: Free Press.

Zinn, C. (1992) Passive smokers win legal victory in Australia, *The Guardian*, 26 May.

Index